Law in a
Business Context

Business in Context Series

Editors

David Needle
Currently Head of the Department
of Business Studies and Languages
The Polytechnic of East London

Professor Eugene McKenna
Currently Director of the School
of Business and Management
The Polytechnic of East London

Accounting Information in a Business Context
Aidan Berry and Robin Jarvis

Behaviour in a Business Context
Richard Turton

Business in Context
David Needle

Economics in a Business Context
Alan Neale and Colin Haslam

Law in a Business Context
Bill Cole, Peter Shears and Jillinda Tiley

Quantitative Techniques in a Business Context
Roger Slater and Peter Ascroft

Law in a Business Context

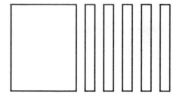

Bill Cole

Peter Shears

and

Jillinda Tiley

CHAPMAN AND HALL

University and Professional Division

LONDON • NEW YORK • TOKYO • MELBOURNE • MADRAS

UK	Chapman and Hall, 11 New Fetter Lane, London EC4P 4EE
USA	Chapman and Hall, 29 West 35th Street, New York NY 10001
JAPAN	Chapman and Hall Japan, Thomson Publishing Japan, Hirakawacho Nemoto Building, 7F, 1-7-11 Hirakawa-cho, Chiyoda-ku, Tokyo 102
AUSTRALIA	Chapman and Hall Australia, Thomas Nelson Australia, 480 La Trobe Street, PO Box 4725, Melbourne 3000
INDIA	Chapman and Hall India, R. Sheshadri, 32 Second Main Road, CIT East, Madras 600 035

First edition 1990

© 1990 Cole, Shears and Tiley

Typeset in 10/11½ pt Times by Best-Set Typesetter Ltd., HK
Printed in England by Clays Ltd, St Ives plc

ISBN 0 412 37520 6

British Library Cataloguing in Publication Data
Cole, Bill
    Law in a business context. – (Business in context series)
    1. England. Business firms. Law
    I. Title   II. Shears, Peter   III. Tiley, Jillinda   IV.
    Series
    344.20665

    ISBN 0–412–37520–6

Contents

Series foreword   vii

Preface   xi

Comparative treatment table   xv

1   **The legal background**   1
    Introduction   1
    Classification of law   2
    Where does law come from?   5
    How and why does law change?   20
    How and by whom is it enforced?   22
    How is the law uscful to business?   34
    What does the law cost?   34
    Summary   36
    Further reading   36
    Exercises   37

2   **The changing legal environment**   38
    Introduction   38
    The role of Government and the increasing scope of legislation   38
    Impact of the common law: constraints of the law of contract   41
    Impact of the common law: constraints of the law of tort   63
    Summary   75
    Further reading   76
    Exercises   76

3   **The organizational context of business**   80
    Introduction   80
    Types of business organization   80
    Setting up a business enterprise   84
    Deciding which form of enterprise to operate   86
    Terminating the enterprise   89
    Summary   93
    Further reading   93
    Exercises   93

4   **Innovation, research and development**   95
    Introduction   95
    Environmental aspects   95
    Strategic aspects   99
    Organizational aspects   110
    Summary   115

	Further reading	115
	Exercises	115
5	**The production process: health, safety and liability**	**117**
	Introduction	117
	The production process	119
	The end product	138
	Summary	142
	Further reading	143
	Exercises	143
6	**Marketing, selling and advertising**	**145**
	Introduction	145
	Attracting business/advertising	145
	The sale	149
	Service and supply contracts	154
	The role of public bodies	155
	Credit	158
	Summary	160
	Further reading	160
	Exercises	161
7	**The personnel function**	**163**
	Introduction	163
	Recruitment and selection	163
	Employee references	168
	Contracts of employment	170
	Termination of employment	182
	The Data Protection Act and personnel records	189
	Trade unions and industrial relations	191
	Union membership agreements (closed shops)	193
	Trade union membership and individual rights	194
	Summary	196
	Further reading	196
	Exercises	197
8	**The finance function**	**198**
	Introduction	198
	Share capital or contributed capital	198
	Loan (or debt) capital	200
	Retained profits and trade credit	202
	Wrongful trading	203
	Insurance and the business enterprise	205
	Summary	210
	Further reading	211
	Exercises	211
	Appendix: Case summaries	**213**
	Table of cases	**226**
	Table of statutes	**230**
	Index	**232**

Series foreword

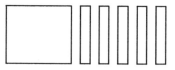

This book is part of the Business in Context series. The books in this series are written by lecturers all with several years experience of teaching on undergraduate business studies programmes. For a number of years we have been conscious that many of the books we were recommending to our students never catered specifically for business studies courses. Although there are some good books covering the different disciplines found in the business studies curriculum, very few of these texts are aimed specifically at the business studies student. Many of the best management texts assume a level of managerial experience and the worst take a simplistic and prescriptive view of business life. The interdisciplinary nature of business studies often means presenting students with a range of books dealing with various specialist topics, which can prove both daunting and expensive.

It is certainly not our intention to offer up our individual texts as a panacea. Indeed, our policy throughout this series is that books are well referenced and the student is guided to further reading on every topic area. However, we do feel that our books provide a focus for the student attempting to seek some meaning in the range of subjects currently offered on business studies programmes.

Business studies has attracted a growing band of students for a number of years and is currently one of the most popular undergraduate courses. Whilst many books have emerged to feed a hungry BTEC market, the undergraduate business studies student has been sadly neglected. One of the causes of that neglect has undoubtedly been the difficulty of many, academics and members of the business community alike, to define business studies, beyond a list of loosely connected subject headings. With this series we hope to make good some of those missing connections.

With the exception of the text, Business in Context, which takes the series title as its theme, all our texts take the approach of a particular discipline traditionally associated with business studies and taught across a wide range of business studies programmes. The first books in our series examine business from the perspectives of economics, behavioural science, law, mathematics and accounting. However, whereas in traditional texts it is the subject itself that is the focus, our texts make business the focus. All the texts are based upon the same specific model of business illustrated in the Figure. We have called our model Business in Context and the text of the same name is an expansion and explanation of that model.

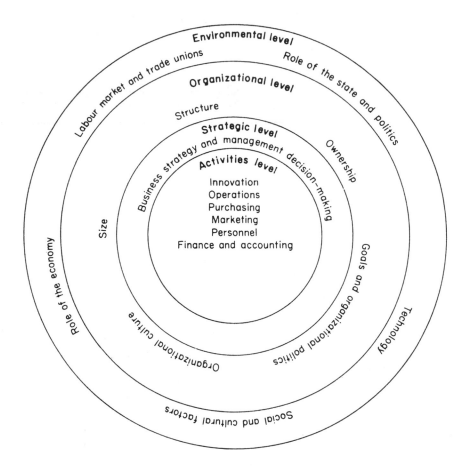

The model comprises four distinct levels. At the core are found the activities which make up what we know as business and include innovation, operations and production, purchasing, marketing, personnel and finance and accounting. We see these activities operating irrespective of the type of business involved, and found in both the manufacturing and service industry as well as in the public and private sectors. The second level of our model is concerned with strategy and management decision–making. It is here that decisions are made which influence the direction of the business activities at our core. The third level of our model is concerned with organizational factors within which business activities and management decisions take place. The organizational issues we examine are structure, size, goals and organizational politics, patterns of ownership, and organizational culture. Clear links can be forged between this and other levels of our model, especially between structure and strategy, goals and management decision–making, and how all aspects both contribute to and are influenced by the organizational culture. The fourth level concerns itself with the environment in which businesses operate. The issues here involve social and cultural factors, the role of the state and politics, the role of the economy, and issues relating to both technology and labour. An important feature of this fourth level of our model is that such elements not only operate as opportunities and constraints for business, but also that they are shaped by the three other levels of our model.

This brief description of the Business in Context model illustrates the key features of our series. We see business as dynamic. It is constantly being shaped by and in turn shaping those managerial, organizational, and environmental contexts within which it operates. Influences go backwards and forwards across the various levels. Moreover, the aspects identified within each level are in constant interaction with one another. Thus the role of the economy cannot be understood without reference to the role of the state; size and structure are inextricably linked; innovation is insepar-able from issues of operations, marketing and finance. The understanding of how this model works is what business studies is all about, and forms the basis for our series.

In proposing this model we are proposing a framework for analysis, and we hope that it will encourage readers to add to and refine the model and so broaden our understanding of business. Each writer in this series has been encouraged to present a personal interpretation of the model. In this way we hope to build up a more complete picture of business initially through the eyes of an economist, a behavioural scientist, a lawyer, a mathematician and an accountant.

Our series therefore aims for a more integrated and realistic apprach to business than has hitherto been the case. The issues are complex but the authors' treatments are not. Each book in this series is built around the Business in Context model, and each displays a number of common features that mark out this series. First we aim to present our ideas in a way that students will find easy to understand and we relate those ideas wherever possible to real business situations. Secondly we hope to stimulate further study both by referencing our material and pointing students towards further reading at the end of each chapter. Thirdly we use the notion of 'key concepts' to highlight the most significant aspects of the subject presented in each chapter. Fourthly we use case studies to illustrate our material and stimulate further discussion. Fifthly we present at the end of each chapter a series of questions, exercises, and discussion topics. To sum up, we feel it most important that each book will stimulate thought and further study, and assist the student in developing powers of analysis, a critical awareness and ultimately a point of view about business issues.

We have already indicated that the series has been devised with the undergraduate business studies student uppermost in our minds. We also maintain that these books are of value wherever there is a need to under-stand business issues and may therefore be used across a range of different courses covering BTEC Higher, and some professional and masters courses.

David Needle and Eugene McKenna
January 1989

Preface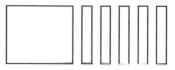

This book is one of the Business in Context series. It has been written by a team of lecturers all of whom are lawyers and involved in teaching law to business studies students. All business studies courses contain a substantial legal input because the law provides not only the environmental framework against which a business operates but also creates some of the range of operational choices which it is the business of management to make. In addition it supplies the organizational framework within which the business must operate.

Despite this, most traditional law texts reproduce the legal rules in greater or lesser depth with no real attempt to show how they integrate with the functions of business. Our purpose in writing this book as part of the series has been to try to fill what we see as a very real gap in the market for business studies students who are seeking an easily intelligible introduction to the business world.

Much of the material presented in a traditional business law book will be found in this book, and the table reproduced on the back cover of this book illustrates where the usual core material can be found. This book is not written as a law textbook and the degree of detail into which it has been possible to go is necessarily limited. At the end of each chapter we have made suggestions for further reading which themselves provide further sources. We are deeply conscious that not all business studies students have access to a comprehensive law library nor would we expect this to be necessary. Emphasis has been placed on principle rather than on too much detail. The references include not only academic texts, cases and statutes, but practical (and sometimes free) guides issued by, for example, trade associations, government departments, banks and the Equal Opportunities Commission.

In the text we have cited a number of cases by way of illustration and as authorities. Where these are essential to enable the student to understand the point being made their facts have been briefly given, and where they are referred to simply as additional reference material their names have been given as a starting point for further research or discussion. It is not intended that the cases cited should be seen as either definitive or exhaustive.

Case studies have been given in all chapters to illustrate the themes under discussion, sometimes with the addition of contemporary newspaper cuttings. Questions for discussion and problems for further consideration are given at the end of each chapter to provoke further thought.

The introductory chapter of the book sets the scene by considering the role and purpose of law, not in the abstract but in terms of its relevance and cost to business. Emphasis is placed on the different ways in which the law can be used by a business to achieve its objectives, including lobbying for change. An attempt is made to evaluate the use of the courts to bring an action as well as outlining other possible alternatives to settle disputes.

The remaining chapters pursue the themes of the business model by considering the interaction of the law with the business at work. The provision of legal environmental constraints reflecting changing economic and social conditions is illustrated by considering some of the rules of contract and tort, though other examples of these occur in later chapters dealing with particular business functions.

The organizational choices affecting a business are discussed not only in the chapter concerned with partnerships and companies, but also at the many points where legal differences make a choice important, for example the choice between employees and independent contractors in the selection of personnel, and the provision of in-house or external credit when considering marketing strategy.

The chapter on research and development deals in more detail than is common in most business law books with the options a business has to protect its inventions. It also draws together some discussion of intellectual property, the enforceability of restrictive covenants in employee contracts and limitations imposed by health and safety legislation on designers and developers.

The chapter on personnel concentrates on the constraints imposed by the employment protection legislation, perhaps soon to be supplemented by the Community's social charter. Illustrations of the impact of the Community on the UK are given in case studies and referred to throughout.

Occupational limitations on the grounds of health and safety, nuisance and occupiers' liability are presented, together with reference to statutory environmental controls increasingly emanating from the EC, as the framework for production. There is also a consideration of product liability and the EC product liability directive implemented in the Consumer Protection Act 1987.

The chapter on marketing considers the sale of goods, and the provision of consumer credit. It also includes a section on advertising, voluntary controls and trade associations, casting a wider net than more traditional texts.

Money is a recurring theme. Most business decisions are related to it. The raising of finance is considered separately from the formation of a company in a chapter devoted to finance which also covers wrongful trading and an outline of insurance, already referred to in the sections on professional and product liability. The issue of taxation as it affects a business is raised several times but not separately covered in the finance chapter. Clearly this is an area which involves social and economic policy and is directly responsible for some of the organizational and strategic choices a business will make. We have alluded to tax at appropriate points to enable the student to see the interrelation of these issues but because the tax regime is all embracing, changes annually and is very complicated it is really not possible in a short book of this nature to give any complete picture of its current structure. With increasing interdependence between the countries of Europe, and the increasing importance of EC directives on fiscal matters, the impact of tax will certainly remain one of the most important elements in a business strategy; businesses must be aware of this and should be prepared to take appropriate professional advice.

No chapter is self-sufficient. For example the advantages of being able to raise capital are discussed in the chapters on finance and organizational structure and the problem of insurance for professional and employers' liability is considered at appropriate points as it arises. Thus the book itself mirrors the Business in Context model of inter-dependent relationships. If this book helps students to appreciate this role of law in business, then it will have achieved its objective.

Comparative treatment table

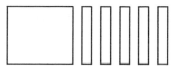

Because the law content of this book is presented in a format designed to illustrate the series model Business in Context and does not follow the usual order of a straightforward legal textbook it was thought useful to offer a table showing where the so-called traditional elements of a business studies law text could be found. Within the book most topics commonly covered by a business law course will be found, perhaps with some others less often discussed.

Nature of law	Chapter 1
Sources of law	Chapter 1
Administration	Chapter 1
Contract	
Offer and acceptance	Chapter 2
Consideration	Chapter 2
Terms	Chapter 2
Mistake	Chapter 2
Misrepresentation	Chapter 2
Restraint of trade	Chapter 4
Breach	Chapter 2
Remedies	Chapter 2
Tort	
General defences	Chapter 2
Negligence	Chapter 2
Nuisance	Chapter 5
Occupier's liability	Chapter 5
Vicarious liability	Chapter 5
Passing-off	Chapter 4
Consumer law	
Sale of goods	Chapter 6
Product liability	Chapter 5
Supply of goods	Chapter 6
Consumer credit	Chapter 6
Trade descriptions	Chapter 6
Business organizations	
Partnerships	Chapter 3
Companies	Chapters 3 and 8
Employment law	

Recruitment	Chapter 7
Making the contract	Chapter 7
Terms	Chapter 7
Dismissal	Chapter 7
Redundancy	Chapter 7
Safety at work	Chapters 4 and 5
Employee inventions	Chapter 4
Trade unions and industrial relations	Chapter 7
Intellectual property	
Patents	Chapter 4
Copyright	Chapter 4
Trade marks	Chapter 4
Insurance	Chapter 8

The legal background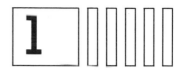

Introduction

Most aspects of life are governed by law, and business is no exception. There is no generally accepted definition of 'law' – in fact its meaning may vary with its context – but to most people 'law' connotes a body or set of rules. These rules not only proscribe certain kinds of conduct by rendering them criminal (imposing a penalty or punishment where the rules are broken) but also, equally important for business, provide an enabling mechanism to allow the achievement of desired business objectives. For example, rules define how to make a legally binding contract, how to set up a new company, or how to register a patent. The only penalty for failure to follow the rules is failure to achieve business objectives.

Any business in determining its strategy must be guided by commercial considerations. In translating the strategy into day-to-day objectives a knowledge of the relevant law is essential both (a) to minimize the risk of breaking the criminal law, with its attendant penal sanctions and potential bad publicity, and (b) to achieve the objectives in the most cost-effective way. The use of tax planning is an obvious example.

The law in England has developed continuously – without major foreign interference or take-over – since the Norman Conquest and before. The range of interests which it has been concerned to balance (Key concept 1.1) has varied enormously in that time.

The potential list might include: *Rival landowners/neighbours*; *Crown/State* v. *People*; *Business* v. *Consumers*; *Employers* v. *Employees*; *Landlords* v. *Tenants*; *Business* v. *Environment*.

From this it can be seen that the law is essentially fluid. In this chapter we will try briefly to lay the essential groundwork by addressing the questions: 'Where does law come from?' 'How and why does it change?' 'How and by whom is it enforced?' 'How is it useful to business?' and 'How much does it cost?'.

One of the strategic purposes of the law may be said to be the creation of a balance between competing interests. The traditional depiction of justice by a pair of scales, or balance, illustrates this very clearly.

KEY CONCEPT 1.1

LAW AS THE BALANCE BETWEEN COMPETING INTERESTS

These questions are central to the Business in Context model as explained in the Series Editors' Foreword – which guides the layout of this book. In Chapters 1 and 2 we deal with the environmental aspects of law pertaining to business by examining those influences which have led to the development of law and the legal process. We will examine the various roles played by the state, the European Community and society in general. In so doing we will develop a clearer idea about how laws are administered in the United Kingdom and also how they change. An issue we will raise here is the way businesses are not simply passive recipients of the law, but will actively seek to influence and change those laws which affect their operation, thus illustrating the two-way process of influence in our model. In Chapter 3 we examine the organizational context of business by focusing upon those laws and legal processes pertaining to the setting up and administration of a business as a legal entity. Chapters 4–8 concentrate on the functional areas of business by examining those laws and legal processes which cover business activity and management strategy related to the innovation, production, marketing, personnel and finance functions. The layout of this book traces the path of the Business in Context model from the outer to the inner levels.

Classification of law

In order to understand the legal system as it regulates business activity it is important to appreciate that, whilst there are several ways to classify the law, there are two fundamental classifications relevant to business.

Public law and private law

Public law consists of those fields of law which are primarily concerned with the state itself, and includes criminal law, constitutional, and administrative and social welfare law. Private law is that body of rules primarily concerned with the rights and duties of individuals towards each other. The areas of law which most affect business transactions, such as those concerning contracts, tort, commerce, employment, etc. are part of private law (Figure 1.1).

Tort A tort is a civil wrong which arises independently of agreement and which is normally remediable by an action for damages.

Contract A contract is an agreement which the law will enforce.

Figure 1.1 Classification of English Law.

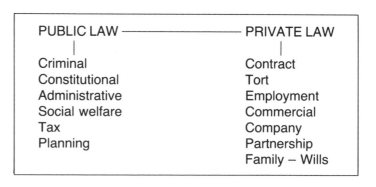

```
PUBLIC LAW ──────────── PRIVATE LAW
     │                        │
Criminal                 Contract
Constitutional           Tort
Administrative           Employment
Social welfare           Commercial
Tax                      Company
Planning                 Partnership
                         Family – Wills
```

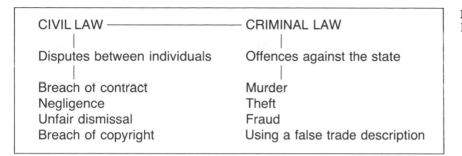

Figure 1.2 Classification of English Law.

Civil law and criminal law

Civil law is concerned with an individual's private rights and duties, whereas criminal law deals with relations between the state and the individual (Figure 1.2). If a criminal prosecution is successful the person found guilty will be punished, by imprisonment, probation, fine, etc. If a civil action is successful, the person bringing the action (the plaintiff) will normally be compensated in damages by the losing party (the defendant), although there are other equitable remedies which are available, such as an order for specific performance, an injunction, or a declaration. We will deal with each of these in turn.

An order of specific performance is an order of the court directing the defendant to carry out the agreed terms of a contract. It will not be granted unless damages (the normal remedy for breach of contract) are inappropriate, nor will it be granted for ordinary items of commerce for which substitutes could readily be purchased. As an example if X contracts to sell Y a particular orginal painting and then refuses to deliver, an order for specific performance could be granted. Damages will not suffice, Y wants that painting and there is no other available for purchase. However, the remedy is not a right, it is an equitable remedy and therefore at the court's discretion. Orders of specific performance will not be granted to enforce personal contracts, such as where Z agreed to sing at a concert but then refused after all the tickets has been sold, because the court is unable to supervise the performance, and even if they could insist that Z performed, they would have no way of ensuring that his or her performance would be of a suitable standard.

Injunctions are also equitable remedies at the discretion of the court. Examples include an order to stop making an unacceptable noise at a certain time (e.g. student discos interfering with neighbours' enjoyment of peaceful evenings at home by the television), or an order not to procure a breach of employment contract (by picketing a certain place of work and persuading the employees not to work).

A declaration is a discretionary court ruling on a point of law at the plaintiff's request usually clarifying the plaintiff's position or a disputed point of law, for example a ruling that a local authority had no legal authority to speculate with ratepayers' money, or that the plaintiff was the subject of sexual discrimination contrary to the Sex Discrimination Act 1975.

It is possible for one act to be both a civil and a criminal wrong. For example, if you take your car to a garage for repair and the garage proprietor steals it, then clearly a crime (theft) has been committed. Additionally the breach of contract by failure to repair according to the terms of the contract will be a civil wrong giving rise to an action for damages. Another example is where an employer's negligence in providing unsafe plant for use by his employee at work causes injury to the employee: the employee will be able to sue in civil law for compensation for his or her injury, and at the same time, the employer may be prosecuted in criminal law for breach of the Health and Safety at Work Act 1974.

The criminal law extends from murder, treason and rape to failing to sign your driving licence, sounding the horn while the car is at rest or conversing with a bus driver.

Likewise, civil law is very wide ranging and still growing! The most important areas within its scope, as far as business is concerned, are contract law, the sale of goods and services, the provision of credit and hire purchase, contracts of employment and leases between landlord and tenant. Civil law also includes the law of tort (Chapter 2), property law, the law of succession, trusts and family law (Figure 1.2).

Where does law come from?

There are many ways of considering this but for simplification there are four main sources of law: custom, precedent, legislation and the European Community. We will deal with each in turn. Custom is the earliest source of law and the European Community the most recent and increasingly important.

Custom

Over the years the established standards became accepted not just as desirable but mandatory of the development of voluntary Codes of Conduct in many industries today. Under the English legal system each time a case comes to court for a decision the judgment of the court forms a pattern or precedent for a later case covering the same legal points. Elementary rules of justice require that like cases be decided alike. Thus an adjudication on the basis of what is customary (Key concept 1.2) becomes an established rule of law or precedent. For example in *Fisher* v. *Bell* (1961) a prosecution was brought under the Offensive Weapons Act 1959 alleging that the defendant in displaying a flick-knife in his shop window had 'offered for sale' an offensive weapon contrary to the provisions of the Act. The prosecution

KEY CONCEPT 1.2	Historically the earliest source of law is custom. Much of what we loosely call commercial or mercantile law owes its origin to *custom*, i.e. the market place developed its own form of what today we would call 'self-regulation'.
CUSTOM AS A SOURCE OF LAW	

failed on the ground that no case had been made out. By mercantile custom displaying goods in a shop window does not amount to offering them for sale but merely to an invitation to the public to treat, i.e. to come in and make an offer which the shopkeeper could then either accept or reject.

It is clear that this rule was widely appreciated by shopkeepers although it was unwritten and no formal source of authority could be produced.

Precedent

Precedent or judge-made law is thus a second source of law. If the facts of a case are similar to an earlier one, particularly one decided by a superior court, then the rule laid down in the previous decision (the *ratio decidendi*) ought to be followed. Where a judge makes a statement of legal principle which is not strictly applicable to the facts before him, the statement is said to be *obiter dicta*. Obiter dicta are not part of the precedent (Key concept 1.3), though they are often of 'persuasive precedent'.

The doctrine of precedent or *stare decisis* is the technical name for the rule that judges must follow the decisions and principles of law declared by superior or earlier courts.	KEY CONCEPT 1.3 **THE DOCTRINE OF PRECEDENT**

The doctrine of precedent (*stare decisis*) depends upon a clear hierarchy of courts and a reliable system of law reporting. The binding nature of a decision works down through the court system (Figure 1.6).

In exactly the same way as a manager making a decision uses past experience to forecast the likely outcome of his or her projections, so a litigant looks to previous decisions for guidance as to the future. Just as it would be seen to be grossly unfair for two employees guilty of the same misconduct to be treated differently – at least without very clearly stated reasons – so it would be inherently unacceptable for the courts to treat similar cases differently without distinguishing carefully their reasons.

This system of custom-based rules recognized and applied by the judges to generations of cases, distinguishing one from another where necessary, is called common law (The Telex: Case study 1.1). The United Kingdom has exported its Common Law system (Key concept 1.4) of pragmatic law-making/adapting to most of the Commonwealth countries and ex-colonies (including the United States of America) though many of these countries additionally have some form of written code providing a Constitution.

Just as any business which has in-house rules or conditions of trade which must normally be adhered to strictly sometimes finds it necessary to introduce a little managerial discretion to deal with a situation which does not easily fit into the established rules, so the law requires some degree of flexibility to ensure that as far as possible justice – or the right balance – is attained in a case where strict application of the rules would not achieve this effect. This is equity.

Ratio decidendi This is a technical phrase meaning the principle or reason for the decision: this portion of the judgement is binding in similar cases which may be subsequently tried by inferior courts.

Obiter dicta These are words delivered by a judge which are not essential to his or her decision, and are not therefore binding on inferior courts.

Stare decisis The doctrine of *stare decisis* is the technical name given to the rule that judges must follow the precedents and principles of law declared by superior courts.

CASE STUDY 1.1

THE TELEX

Entores Ltd, metal brokers in London, entered into discussions with Miles Far East Corporation in Amsterdam. Negotiations were conducted by Telex. Eventually an offer was made by Entores Ltd to Miles Far East Corporation which Miles Far East Corporation accepted. According to the established rules of precedent, based on custom, a contract is complete when an offer is accepted. In a case where the parties are at a distance and the post is used, acceptance is taken to be complete when a correctly addressed and stamped letter is consigned to the Post Office. The Court in London had here to rule on when an agreement made by Telex became complete – essentially whether on *receipt* of the letter of agreement by the offeror or on despatch by the offeree? In the absence of any precise precedent, Telex being distinguishable from letter post, the court ruled on the basis of commercial convenience in favour of receipt. There is, as far as we know, no precedent for FAX messages but presumably custom would now dictate the same answer.

NB   Realizing the drawbacks of the postal system many businesses, knowing the law, choose to make it a condition of their offers that acceptance is NOT effective until *received*, thus avoiding the inconvenience of not knowing and shifting the risk of postal delay or loss to the sender.

(*Entores Ltd* v. *Miles Far East Corporation* (1952))

KEY CONCEPT 1.4

COMMON LAW

Common Law means law based on unwritten custom or judge-made decisions as opposed to a system based on written rules or exhaustive codes. Such a code-based system is called a Civil Law system. Most of Continental Europe uses civil law based originally on the old Roman Law Code.

Parallel with the customary or common law rules there grew up rules of equity (Key concept 1.5) where special relief was asked for, not as of right but as seemed appropriate in all the circumstances (Figure 1.3). Originally, equity was the prerogative of the King, dispensed through his Chancellor and later the Court of Chancery.

Today, equitable relief may be sought in all courts but it is still discretionary and depends on the fair play of the plaintiff – 'He who comes to equity must come with clean hands'. Numerous illustrations of equitable relief will be found in the course of the book, e.g. the common law normally provides only monetary compensation by way of redress, and the provision of the remedies of specific performance – an order to a contracting party actually to perform his or her contract – or an injunction, an order to stop a threatened or continuing wrong, e.g. an illegal strike or publication of a damaging libel, is an addition of equity.

Very often for a business the ability to *stop* a strike before it happens or to prevent a breach of copyright or confidence before the damage occurs is

> Equity in a literal sense means fairness; in a technical sense those rules of law derived from petitions to the King or his Chancellor for relief from the inadequacy or harshness of the Common Law on the grounds of conscience.

KEY CONCEPT 1.5

EQUITY

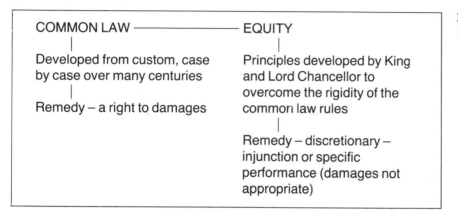

Figure 1.3 Classification of English Law.

far more valuable than claiming damages of an indeterminate amount from an errant or impecunious defendant after the event. To understand what remedies are available and the conditions necessary to secure them is an invaluable tool.

Legislation

The third source of law is *legislation*, or the rules enacted by Parliament in the form of Statutes (Figure 1.4). Today most new law is made by Parliament. One of the characteristics of the second half of this century has been the growth of legislation, particularly in the field of business regulation. Unlike judicial decisions which are haphazard, in the sense that the courts have no choice over the issues that come up before them for decision, legislation epitomizes the strategic use of the law. Statutes are passed to implement defined government policy often after prolonged discussion and debate. At this point the role of the parliamentary lobbyist becomes crucial, the ability of business to influence the future course of the law depends firstly on knowing what is proposed or projected and secondly being able to bring pressure to bear on the outcome. The ability of the City of London to persuade the government to permit self-regulation of the Stock Exchange rather than submit to external controls is a recent example of such success.

The purpose of statute can be:

☐ To introduce new law, e.g. The Transport Act 1981 which introduced the compulsory wearing of seat belts in cars; or

☐ To repeal existing law, e.g. The Trade Union and Labour Relations Act 1974 which repealed in its entirety the controversial Industrial Relations Act 1971; or

Figure 1.4 Enactment of a Statute.

1. 1st Reading — Formal introduction of the Bill – no debate.

2. 2nd Reading — Examination and debate of principles behind the Bill. This debate is, in theory, according to Erskine May (the leading expert in parliamentary procedures), 'the most important stage through which the Bill is required to pass; for its whole principle is then at issue, and is affirmed or denied by a vote of the House'.

3. Committee stage — All party committee examines Bill in detail, clause by clause, and re-assembles it.

4. Report stage — Report back to the whole House of the changes made.

5. 3rd reading — The last opportunity for the House to reject the Bill before it passes to the House of Lords, where it goes through substantially the same stages again, returning for further consideration of any amendments made by the House of Lords.

Final stage
Royal Assent — This is a pure formality today, the usual procedure being the Speaker and the Lord Chancellor notifying the assent in each House. The words of the Royal Assent are 'la reyne le veult' (for Public Bills), and 'la reyne remercie ses bon sujets, accepte leur bene volence et ainsi le veult' (for Financial Bills). Once Royal Assent has been given the Bill becomes an Act of Parliament.

☐ To consolidate various Acts into one for the sake of simplicity, e.g. The Employment Protection (Consolidation) Act 1978, which drew together all Acts and Regulations concerning the employment of individuals. A consolidating Statute also repeals existing law; or

☐ To implement government policy in the area of business competition and economy, e.g. The Telecommunications Act 1984; or

☐ To implement obligations entered into by the government under international convention or treaty, e.g. The Data Protection Act 1984.

Parliament is the supreme law-maker in the UK and once an Act has received Royal Assent the judiciary cannot challenge its validity, they must implement it.

The government of the day, with a working majority, will dominate law-making in Parliament. Manifesto promises may become Green or White Papers, which in turn may become Bills. Bills can either be Government Bills or Private Member's Bills. The majority of Bills, however, originate not from manifesto promises but from government departments.

Normally a Bill is first introduced into the House of Commons. It then has to pass through five stages before passing to the House of Lords and receiving Royal Assent before it becomes an Act of Parliament. This pass-age from introduction to Royal Assent is detailed in Figure 1.4.

Private Member's Bills have to go through the same stages, though they usually fall by the wayside during the Second Reading, because most are not supported by the Government. Each year there is a ballot of those MPs who wish to introduce Bills and the top twenty names are guaranteed time to introduce their Bill.

Pressure groups, such as the Consumers' Association, National Caravan Council, British Institute of Management, etc. bring pressure upon MPs, especially during the private members' ballot, although they also represent their members' views to all MPs during the course of the year. The activity of business as a pressure group is a good illustration of the Business in Context model in action. It is not just the state that sets laws for business to follow, but businesses themselves attempt to influence the law-making activity of the state. Influences therefore flow both ways across the various levels of the model.

Sectional or interest groups	Promotional or 'cause' groups
CBI	RSPCA
BIM	Howard League for Penal Reform
NFU	Lord's Day Observance Society
The Consumers' Association	NSPCC

CBI Confederation of British Industry.

BIM British Institute of Management.

NFU National Farmers' Union.

RSPCA Royal Society for Prevention of Cruelty to Animals.

NSPCC National Society for Prevention of Cruelty to Children.

The degree of influence wielded by any particular pressure group will vary according to whether we have a Conservative or Labour Government. The TUC will usually have more influence on a Labour Government, and the CBI more influence on a Conservative Government. Many pressure groups even sponsor their own MPs to ensure their members' views are well represented in Parliament.

Delegated legislation

Modern government is very complex, and with the increased amount of social and economic change in the past years, Parliament has had to resort more and more to 'delegated legislation'. 'Delegated legislation' is where Parliament delegates legislative duties to a variety of nominees: for example Secretaries of State who enact Statutory Instruments (SIs) to cover matters handled by their departments, or completing a scheme of legislation; for example: S.2(4) Health and Safety at Work Act 1974:

> Regulations made by the Secretary of State may provide for the appoint-ment in prescribed cases by recognised trade unions (within the meaning of the regulations) of safety representatives from amongst the employees, and those representatives shall represent the employees in consultations with the employers ... and shall have such other functions as may be prescribed.

The Secretary of State did in fact draft the regulations and they are now in force as The Safety Representatives and Safety Committees Regulations 1977 (SI 1977 No. 500).

Local authorities can pass byelaws for the control of their areas (Figure 1.5, for example), e.g. relating to planning controls, parking, etc., and various other bodies have power to lay down rules to govern themselves and their members; e.g. The Law Society, The General Medical Council, etc. This form of delegated legislation requires the consent of the appropriate Minister of State.

Delegated legislation has considerable advantages:

☐ A great saving on Parliamentary time.
☐ Greater flexibility which makes it easier to respond quickly to necessary change.
☐ Speed in emergency situations.
☐ Increased technicality of legislation, beyond the expertise of most MPs, can be dealt with by experts in a particular field.
☐ Local knowledge is required to make useful local byelaws.

Figure 1.5 Cambridgeshire County Council Byelaws.

Byelaws with respect to the employment of children, under the Children and Young Persons Acts, 1933 to 1963 (as amended by the Education Acts, 1944 to 1976 and the Children Act, 1972).

Employment of Children

Interpretation of terms

1. For the purposes of these byelaws
   (a) The expression 'child' means a person who is not over compulsory school age.
   (b) The expression 'guardian' in relation to a child includes any person who, in the opinion of the Court having cognizance of any case in relation to the child or in which the child is concerned, has for the time being the charge of or control over the child.
   (c) A person who assists in a trade or occupation carried on for profit shall be deemed to be employed notwithstanding that he or she receives no reward for his or her labour.
   (d) The expression 'local authority' means the Country Council of the Administrative Country of Cambridgeshire.

   Notes

   (i) A child whose 16th birthday falls between 1st September and 31st January (both dates inclusive) ceases to be of compulsory school age at the end of the Spring Term which includes such month of January.
   (ii) A child whose 16th birthday occurs between 1st February and 31st August, (both dates inclusive) ceases to be of compulsory school age on the Friday before the last Monday in May.

Prohibited employments

2. No child shall be employed in any of the following occupations:
    (a) In commercial (but not domestic) kitchens.
    (b) In clubs licensed for gambling.
    (c) In or in connection with the sale of intoxicating liquors, except in places where such liquors are sold exclusively in sealed vessels.
    (d) In cinemas, dance halls, discotheques, or theatres or other places of public entertainment except when performances are entirely by children.
    (e) In collecting or sorting rags or refuse other than tidying or sweeping up.
    (f) In any slaughter house.
    (g) In or in connection with any racing course or track or other place where any like sport is carried on, or as an assistant in any business conducted therein.
    (h) In any agricultural work involving heavy strain or danger.
    (i) In the delivery of fuel oils.
    (j) Employment at any machine prescribed as dangerous in an order made under section 19 of the Offices, Shops and Railways Premises Act, 1963.
    (k) In outside window cleaning more than 3 metres above ground level.

    ### Note

    By Section 18 (i) (f) of the Children and Young Persons Act 1933 no child may be employed to lift, carry or move anything so heavy as to be likely to cause injury to him.

Regulation of employment

3. No child under the age of 13 shall be employed: provided that a child who has attained the age of 10 may be employed by his parent or guardian under the direct supervision of a responsible person in light agricultural or horticultural work but only on the agricultural or horticultural holding of such parent or guardian.

4. No child shall be employed on school days for more than two hours a day and this employment will be limited to either one hour between 7.00 a.m. and 8.30 a.m. and one hour between end of school and 7.00 p.m. or two hours between end of school and 7.00 p.m. Employment of children who work both morning and evenings must be confined to the same employer.

5. Employment on Sundays shall be limited to two hours between 7.00 a.m. and 11.00 a.m.

6. On non-school week days, i.e. Saturdays and week days during holidays employment of children under 15, shall be limited to a

maximum of 5 hours net a day and subject to a maximum of 25 hours per week. Employment of children aged 15 and over shall be limited to a maximum of 8 hours net a day and subject to a maximum of 35 hours per week. The hours worked net are exclusive of intervals of 15 minutes or more for rest.

7. For harvest work during harvest periods in school holidays only, children over 13 and under 15 may work a maximum of 8 hours a day subject to a maximum of 25 hours a week and children aged 15 and over to work a maximum of 8 hours a day, subject to a maximum of 35 hours a week.

8. No child shall be employed for more than four hours continuously without a period of one hour or more for rest and recreation.

9. No child shall be employed in any work out of doors unless he or she is suitably shod and is suitably clad for protection against inclement weather.

10. Where a bicycle is used in connection with the child's employment the employer shall see that the bicycle is kept in good working order and is suitable to the child.

11. No child taking part in any entertainment in pursuance of a licence under Section 37 of the Children and Young Persons Act, 1963 shall be employed on the day or days of, or the day following, such entertainment, in any other employment.

Administrative arrangements

12. Except where children are employed under the provisions of byelaw 3 or byelaw 7 above no child shall be employed in the Administrative County of Cambridgeshire except subject to the following conditions:

    (a) The employer shall send a written notification before employment begins to the Local Authority in a form prescribed by the Authority, endorsed by the signature of the parent or guardian and Head of the school at which the child is a registered pupil to indicate their assent to the proposed employment, stating the employer's name and address, the name and address and date of birth of the child, the occupation in which, and the place at which it is proposed to employ the child and the times at which the employment will begin and end.

    (b) No child may be employed unless he has been granted an authorised permit issued by the Authority after consideration of such notification. The child must lodge it with his employer. The permit must be produced by the employer for inspection when required to do so by a police officer or any authorised officer of the Local Authority.

    (c) The Local Authority shall enter on the permit the name and address and date of birth of the child, the occupation in which, and the times between which the employment of the child is approved.

The times so entered shall be such as the employer may choose, provided they are such as are allowed by these byelaws, and they may be altered by the Local Authority from time to time on the application of the employer.

(d) A child to whom a permit has been issued in accordance with the provisions of these byelaws shall be employed only within the times entered thereon by the Local Authority.

13. The proposed employment of a child shall be notified by the Local Authority to the Specialist in Community Medicine – Child Health for the Area. Any permit shall be refused, withdrawn or amended if at any time in the opinion of the Specialist in Community Medicine-Child Health such employment is considered to be prejudicial to the health or physical development of the child.

14. Any permit may be withdrawn or amended at any time if in the opinion of the Chief Education Officer either by reason of late arrival at, or absence from, school or any other reason such employment is likely to render the child unfit to obtain benefit from his or her education.

15. These byelaws do not apply in the case of work experience under the Education (Work Experience) Act 1973.

Note: Penalties

Section 21 of the Children and Young Persons Act 1933 provides: If a person is employed in contravention of any of the provisions of Section 18 of the Act or of the provisions of any byelaw made thereunder, the employer and any person (other than the person employed) to whose act or default the contravention if attributable shall be liable on summary conviction to a fine not exceeding £20.00 or in the case of a second or subsequent offence not exceeding £50.00.

Revocations

The byelaws made by the Cambridgeshire County Council and confirmed by the Secretary of State on 25th June, 1955, by the Isle of Ely County Council and confirmed by the Secretary of State on 12th November, 1951, by the Huntingdon County Council and confirmed by the Secretary of State on 24th May, 1951, and by the Peterborough County Council and confirmed by the Secretary of State 15th March, 1955, are hereby revoked.

The Common Seal of Cambridgeshire
Country Council was hereunto affixed
on the   day of
                                1978 in the
presence of

County Secretary

There are considerable controls over the use and abuse of delegated legislation. Parliament can revoke the grant of power or it can legislate to change bad law. Most forms of statutory instruments have to 'lie on the table' in the House of Commons for 40 days, during which time they can be challenged. There is a Joint Scrutiny Committee which has responsibility for keeping an eye on the use of the delegated authority and drawing the attention of Parliament to any controversial measures.

Parliament can also call the responsible minister to account at Question Time where he or she will have to answer for their department's activities. Finally the courts are able to veto any item of delegated legislation by ruling it has been drafted outside the limits of the delegated power (*ultra vires*).

Ultra vires   A thing is done by a Government Minister or a public authority or a company *ultra vires* when it is not within the scope of the powers entrusted to such authority or company.

Statutory interpretation

If a dispute arises between two parties as to the exact meaning of the words of a statute, settlement of that dispute can only be brought about by a court action, and the judge will need to interpret and construe the words used by Parliament to ascertain the true intention of the legislature. Judges will, in these circumstances, follow the rules of statutory interpretation evolved over centuries by the courts (The Estate Agents: Case study 1.2).

CASE STUDY 1.2

THE ESTATE AGENTS: THE RULES OF STATUTORY INTERPRETATION

Porter was an estate agent. In accordance with normal business practice he erected 'For Sale' or 'To Let' boards outside the properties whose owners he represented, to advertise both the availability of the property and his own services. Under the Town and County Planning Act 1971, and 1984 Regulations made under them, the consent of the local planning authority is normally required for the display of advertisements. However, the regulations provide for a number of cases where such express consent is dispensed with and is deemed to have been given. Breach of the regulations is a criminal offence, punishable by the magistrates with a fine. One of the cases where consent is not required, because 'deemed' to have been given, is the display at a property of a single 'For Sale' board, provided it is within permitted size limits. Mr. Porter duly erected his board outside the property and waited for customers. However, the customers did not instantly materialize and the would-be vendor instructed a second agent to seek a purchaser. The second agent then erected his board. Thus two boards were displayed outside the same premises. A prosecution of both agents for breach of planning regulations resulted in both being fined. However, Mr. Porter appealed unsuccessfully to the Divisional Court and subsequently to the House of Lords on the meaning of the Regulations.

The Regulations, it was argued, could be interpreted in a number of ways:

☐ They permitted one board per advertiser, not one per house.
☐ No offence is committed unless the defendant *knew* two boards were displayed.

□ Deemed consent is given to one advertisment, therefore if there are two in respect of the same sale, there is no deemed consent in respect of either or them.

□ Deemed consent is given to one advertisement, that is the first to be displayed. Such deemed consent continues even if further unauthorized boards are erected.

The House of Lords chose the last of these, while accepting Parliament's desire to 'reduce the unsightly proliferation of estate agents' boards that now deface many streets' (Lord Griffiths at p. 1049), their Lordships held the regulations had to be interpreted to avoid an unjust rule being introduced by delegated legislation without the express will of Parliament. To hold that a criminal offence had been committed by the first agent, because another person over whom he had no control acted unlawfully in erecting an unauthorized second board, would be undesirable.

Mr. Porter succeeded in his appeal and was awarded costs.

(*Porter* v. *Honey* [1988] 3 All E.R. 1045 House of Lords)

Where the words of a statute are clear and unambiguous when read as a whole, the courts must apply the statute. The court should refer to the wording of the statute (together with its Schedules, if any) and all words and phrases must be interpreted according to any definitions contained in the statute itself and in the Interpretation Act 1978.

A good example of a detailed definition section is contained in the Sex Discrimination Act 1975: S.82(1).

S.38(1) Sex Discrimination Act 1975 states:

It is unlawful to publish or cause to be published an advertisement which indicates, or might reasonably be understood as indicating, an intention . . . (to discriminate)

Will a handwritten postcard on a farm gate stating 'Strong man required for heavy farm labouring' be unlawful? Will the card be an 'advertisement' within the meaning of S.38(1)? S.82(1) provides:

'advertisement' includes every form of advertisement, whether to the public or not, and whether in a newspaper or other publication, by television or radio, by display of notices, signs, labels, showcards or goods, by distribution of samples, circulars, catalogues, price lists or other material, by exhibition of pictures, models or films, or in any other way, and references to the publishing of advertisements shall be construed accordingly.

This example clearly demonstrates that a card pinned to a farm gate will be an 'advertisement' for the purposes of the Act, and it is clearly therefore an unlawful advertisement.

If there is ambiguity or uncertainty, however, the court will have to refer to extrinsic aids such as the long title, headings, side notes or other statutes to discover the 'intention of Parliament'. Over the years the courts have developed a clumsy collection of so called 'rules' of statutory interpretation, including the following:

(a)   The literal rule

The intention of Parliament is found in the ordinary and natural meaning of the words used, and they should be applied strictly and literally. This rule was applied in *Whiteley* v. *Chappell* (1868) where the statute in question made it a criminal offence to pretend to be 'any person entitled to vote' at an election. The accused had masqueraded as someone whose name was still on the list but who had died. The 'literal rule' applied here disclosed no offence, because the dead person was no longer 'entitled to vote'!

The Law Commission have criticized this rule on the grounds that it assumes an unattainable perfection in draftsmanship. The literal rule will not be applied if it produces a manifest absurdity.

(b)   The golden rule

This covers the case where the words of a statute are capable of two or more meanings. By the golden rule a court must adopt the interpretation which produces the least absurd result.

For example, in *R.* v. *Allen* (1872) L.R. 1 C.C.R. 367 the accused was charged with bigamy, contrary to the Offences Against The Person Act 1861. S.57 stated: '... Whosoever, being married, shall marry any other person ...'. In the arguments the point was made that, marriage being a change of legal status, a person cannot 'marry' whilst married because he is already married. The court felt able to interpret the phrase 'shall marry' as meaning 'go through a ceremony of marriage'. The accused was therefore convicted after the golden rule was applied.

(c)   The mischief rule

It is a rule that a judge may look at the mischief covered by the Act to discover the intention of Parliament. In *Smith* v. *Hughes* (1960) the court had to consider the interpretation of the Street Offences Act 1959, which made it an offence for a common prostitute to loiter or solicit in a street or public place for her professional purposes. In this case the ladies were soliciting from a first floor window, and were clearly not in the street. Parker C.J. said:

> Everybody knows that this was an Act intended to clean up the streets, to enable people to walk along the streets without being molested or solicited by common prostitutes. Viewed in that way, it can matter little whether the prostitute is soliciting while in the street or is standing in a doorway or on a balcony, or at a window, or whether the window is shut or open or half-open. In each case her solicitation is projected to and addressed to somebody walking in the street.

The mischief rule was applied and it was held that soliciting from behind a window was 'soliciting in the street', i.e. solicitation takes place where it is received by the client.

(d)   Other rules of interpretation

The further rules of interpretation are usually expressed as presumptions or on the basis that Parliament must be presumed not to have intended to make certain kinds of law except by express provision:

- ☐ *Expressio unius, exclusio alterius* – 'what is included, excludes that which is not', e.g. if particular words like 'school' and 'museum' are not followed by general words like 'other buildings', then other buildings will be excluded.
- ☐ *Ejusdem generis* – 'of the same kind'. Where general words do follow particular ones, they must be interpreted to include only things 'of the same kind', e.g. the 1853 Betting Act, S.1 prohibited the keeping of a 'house, office, room or other place' for betting purposes. In *Powell* v. *Kempton Park Racecourse Co.* (1899) the House of Lords held that Tattersall's ring at the racecourse was not 'another place' within the meaning of the Act, as the words 'house, office, room' created a 'genus' of indoor places within which a racecourse, being outdoor, did not fall.
- ☐ There is a presumption against altering the existing case law and statute law; thus if an Act is inconsistent with a previous Act, the two must be construed and reconciled.
- ☐ There is a presumption that a statute does not bind the Crown, for example Crown property in the form of NHS hospitals, was not subject to health and hygiene legislation until expressly included.
- ☐ There is a presumption against retrospective operation of a statute.
- ☐ There is a presumption that a statute will apply to the whole of the UK.
- ☐ There is a presumption that an owner will not be deprived of his or her property.
- ☐ There is a presumption that strict liability offences will not be created.

These rules may seem technical and far removed from the needs of a business but when so much activity is now governed by statute, or regulations made under them, a correct understanding of their meaning and application is vital.

Rules on interpretation of statutes are necessary because it is often very difficult to present a rule in language which is clear, unambiguous and intelligible to the layman or woman. Equally in a business context it is often difficult to draft an agreement or contract which is incapable of being misinterpreted. It is a great advantage to be aware first of all of the problem of communication and secondly of the objective rules which should be applied to resolve disputes.

Strict liability This is liability without proof of wrongful intent or negligence on the part of the defendant. The doing of the act itself is sufficient to attract liability, no matter that the wrongdoer did not intend to break the law.

The European Community

The most recent source of UK law is the European Community. The UK became a member of the European Community on 1 January 1973 by acceding to the Treaty of Rome originally signed by the six founder member states in 1957. Under the European Communities Act 1972 all the obligations and laws made or to be made under the Treaty of Rome were directly incorporated into English law with a provision that where there is conflict

CASE STUDY 1.3

EQUAL TREATMENT

Article 119 of the Treaty of Rome requires that men and women should receive equal pay for equal work. EC Directives have extended this to cover conditions of work including incidental benefits such as travel concessions for employees. British Rail's policy was to allow their concession to widows of male employees but not to widowers of their female employees. Mrs. Garland challenged this policy. Under the UK legislation then in force, the Sex Discrimination Act 1975, provisions relating to death and retirement were specifically excluded from the requirements to provide equal treatment. Despite this exception Mrs. Garland was held entitled to equal treatment under the Community provision which had to prevail.

(BREL 1983 (1982) I.R.L.R. III E.C.J. (1982) I.R.L.R. 257 (H.L.))

CASE STUDY 1.4

THE AGE OF RETIREMENT

Miss Enid Marshall was employed as a senior dietician by the health authority. In common with other UK employers, the authority operated a retirement policy of age 60 for women and 65 for men. By agreement Miss Marshall continued working until she was 62 and was then dismissed. She challenged the legality of the company's policy in the Industrial Tribunal on the grounds that it constituted unlawful discrimination on the grounds of sex. The Industrial Tribunal found she had no case under the Sex Discrimination Act 1975 but could claim directly under the Equal Treatment Directive. The case went to appeal and application was made to the European Court in Luxembourg for a preliminary ruling on the effect of the Community directive requiring equal treatment. The Court held the directive was not binding on individual citizens/companies until implemented by national laws of member states but *was* binding directly on member states. Since the health authority was effectively an arm of the UK Government the authority was bound and was therefore in breach. The case was remitted to the Industrial Tribunal who applied Community Law and found in favour of Miss Marshall, awarding her damages within the limits provided. A subsequent appeal by Miss Marshall against the statutory limit of damages provided by the Sex Discrimination Act 1975 has also succeeded. The Court applying European Community law again, held that the limit of damages available broke the Treaty requirement that adequate compensation be recoverable by individuals for breach of their Treaty rights.

Parliament has since amended UK law to conform with the European Community Directive. Under the Sex Discrimination Act 1986 it is now illegal for a firm to distinguish on the grounds of sex in its provision for a retirement age. This is notwithstanding the current provision of a state pension at age 60 for women and 65 for men. This is itself the subject of contention; clearly economic repercussions play a major part in the introduction of appropriate amendments.

(*Marshall* v. *Southampton and S.W. Hants Health Authority* (1986) 2 All E.R. 584) between Community law and UK law, Community law is to prevail (Equal Treatment: Case study 1.3; The Age of Retirement: Case study 1.4).

The Single European Act 1986 has since been agreed by all member states. This has amended the founding Treaty of Rome in particular by extending the original objectives of the Community and by increasing the use of majority voting.

(a) The organizational structure of the community

The Treaty of Rome set up four main Community institutions.

The Commission
This proposes Community policy and legislation. There are 17 Commissioners, appointed by the Community Governments, and they act, not as national delegates, but in the interests of the Community as a whole.

The Council
This is the Community's decision-making body. It agrees legislation on the basis of the proposals from the Commission and consists of Ministers from each member state, supported by various working groups and officials from member states.

The European Parliament
This is a directly elected body of 518 members, and under the EC Treaties its formal opinion is required on most proposals before they can be adopted by the Council. Members are elected for a period of five years.

The European Court of Justice
The court rules on the interpretation and application of Community laws. It has 13 judges, one from each Community country, and judgments are binding in each member state.

In addition to these four formal bodies regular meetings of Heads of State at so-called Euro Summits were recognized formally in the Single European Act 1986 as the European Council.

The European Council
The European Council consists of Heads of member states or Governments and the President of the Commission. It is required to meet at least twice a year. The European Council has no law-making power as such; it acts as a summit or board meeting to discuss long-term strategy and to resolve disputes.

(b) Executive powers of Community institutions

The Treaty of Rome having set out the agreed objectives of the Community and established its organizational structure gave powers to the various institutions to implement its policy by making regulations, issuing directives, taking decisions or making recommendations and delivering opinions.

These are terms of art and each has a different legal effect.

Regulations

These are binding and directly applicable in all member states. They do not have to be confirmed by national Parliaments in order to have binding legal effect. If there is a conflict between a regulation and existing national law, the regulation prevails.

Directives

These are instructions to member states to change their law within a stated period of time to give effect to the directive. In the UK directives are implemented either by statute or by delegated legislation, for example, the Transfer of Undertakings (Protection of Employment) Regulations 1981 which were passed to give effect to the EEC Directive 77/187, the 'Acquired Rights' Directive (The Age of Retirement: Case study 1.4).

Decisions

These are specific to particular parties and are binding in their entirety on those to whom they are addressed, whether member states, companies or individuals. Decisions imposing financial obligations are enforceable in national courts.

Recommendations and Opinions

These have no binding force but merely state the view of the institution that issues them (Figure 1.6).

Increasingly at all levels the impact of the European Community legislation will be felt, as Lord Denning said with some foresight in 1974 in *Bulmer* v. *Bollinger* (1974) 2 All E.R. at 1231. 'The Treaty is like an incoming tide. It flows into the estuaries and up the rivers. It cannot be held back.... We must speak and think of Community law, of Community rights and obligations and we must give effect to them'.

Business will be ever more aware of the advantages of common standards for their products as 1992 draws nearer, for example the Common European Safety Standard for Consumer goods and prospective common standards for food and labelling. The impact of the Community is also increasingly apparent on environmental issues, for example the purity of water and the discharge of industrial waste.

How and why does law change?

The law changes imperceptibly and dramatically! Each time a court decides a case by applying a precedent or previous judgment to a new situation or distinguishes a previous decision in the case before it, it almost imperceptibly adds to the body of the law by laying down another example to be taken into account. The illustration in the law of contract on when acceptance takes effect is a simple example of the process at work. The earliest rule based on custom is that acceptance takes effect when it is received; but in the case of posting, for commercial convenience and to ensure certainty, the courts found an exception to the basic rule and held that acceptance takes effect when it is posted; with the introduction of electronic mail the courts distinguished the postal rule and held that in the case of a telex

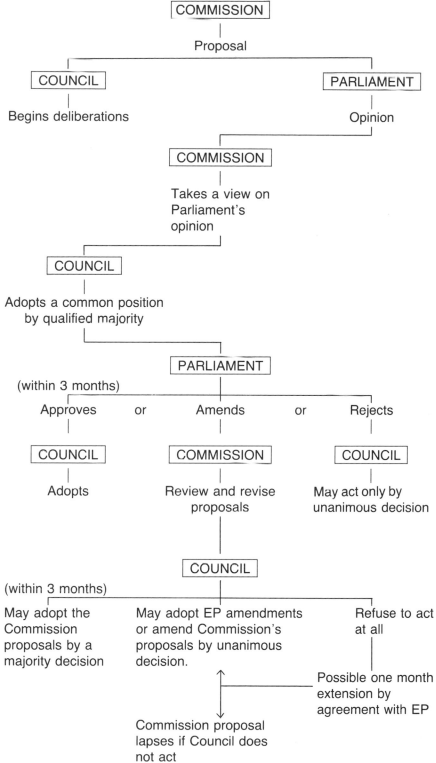

COMMISSION

Proposal

COUNCIL   PARLIAMENT

Begins deliberations   Opinion

COMMISSION

Takes a view on
Parliament's
opinion

COUNCIL

Adopts a common position
by qualified majority

PARLIAMENT

(within 3 months)

Approves   or   Amends   or   Rejects

COUNCIL   COMMISSION   COUNCIL

Adopts   Review and revise   May act only by
            proposals   unanimous decision

COUNCIL

(within 3 months)

May adopt the   May adopt EP amendments   Refuse to act
Commission   or amend Commission's   at all
proposals by a   proposals by unanimous
majority decision   decision.
                                                    Possible one month
                                                    extension by
                     Commission proposal   agreement with EP
                     lapses if Council does
                     not act

Figure 1.6 Community
Legislative Process.

commercial convenience dictates that acceptance is complete on receipt (Telex: Case study 1.1).

By contrast much law today is introduced by Parliament. Each statute, or sometimes individual sections of an Act, is brought into force on a specific day, e.g. the accession to the European Community took effect from 1 January 1973. From 1 August 1989 the lower limit to bring in the regulation imposed by the Consumer Credit Act 1974 was abolished.

The actual mechanism of judicial decision and the parliamentary process has been briefly outlined above. More detailed discussion of the workings of these bodies and of the European Community institutions should be sought in the further reading recommended at the end of this chapter.

Why the law changes is essentially the product of the environmental forces in which it operates. In principle the law referred to in this book is the law of England and Wales. For legal purposes Scotland is a separate jurisdiction although in some cases legislation embraces the whole of the United Kingdom. The accession to the Treaty of Rome and the consequent exposure to the far wider influences of Europe have already had a profound effect on the way the law has developed, not only in that specific rules have emanated from Brussels, but in the way our courts and Parliament have to consider the *purposes* of the Treaty at all times in carrying out their functions. The most literal forms of statutory interpretation to which we have become accustomed are having to give way to wider considerations in order to ensure that an interpretation given to a UK Statute does not break the Treaty of Rome (Case studies 1.3 and 1.4).

Social, political and economic reasons are all easily identifiable as factors instigating change. The ability of the Chancellor to manipulate business activity by (for example) credit controls, exchange rates, interest rates and taxation illustrates the point. In social terms the primary object of the European Community is to draw a balance between the interests of its citizens – the promotion of a fair competition policy, a workers' charter (so resisted by the present Government) and increasing concern for the pollution of the environment are all evidence of this. Straightforward Party politics is behind a large part of new law introduced each year, e.g. the introduction of the Community Charge (called the 'Poll Tax' by many of its opponents) to replace the rates, the reform of the education and NHS management systems and the current wave of industry privatizations.

The size of the Government majority in Parliament may cast some doubt on the value of debate but the ability of business – and other pressure groups – to lobby effectively is clearly proven. MPs are ultimately dependent on the electorate for their seats. A good political intelligence is an essential for any business to enable it to plan effectively.

How and by whom is it enforced?

There is clearly no point in having rules and regulations if they are not kept. The state provides an organized structure or hierarchy of courts to hear and resolve disputes if all else fails.

The settlement of disputes

Given the nature and complexity of business activity it is inevitable that disputes arise. Disputes may be between the two parties to a commercial contract, or between partners in a business, or between a business and the state; and it is essential in the interests of justice and the efficient use of economic resources, that good machinery exists to settle the dispute. It is now necessary to examine the variety of ways that exist to settle a business dispute; these include:

☐ Negotiation between the parties.
☐ Via state machinery to help settlement, e.g. Advisory, Conciliation and Arbitration Service (ACAS) for industrial disputes.
☐ Arbitration.
☐ Other methods of dispute resolution.
☐ Litigation.

(a) Negotiation

A difference of opinion between two parties about (for example) the delivery of goods of the wrong colour, or the wrong size, might escalate into a full blown legal dispute, settled in court by a judge interpreting the exact meaning of certain contractual terms. However, as with most minor family arguments, the two sides will probably sort the problem out themselves and, after negotiation, reach an amicable agreement, acceptable to both sides.

(b) State machinery for the settlement of disputes

The policy of recent employment statutes has been to exclude trade disputes, i.e. disputes between employers and workers (usually via trade unions), from judicial review and aid settlement via the use of the Advisory, Conciliation and Arbitration Service (ACAS).

ACAS was set up in 1974 and was given the duty

> ... of promoting the improvement of industrial relations, and in particular of encouraging the extension of collective bargaining and the development, and where necessary, the reform of collective bargaining machinery.

ACAS is independent of both employer and trade union influence, and of the Government, and the Employment Protection Act 1975 clearly provides that it is not to be 'subject to directions of any kind from any Minister of the Crown as to the manner in which it is to exercise any of its functions under any enactment'.

As well as its role in aiding the settlement of collective disputes, ACAS also receives copies of all industrial tribunal applications by individuals. A conciliation officer will then offer his or her services to the parties, usually employer and employee, to help them reach a settlement without the need to proceed to a full tribunal hearing. Since 1972, 60% of all unfair dismissal cases have been settled at this stage. (Further details on the law relating to unfair dismissal are given in Chapter 7).

(c)   Arbitration

It is quite common today for parties to agree when entering into a business transaction that in the event of any disagreement the dispute will be resolved by the ruling of a third party. This is the process known as 'arbitration', and it is of considerable importance in the commercial world.

Once the parties have agreed to a 'reference' to an arbitrator, this agreement operates as a separate contract between them and if one party breaches this agreement, e.g. by taking the matter to the courts, then the other party can sue for this breach.

The arbitrator may be anyone whom the parties choose, but he or she is usually a lawyer or a specialist in the particular industry and/or area of the dispute. Once appointed the arbitrator has the power to examine witnesses, inspect documents and to reach a decision on the issue. His or her decision can be enforced by the successful party as if it were a court decision.

The courts will normally only set aside an arbitrator's award where it can be shown that some exceptional circumstances existed, e.g. a proven bias on the arbitrator's behalf, or fraud by one of the parties. Under the Arbitration Act 1979, questions of law arising during the arbitration which could substantially affect the rights of either party, may be referred to the High Court on agreement of both parties, or with leave of the Court.

The obvious advantages in arbitration are that it is cheaper, quicker and less formal than litigation, and perhaps more importantly, the arbitrator is usually an expert in the particular industry or area of dispute (unlike the judge). Professor Schmitthoff said in 1985:

> . . . In international disputes the parties are sometimes disinclined to go to the national courts. They prefer their dispute to be settled by persons with an international outlook.

Arbitration also avoids the publicity of court hearings as it is usually held in private. Arbitration agreements are particularly prevalent in the insurance, construction, civil engineering and shipping industries.

(d)   Other methods of dispute resolution

In recent years other methods of dispute resolution have emerged; though in general they are simply variants on litigation or arbitration.

- ☐ The Director General of Fair Trading has encouraged trade associations to introduce Codes of Practice, most of which include conciliation and arbitration schemes for consumers (Chapter 6).
- ☐ Ombudsmen have been introduced by many professional organizations to adjudicate on disputes, e.g. Insurance Ombudsman introduced in 1981. The Banking Ombudsman (1986) was introduced by the five major clearing banks and deals with disputes between individual customers and partnerships and the banks concerned. He or she can make awards of up to £50 000 which are binding on the bank but not on the complainant.
- ☐ Judicial review is a method whereby the courts can examine the activities of the executive in order to ensure compliance with the law. High Court

judges can scrutinize the decision-making process of government departments, local authorities and other agencies of the state. A simplified procedure for judicial review was introduced in 1977 and has led to a considerable increase in the number of applications, viz. from 533 applications in 1981 to 1230 in 1985.

(e) Litigation

Unfortunately for the parties concerned (but not for the lawyers) some disputes are not settled by the above means and the only result is litigation by the 'wronged' party seeking redress in the appropriate court. It is the function of the court to establish the facts of the case, identify the legal rules to be applied and via its decision, uphold the law and the rights and obligations of the parties. To understand the role of courts in dispute settlement it is now necessary to outline the existing criminal and civil court systems.

The court system

Every business enterprise needs access to legal services: a large business will often have a legal department, a smaller concern will have a solicitor whose services they regularly call upon. One function of an experienced business person is to be able to spot when a legal problem is likely to arise, and when it is time to call for professional advice. One of the main functions of a business lawyer is to keep his or her clients out of court to avoid the expense, in time and in money, of going to court to settle a problem.

However, the time will come when such a resort to the formal arenas of the legal system is inevitable. It may be because the other party will not answer letters, or settle his or her account; it may be because the other party believes that he or she is in the right just as fervently as the lawyer's client. Whatever the circumstances, it is important for the student of business to have a grasp of the outline, at least, of the English Court system (Figure 1.7), in which many of these business disputes will, unfortunately, have to be settled.

(a) Classifying the courts

The courts within the English legal system are not designed for ease of academic exposition. There are at least two ways in which they can be classified:

Courts of first instance and courts of appeal

A court of first instance is the arena in which the disputed matter is first heard. A court of appeal is where the result of that first consideration is challenged by the loser at first instance. The magistrates' courts, the county courts, the High Court and the Crown Court are all courts of first instance. The Court of Appeal and the House of Lords are courts of appeal. However, this classification is not watertight: the High court and the Crown Court are also courts of appeal under certain circumstances.

Figure 1.7 The Court System.

Civil courts

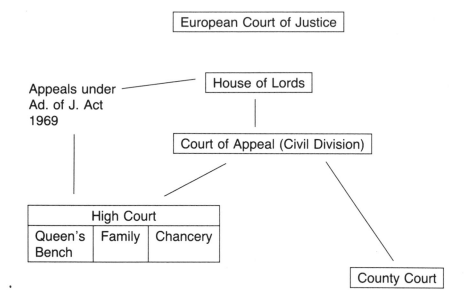

Criminal courts

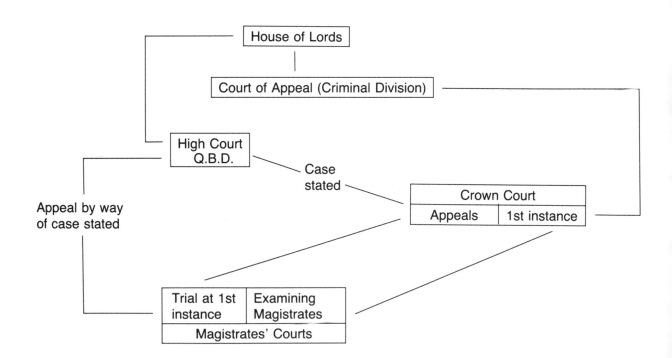

Civil courts and criminal courts

The county courts, High Court and the Court of Appeal (Civil Division) are civil courts. The magistrates' courts, the Crown Court and the Court of Appeal (Criminal Division) are criminal courts. But once again the classification is not watertight; the magistrates' courts act as a civil court sometimes, and the House of Lords is both a civil and a criminal court.

(b)   The jurisdiction of the main English courts

The county courts

There are about 400 county courts in England and Wales. They are local civil courts, established by the County Courts Act 1846, to provide cheap, speedy, local justice in the resolution of relatively small civil disputes, and the case is usually heard by a single judge. Matters involving less than £500 can be dealt with by an 'assistant' judge called a Registrar. Broadly the county courts can deal with virtually any civil case (except defended divorces and defamation) but only up to a set limit; the level of which is currently under review and it is proposed this might be raised as high as £25 000.

Defamation This is the publication of a statement which exposes a person to hatred, ridicule or contempt or causes him or her to be shunned or avoided by right-thinking members of society generally.

For example:

- ☐ Actions in contract and tort (other than defamation, unless both parties agree), where the sum involved does not exceed £5000.
- ☐ Equity matters like trusts, mortgages and partnerships.
- ☐ Actions over the title to land, where the rateable value does not exceed £1000 (this covers most domestic property);
- ☐ Probate and the administration of estates up to £30 000.
- ☐ The winding-up of companies with capital up to £120 000.
- ☐ Undefended divorces (all divorces start here, defended cases are transferred to the High Court).
- ☐ Adoption and custodianship of children.
- ☐ Landlord and tenant disputes.
- ☐ Race relations.
- ☐ Consumer credit.
- ☐ Arbitration, using the small claims arbitration procedure, up to £500 limit.
- ☐ Bankruptcy.

Small claims arbitration is of great (and increasing) importance in the business context. In 1986 over 45 000 cases were dealt with under the Small Claims Procedure. It might be very important for a businessman or woman to know that he or she can pursue the collection of debts of up to £500 without the problem of a full court hearing and the consequent deterrent of payment of the other side's legal costs if the action is unsuccessful, which is the normal rule in civil cases ('costs go with the cause').

The small claims arbitration procedure was first set up in 1973, with a jurisdictional limit of £75. The idea was to set the limit at the average cost of consumer durables (other than cars). Inflation has resulted in the setting of the limit at £500 today, and there is pressure for an increase to £1000. The Procedure is usually informal, in private and by appointment. It is an increasingly popular method of small debt collection for the businessman or woman.

The introduction to the free booklet, *Small claims in the county court* (available from any county court office) states:

> Have you ever lost money because someone has either sold you an appliance that does not work or done a job so badly that you have had to pay someone else to put it right? Maybe you have had your car slightly damaged by a careless driver or lent money that has never been repaid. These problems are often resolved by agreement but sometimes complaints are rejected or ignored. So what do you do? The answer is simple; you either give up or take court proceedings. Unfortunately many people in the past did nothing because they could not afford the risk of having to pay legal costs and were afraid to take court proceedings on their own. Court procedure has now been simplified so that ordinary people can bring small claims before the courts without any legal knowledge or professional assistance.

The clearly stated objective of making legal proceedings simple, cheap and easy for consumers in the county courts has slightly back-fired in that most cases brought for small claims are brought by businesses and not by the consumer. The booklet also contains the 'health warning':

> A word of warning. The principal purpose of this guide is to tell you how to sue in the county court. Whether it is worth your while to do so is another matter. There is little satisfaction to be gained from winning an action if your opponent has no money to pay the judgment debt. You should consider this question carefully before you start proceedings.

The High Court

The High Court, in its present form, dates from 1971, although it was first set up in 1873. The Court sits every day at the Royal Courts of Justice in the Strand in London, as well as a number of High Court centres throughout the country. The judges visit these centres in turn, 'on circuit'; there are six circuits in England and Wales.

The jurisdiction of the High Court is similar to that of the county courts, and it can deal with every kind of civil matter at first instance. There is, however, no maximum limit to the amount of the claim that can be brought. For convenience and for the focus of expertise, the work of this Court is split between three divisions: the Chancery Division, the Family Division and the Queen's Bench Division (Figure 1.8).

In order to discourage the use of the High Court for actions which could be brought before the county courts, rules of court provided that if less than £3000 is recovered in a High Court action, costs will only be awarded to the successful litigant on a scale appropriate to the county courts, he or she will probably, therefore, be substantially out of pocket. The rules of court also provide, contrary to the usual rule of the loser paying the costs of both sides, that if less than £600 is recovered in the High Court, the winner will normally recover no costs at all.

Within the Queen's Bench Division, jurisdiction over commercial matters is exercised by a Commercial Court, which sits in London, Liverpool and Manchester. The Commercial Court has the advantage of speed, simplicity and flexibility in terms of procedure. The strict rules of evidence may be

High Court

Figure 1.8 The High Court.

Queen's Bench Division
Deals with all contract
and tort claims above
County Court limits.

Slower and more costly
than County Court.

Barristers right of
audience.

Good enforcement of
judgements.

Family Division
Deals with all family
matters, e.g. divorce,
marriage, wardship,
adoption,
guardianship, family
property disputes,
etc.

Chancery Division
Deals with trusts,
partnerships, the
winding up of
companies, revenue,
bankruptcy, planning,
landlord and tenant,
etc.

relaxed and the judges are available at short notice at any stage of the action on the initiative of either party, thus disputes can be dealt with more easily and quickly.

The Division also has an Admiralty Court which deals with claims for damage, loss of life, or personal injury arising out of collisions at sea, claims for loss of or damage to goods carried in a ship, and disputes concerning ownership or possession of ships.

The criminal jurisdiction of the Queen's Bench Division is entirely appellate and is exercised by a divisional court, usually consisting of three judges, and often including the Lord Chief Justice. Appeals are heard from the magistrates' courts and the Crown Court by way of case stated. The divisional court also exercises a *supervisory jurisdiction*, and it may issue the prerogative writ of habeas corpus, as well as orders of mandamus, prohibition, and *certiorari* by which inferior courts and tribunals are compelled to exercise their powers properly and in accord with 'natural justice' and are also restrained from exceeding their jurisdiction.

The magistrates' courts
These are the local criminal courts. The office of 'justice of the peace' dates from the twelfth century, and today magistrates (or JPs) are local people, not necessarily qualified in law, who are nominated by local advisory committees and appointed by the Lord Chancellor. The right to 'time-off' work for public duties (contained in the Employment Protection (Consolidation) Act 1978) (Chapter 7) has resulted in the composition of the magistrates' bench changing in the past few years. Now many working people are able to accept the invitation to become a magistrate and the bench is now truly drawn from a very wide cross-section of society.

The jurisdiction of the court consists of:

☐ *Summary trial*, of those minor, statutory offences which are only triable 'summarily' (i.e. sitting without a jury), for example, many motoring offences; and summary trial of those more serious offences where the accused has the choice of trial before the magistrates, or on indictment in the Crown Court, for example, shoplifting. Every year the magistrates deal with 98% of all criminal trials.

Case stated An appeal on the basis, not that the facts found were wrong, but that either the decision as to the law relating to those facts was wrong or the decision-makers were acting beyond their jurisdiction.

Habeas corpus The writ is issued to obtain the release of someone imprisoned or restrained illegally. The court will require the imprisoner to justify the restraint, and if he cannot, the individual will be freed.

Mandamus An order commanding (*mandamus = we command*) a person or body to perform a duty imposed by common law or statute, e.g. compelling a local authority to produce its accounts for inspection by a ratepayer.

Prohibition An order prohibiting an inferior court or tribunal from continuing to exceed its jurisdiction.

Certiorari An order removing the decision of an inferior court taken without jurisdiction, or contrary to natural justice, or where there is an error of law actually in the written record of the case.

Natural justice As per Megarry J. in *John* v. *Rees* [1970] Ch 345 at 399: '. . . justice that is simple or elementary as distinct from justice that is complex, sophisticated and technical . . .'. It represents the basic irreducible procedural standard with which administrators, judges, employers, etc. are required to comply (Chapter 8, *Foulkes' Administrative Law*, 6th edn [Butterworths]).

□ *Committal proceedings*, whereby the more serious criminal offences (murder, rape, etc.), which are only triable by jury in the Crown Court, are brought before the magistrates to ensure that there is a sufficient case for the accused to answer. If the magistrates find there is a case to answer then the accused will be committed for trial in the Crown Court.

□ *Juvenile work*, where specially trained magistrates deal with children (10–14 years) and young persons (14–17 years). Such courts will usually meet either at a different place or at a different time to the adult court, and so reduce the theatrical and intimidating aspects of an appearance in court.

□ *Civil work*, where certain civil matters, such as affiliation, maintenance, some adoption and guardianship of children, and a variety of other matters including some important business matters like licensing and rate enforcement.

The Crown Court

The Crown Court was set up by the Courts Act 1971, and it may sit anywhere in England and Wales; when sitting in the City of London it is known as The Central Criminal Court (The Old Bailey). The Crown Court has some minor civil jurisdiction, but its main business concerns all criminal proceedings upon 'indictment', i.e. the trial, by jury, of serious criminal offences, such as murder, rape, fraud, etc.

The structure of the Crown Court is complicated by the fact that it has three kinds of judges, High Court judges, Circuit judges and Recorders. Which judge sits normally depends upon the gravity of the offence involved, with the most serious offences tried before a High Court judge, and the least serious by a Recorder, or part-time judge.

The Court of Appeal

The Court of Appeal is split into two divisions: civil and criminal, and will only sit at the Royal Courts of Justice in the Strand. The Civil Division of the Court of Appeal is presided over by the Master of the Rolls, and the Criminal Division by the Lord Chief Justice. This Court can deal with appeals on facts, on law, against sentence, or on the size of an award of damages. It can reconsider cases if asked to do so by the Home Secretary, and, after an acquittal, the Court can be asked by the Attorney-General to consider the points of law in the case. (This, of course, will not affect the outcome of that case, but it might change the law, or the courts' interpretation of the law in future similar cases.)

The House of Lords

This is the final court of appeal in England and Wales, and also for Northern Ireland (where the legal system is slightly different) and for Scotland (where the legal system is very different). The Court sits within the Palace of Westminster, and deals with only about 80 cases each year. Most of these cases are civil matters, and many of them involve statutory interpretation, each case usually being heard by five Lords of Appeal in Ordinary. There is no right to appeal to the House of Lords, in contrast to the Court of Appeal where such a right does exist. Permission ('leave') to appeal must be obtained from the court below, or from the House of Lords itself.

The Law Lords are the senior judges within the English legal system; some people regard them as the finest judges in the world. They have the last word in matters of English, Welsh, Northern Irish and Scots law – but not in matters of European Community law which they must apply according to the European Court of Justice's interpretation.

The Court of Justice of the European Communities

This Court sits in Luxembourg, and it has the last word in matters involving the law of the European Communities. Where such a case arises in an English court it may be referred to Luxembourg for interpretation, or if it arises in the House of Lords, it must be referred to Luxembourg (Article 177(3) Treaty of Rome). The idea, of course, is to attain a uniformity of interpretation.

The importance of this Court's decisions in changing English law is clearly illustrated by the recent case (Case study 1.4) of *Marshall* v. *Southampton and South West Hampshire Health Authority* [1986] I.R.L.R. 140, concerning compulsory retirement ages from employment. The judgment of the Court, delivered on 26 February 1986, led to the passing, by Parliament, of the Sex Discrimination Act 1986 (on 7 November 1986), and the relevant provisions came into force, changing English law, on 7 November 1987.

Courts and tribunals with special jurisdiction

There are a number of other courts and tribunals which have particular importance in defined areas of the law: the Employment Appeal Tribunal, the Coroners' Court, the Restrictive Practices' Court, the courts-martial, the Naval courts, the Ecclesiastical courts, the Court of Chivalry and the Judicial Committee of the Privy Council. (Space does not permit discussion of these courts, but further reference should be made to *The English Legal System* by Walker and Walker (Butterworths, latest edition).

Some writers suggest that the entire system of law courts in the UK (based on tradition, complicated and obscure rules of procedure and evidence, and extremely expensive) could be replaced by a tribunal type of court. Here one judge, an expert in that particular area of law, would be aided by two or more lay people, knowledgeable in the practical aspects of the dispute. This system could replace both the civil and criminal court systems, and result in the abolition of the jury system, which research has tended to suggest is outdated and does not work as well as it should, and remove the idea that a judge is an expert in all aspects of law and life.

The Industrial Tribunal is a good example, where a legally qualified chairman, usually a solicitor who has specialized knowledge of employment law, is aided by two lay persons: one drawn from the list of nominees by trade unions in the area, and one drawn from the list of nominees of employers in the area. The bench of three thus combine legal expertise and practical experience in employment matters: a typical bench consisting of a local solicitor, the personnel manager of a local company, and an official (full-time or shop-steward) of a trade union working (or retired) in the locality.

All criminal cases could be tried by a similar bench. The magistrates' courts are described on p. 29, each bench consists of a minimum of three local lay persons. Magistrates' courts are currently dealing with 98% of all criminal cases in England and Wales in a cheap, speedy and efficient manner. A more serious criminal case, currently tried by judge and jury in the Crown Court, might, under this system, be tried by a judge (why not a solicitor as chairman?), a social worker and a psychiatrist, for example; shop-lifting cases could be tried by a judge (or solicitor), shop keeper and social worker. In civil law, a consumer action could be tried by a judge, a manufacturer and a consumer.

The legal profession

It is important in practical terms for the businessman or woman to understand how the legal profession works so that he or she will be aware of what is happening when they need to seek legal advice. It is therefore necessary for us now to examine briefly the legal profession: a profession which is steeped in tradition. It may be very hard for the layman or woman to understand what is going on when he or she first seeks legal advice: should they consult solicitors, legal executives, articled clerks, licensed conveyancers, barristers or barristers' clerks? The term 'lawyer' could refer to any of these, as well as to academic lawyers, or simply to someone who knows something about law.

The basic division, between solicitors and barristers, is one which is not seen in other legal systems, such as in the United States, but some split of function and specialization is common to most legal professions in the western world.

(a) Solicitors

Solicitors are the 'general practitioners' of the legal profession: they have their offices in the high streets of all major towns and cities, and are usually organized into partnerships, with partners specializing in different fields of law. It is to the solicitor the businessman or woman must go if he or she wishes to seek legal advice.

A solicitor will advise his or her client on all aspects of law, often taking advice from a barrister (called an 'opinion') on a particularly complicated problem. He or she will draft agreements, leases, contracts of employment, wills, etc. and convey property. (The long-established solicitors' monopoly over conveyancing work has now been broken and this can be carried out by either a solicitor or a licensed conveyancer.) Solicitors can also represent their clients in court, but they have a 'right of audience' generally only in the county courts, magistrates' courts and in the various types of tribunals, such as industrial tribunals and rent tribunals, not the High Court.

Where a case is a High Court matter the main role of the solicitor would be:

☐ To advise his or her client as to the merits of continuing the action in court.
☐ If the action is to be continued, to engage a suitable barrister to conduct the case in court.
☐ To prepare the brief, which is a bundle of documents which instruct the

barrister to act, outlining the nature and history of the case, and including all relevant documents and witness statements, etc.

(b) Barristers

Barristers are the specialists of the legal profession: they specialize in certain fields of law, and in advocacy, i.e. the presentation of cases in court. Barristers have the right of audience in *all* courts and tribunals.

This branch of the profession is subject to rules of procedure and etiquette which restrict the ways in which a barrister can carry on his practice. The principal rules are:

☐ Barristers must work as sole practitioners; they cannot currently form partnerships. They work from a 'set of chambers' where, with other barristers, they share the services of a barristers' clerk.

☐ Barristers cannot normally accept work direct from their clients; they can only be engaged by solicitors.

☐ Barristers' fees can only be negotiated by their clerk.

☐ When a leading barrister (called a Queen's Counsel) is engaged he or she will normally only act if aided by a 'junior barrister'; both then command substantial fees. (It is only recently that the rule that QCs could not be hired without a 'junior' has been relaxed.)

The consequence of all this to the businessman or woman is that if they wish to obtain advice on a complicated legal problem they will not be able to consult a barrister direct, but only through a solicitor. They have therefore to employ two lawyers! If they become involved in a dispute that involves High Court litigation, they will again have to engage the services of both a solicitor and a barrister, as will the other party to the action. If they wish to be represented by a Queen's Counsel, their solicitor will probably also have to engage a junior barrister! As the barristers' clerk is paid purely by a percentage of the fees he or she negotiates for their barristers, it will be in his or her best interests to negotiate the highest possible fees, thereby putting costs up considerably! Finally, the normal rule in English law is that in civil cases 'costs go with the cause', i.e. the loser normally pays the costs of both sides!

There are strong arguments today that the distinction between the two arms of the profession should disappear, and that one person should perform both the functions of a solicitor and an advocate, as in the United States. On the other hand, the particular expertise and independence of the barrister is of enormous value and there is great concern that fusion might erode this.

Lord Mackay's Green discussion Paper on the reform of the legal profession was very widely aired in 1989, leading to a White Paper with positive proposals aimed at reducing the cost and delay involved in bringing a case to court. The Courts and Legal Services Bill implementing some of these proposals is to be debated during the 1989/90 Parliamentary Session. Under these, solicitors would acquire wider rights of audience than at present and direct access to barristers would be permitted by other professionals more freely than currently. In certain circumstances partnerships between barristers or barristers and solicitors or other professionals might also be permitted. The raising of the County Court limit would mean much litigation being removed from the High Court to the County Court and therefore automatically increasing the scope for solicitors to deal single handedly with a case.

(c)   Other legal personnel

Much of the work done in a solicitor's office is carried out by clerks, who are not qualified lawyers. Some of these clerks are 'articled clerks', i.e. 'trainee solicitors' who are completing their period of practical training after (or before) taking their final professional examinations in order to be 'admitted' to the profession. Other clerks will be 'legal executives', which means they have passed certain compulsory examinations in law and have been admitted to the Institute of Legal Executives (ILEX). Legal executives are often very skilled, highly experienced people, but they are not qualified lawyers and cannot therefore represent clients in court, or complete a conveyance in their own name, unless licensed conveyancers.

Now there is also the new breed of professional, the Licensed Conveyancer, who, after passing the stipulated examinations, is able to convey property in his or her own name in the same way as a qualified solicitor. The long established solicitors' monopoly on conveyancing was finally broken in 1986, and the growth in numbers of licensed conveyancers has already led to a fall in the cost of buying a house.

How is the law useful to business?

Apart from creating a stable social/economic and political environment in which to operate – in at least two ways.

First, by making clear the parameters of acceptable conduct, a knowledge of the law enables a business to avoid breaches which would incur sanctions. For most business there is, of course, normally no 'criminal intent' in the popularly understood way, but the maze of regulations covering (for example) employment, health and safety, hygiene, credit provision and advertisements of all kinds create something of a minefield which merits careful attention.

Secondly, knowing how to achieve an objective in the quickest, most effective way is going to save money and generate profit, objects surely at the heart of every business! A clearly drafted contract excludes argument, a properly submitted patent application may result in a lucrative monopoly, a thorough consideration of the current tax position can generate great saving.

Where there is dispute or doubt, recourse to an expert is always sensible. It is a case of 'a stitch in time saves nine' – knowing the choices and their legal consequences/costs is a prerequisite to effective commercial decision-making.

What does the law cost?

For most businesses recourse to a law court is the last resort, although recourse to a lawyer may be extremely profitable! In deciding what course of action to pursue a business must be aware of the cost/benefits involved. No true analysis can be made without an accurate estimate of the cost of the proceedings; the likelihood of success; the chance of recovering any compensation awarded; and the cost of *not* pursuing the action in terms of false signals given to customers/competitors which may itself result in further costs.

Put at its simplest, the ability to bargain is only as strong as the ability to put the case. Notoriously the rules of evidence are crucial. 'Knowing' something is no use unless objective evidence can be found to stand up in court. Hence the requirement of keeping written records, receipts, memoranda etc. may be justified as good business practice. Memory is often unintentionally fickle.

Nobody is going to fight a case which they are clearly going to lose. An opinion from a leading Counsel strongly in your favour may well encourage the opposition to settle at an early stage; thus money spent on his or her fee is really well spent. Equally if on the balance of available evidence it seems more prudent to give in gracefully this will be much cheaper than being pursued to the bitter end and – from a business point of view often just as important – potential bad publicity will be avoided. In the case of Distillers and Thalidomide, the Company were never found legally liable for the birth defects of the drug victims and so avoided some of the odium that might otherwise have attached to them. The *ex gratia* – or voluntary – payment they made to the trust fund for the victims may have been seen as 'conscience money' by many or even an admission of liability for their product, but in the absence of any compulsion to pay it was certainly good public relations (Out-of-Court Settlement: The Piper Alpha Disaster: Case study 1.5).

Even if the case is considered sufficiently open to fight and neither side will compromise it is still a matter of policy whether a fight is worth it. The present practice, as has been referred to before, is that costs follow the action i.e. the losing party pays not only his or her own costs but also those of the opposition. The stakes are high! Although this is generally bemoaned, it has the one advantage that a litigant does not lightly enter the lists. The introduction of a 'no win no fee' or contingent fee system along the lines of the American practice not only opens the doors to potential litigants who may be discouraged or even prevented from suing at present but may also open the floodgates to vast numbers of disgruntled people prepared to argue the toss but not at their expense. Whereas the plaintiff has the choice whether to sue or not, a business which is sued has very little choice whether to defend or not. Not to defend may result in judgment by default, and

In the case of the disastrous fire and explosion on the Piper Alpha oil rig off Scotland in 1988, Occidental Petroleum, the rig's owners, were quick to accept legal liability and to seek an out-of-court settlement. Likewise, British Transport in the case of the 1988 King's Cross underground fire, British Rail in the case of the 1989 Clapham rail crash, and P and O in the case of the Zeebrugge ferry disaster in 1987, were all ready to admit their liability.

CASE STUDY 1.5

OUT-OF-COURT SETTLEMENT: THE PIPER ALPHA DISASTER

even winning is of little consolation where the plaintiff has no means to cover your costs.

There was a time when many businesses felt held to random in just this way by applicants to the Industrial Tribunal. An improved preliminary procedure and the ability to require a minimum deposit by a plaintiff in doubtful cases have been introduced to combat this.

There can be no doubt that the best policy is to be as clear as possible on what the law is and how it applies. This is best achieved by consulting legal advice at various stages of any business operation, including the planning stage not merely the aftermath of a disaster! In the event of a finely balanced dispute commercial considerations – public relations, customer satisfaction, company image – may well dictate the choice of settling quietly, referring to arbitration or fighting publicly.

Summary

It has been necessary in this chapter to lay the foundation for the rest of this book on law in a business context. Inevitably businesses and business persons will become involved in disputes, and often these can only be resolved by recourse to law. This chapter has therefore sought to explain the nature of law and the environment within which it has to operate. Having identified the differences between civil and criminal law, and between statute and common law, we examined the way that laws are made and changed, including the growth of delegated legislation. A brief outline of the civil and criminal court system, the judiciary and the various members of the legal profession with whom business persons may come into contact, illustrated the dangers of going to Court, particularly the time and cost involved. The pressure is definitely on settling outside the Court System!

Further reading

James, *Introduction to English Law* (Butterworths) contains a more detailed description of the English legal system than is possible in this book, but it was written for law students so it contains more detail than is necessary for business students. A book written for non-law students, but again perhaps more detailed than is necessary in some sections is Savage and Bradgate, *Business Law*, (Butterworths). Walker and Walker, *The English Legal System* (Butterworths) is a traditional law book so it contains all the detail (usually too much) ever needed about the introductory material contained in this chapter. Ranking, Spicer and Pegler's, *Business Law for Accountants* (Butterworths), although written for accountancy students, contains a good chapter on arbitration and the settling of commercial disputes. Other good texts for the introductory material are Card and James, *Law for Accountancy Students* (Sweet and Maxwell) and Hartley, *The Foundations of European Community Law* (Clarendon Press, latest edition).

Exercises

1. What are the main sources of English law?

2. What do the following mean? (a) *ratio decidendi* (b) *obiter dicta* (c) *stare decisis*.

3. Outline the main stages through which a Bill has to pass before it becomes an Act of Parliament.

4. Why would the parties to a dispute choose (a) arbitration, and (b) settlement out of court, rather than litigation as the way to settle their differences?

5. Your employer has been served with a writ in which Fixit Ltd are claiming £10 000 for breach of contract. Your employer wishes to know how he or she should go about defending the action. Where should he or she go to seek legal advice? Who will represent him or her? In which court will the action be taken? How costly will it be? Prepare a report for your employer.

6. How has Britain's membership of the European Community affected the English legal system?

2 The changing legal environment

Introduction

In this chapter we will outline the legal environment within which a business organization operates; this includes the role of government through the increasing use of legislation, and the development of the common law areas of contract and tort.

Law both provides an external environment within which business has to operate and itself responds to and reflects external environmental pressures from society and the market place and so operates in accordance with the Business in Context model. Legislation now covers all kinds of business functions. It is clearly impossible to itemize them exhaustively, so we will sketch in the framework, and detailed reference should be made for particular regulations. Trade associations and trade unions provide excellent practical guidance on the matters which concern them and Government departments produce many free publications to explain and illustrate current rules.

In the field of common law the areas of contract and tort have been selected to reflect the less perceptible changes in the legal environment. This is the field of private law which most affects business. The bulk of commercial law governing the making and breaking of agreements is based on custom/common law. Legislation, where it applies, is piecemeal.

The role of Government and the increasing scope of legislation

The twentieth century has seen a massive growth in the state regulation of the business enterprise. From the *laissez-faire* attitudes of the nineteenth century we have 'progressed' to a new legal and administrative framework which regulates most closely the environment within which a business has to operate. The two World Wars accelerated the growth in governmental control and intervention although under the policies of central Government since 1979 there has been a movement away from centralized manipulation of the economy.

A good example of the dramatic increase in legislation affecting the way a business is run is provided by employment law. Before the Second World War the notions of freedom and equality resulted in contracts of employment which could be terminated at will, giving much flexibility to business but little security to workers. The exploitation of labour after the war, the growth of the trade unions and the beginnings of the 'individual rights' movements, all led to government intervention in employment relationships.

The year 1963 saw the first major Act of Parliament controlling the contract of employment, requiring employers to provide written information to all full-time employees regarding the major terms of their employment contracts, and providing for the first time a statutory minimum notice period to terminate the contract. Since 1963 the floodgates have opened and there has been so much legislation regulating the employer/employee relationship that there is virtually nothing left for the parties to bargain over.

A list (Table 2.1) of the relevant statutes regulating the employment relationship illustrates the point. For further discussion, see Chapter 7.

If one then considers the increase in legislative activity in other fields, e.g. Company and Securities, Taxation, Customs and Excise, Planning, the Environment, Consumer Protection and Competition, it is easy to see that the legal and administrative framework regulating business activity today is both massive and restrictive. The European Community will be responsible for further regulation with the harmonization of standards.

Table 2.1 Employment legislation

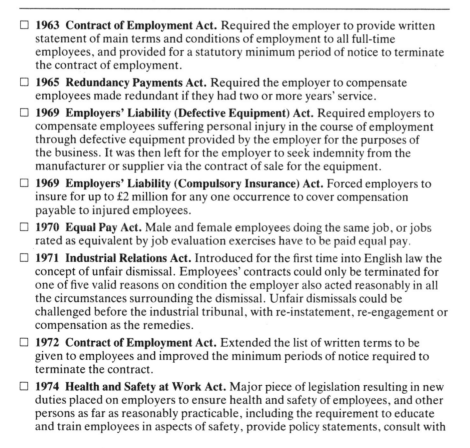

☐ **1963 Contract of Employment Act.** Required the employer to provide written statement of main terms and conditions of employment to all full-time employees, and provided for a statutory minimum period of notice to terminate the contract of employment.

☐ **1965 Redundancy Payments Act.** Required the employer to compensate employees made redundant if they had two or more years' service.

☐ **1969 Employers' Liability (Defective Equipment) Act.** Required employers to compensate employees suffering personal injury in the course of employment through defective equipment provided by the employer for the purposes of the business. It was then left for the employer to seek indemnity from the manufacturer or supplier via the contract of sale for the equipment.

☐ **1969 Employers' Liability (Compulsory Insurance) Act.** Forced employers to insure for up to £2 million for any one occurrence to cover compensation payable to injured employees.

☐ **1970 Equal Pay Act.** Male and female employees doing the same job, or jobs rated as equivalent by job evaluation exercises have to be paid equal pay.

☐ **1971 Industrial Relations Act.** Introduced for the first time into English law the concept of unfair dismissal. Employees' contracts could only be terminated for one of five valid reasons on condition the employer also acted reasonably in all the circumstances surrounding the dismissal. Unfair dismissals could be challenged before the industrial tribunal, with re-instatement, re-engagement or compensation as the remedies.

☐ **1972 Contract of Employment Act.** Extended the list of written terms to be given to employees and improved the minimum periods of notice required to terminate the contract.

☐ **1974 Health and Safety at Work Act.** Major piece of legislation resulting in new duties placed on employers to ensure health and safety of employees, and other persons as far as reasonably practicable, including the requirement to educate and train employees in aspects of safety, provide policy statements, consult with

Table 2.1 Continued

the trade unions over safety, etc. This is a criminal statute and non-compliance can lead to prosecutions in the criminal courts.

☐ **1974 Trade Union and Labour Relations Act.** Repealed the Industrial Relations Act and re-enacted the unfair dismissal provisions.

☐ **1974 Rehabilitation of Offenders Act.** Restricted the employer's right to refuse to employ ex-offenders or to ask for criminal records of new employees or applicants.

☐ **1975 Sex Discrimination Act.** Made it unlawful to discriminate on the grounds of sex or marital status in job advertising, short-listing, interviewing, terms of employment and reasons for dismissal. Employers could no longer decide to have an all-male workforce.

☐ **1975 Employment Protection Act.** Major piece of legislation introducing many new employment rights for workers, including maternity pay, leave and the right to return to work after maternity leave, right to time off work for certain duties, rights against the employer in an insolvency situation, rights to guarantee payments, right to receive properly itemized pay statements and written reasons for dismissal. The employers were also fettered in a redundancy situation by this legislation as they had to consult with any recognized trade unions before they could make any workers redundant.

☐ **1976 Race Relations Act.** Made it unlawful to discriminate in all aspects of employment on the grounds of race, colour, ethnic, nationality or national origins.

☐ **1978 Employment Protection (Consolidation) Act.** No new law but tried to consolidate all provisions relating to the employment of individuals into one statute.

☐ **1981 Transfer of Undertakings (Protection of Employment) Regulation.** Employers taking over a business as a going concern become responsible for all past service with previous owner of employees taken over. They also have to take over the contractual obligations of the previous employer, and even any trade union recognition on behalf of those workers.

☐ **1982 Employment Act.** Tightened the rules on termination of employment of employees in relation to trade union membership and closed shop situations.

☐ **1982 Social Security and Housing Benefits Act.** Made employers responsible for paying sick employees for the first 8 weeks of sickness, to replace the former system administered by the DHSS. The period has since been amended and employers are now responsible for paying for the first 28 weeks of sickness.

☐ **1983 Equal Pay (Amendment) Regulations.** Equal pay legislation extended to permit comparisons with other workers in different jobs, and the right of workers to take the employer to an industrial tribunal if no job evaluation exercise has been carried out. The tribunal can appoint an 'independent expert' to carry out the exercise.

☐ **1984 Data Protection Act.** Employers have to register with the Data Protection Registrar if they have computerized personnel systems, and employees now have the right to inspect these records and have them corrected if they are wrong in any way.

☐ **1986 Wages Act.** Permits cashless pay, except to those existing employees on 1 January 1987 who had the right to payment in cash under their contracts. Abolished the redundancy rebate system except for small employers with less than 10 employees.

☐ **1986 Sex Discrimination Act.** Further restrictions in relation to discrimination in

Table 2.1 Continued

employment, including that it is now unlawful to require men and women doing the same job to retire at different ages.

☐ **1986 Social Security Act.** Employers now responsible for paying statutory maternity pay for 18 weeks, again to replace the former system of grants and allowances administered by the DHSS.

☐ **1988 Employment Act.** Increased the rights of trade union members in relation to their union, made closed shop provisions unenforceable.

   These major legislative provisions have been added to by many sets of Regulations, all undermining the traditional concept of freedom of contract between the employer and employee, and clearly illustrating the dramatic increase in legislation affecting business activity.

Impact of the common law: constraints of the law of contract

Introduction

The law of contract provides the mechanism within which all commercial life operates. Nothing is bought or sold, lent, hired or leased without a contract being formed. The spectrum runs from throwing down 30p and picking up a newspaper whilst running for a train to negotiating for months for an oil rig (or whatever!). This is an area of law where the judges can be seen responding to the needs of business both in their interpretation of clauses and in their recognition of new forms of technology (Case study 1.1), and at the same time seeking to protect consumers in their approach to exemption clauses and the expansion of 'economic duress'. A grasp of the essentials of the law of contract is centrally important for those who operate a business enterprise. We shall identify each of the main elements and consider them briefly in turn.

(a)   Intention to be legally bound

There are some agreements which are not contractually binding, such as an arrangement between friends, or between husband and wife. They do not intend to make a contract (Key concept 2.1) out of their social dealings, so they are not deemed to have done so.

A contract is an agreement intended to be legally binding and supported by consideration. It is a legally enforceable agreement.

KEY CONCEPT 2.1

A CONTRACT

***Balfour v. Balfour* (1919)**
A civil servant, working in Sri Lanka, promised to pay his wife £30 each month, but he was held not to be contractually bound to do so. As Atkin L.J. said:

... the small courts of this country would have to be multiplied one hundredfold if these arrangements were held to result in legal obligations. They are not sued upon, not because the parties are reluctant to enforce their legal rights when the agreement is broken, but because the parties, in the inception of the arrangement, never intended that they should be sued upon. Agreements such as these are outside the realm of contracts altogether.

But cf. *Simpkins* v. *Pays* (1955) where a domestic agreement to enter a newspaper competition was held to be enforceable, requiring the winnings to be shared. However, in a business context it is assumed that the parties are more serious in their intentions towards one another (*Edwards* v. *Skyways* (1964)).

(b)   The agreement

The essence of all contracts is the agreement – in law this is not a subjective matter, i.e. does not depend on what the parties individually thought or meant but whether their actions legally amounted to an offer which was unconditionally accepted. We shall consider briefly the legal rules on offer and acceptance.

Offers

It is important to distinguish between an offer and an invitation to treat or advertisement for custom. When a retail outlet emblazons its windows with 'cut price offers', 'this week's extra special good deal offer', and so on, they are not making an offer at all, but extending an invitation to passers-by to call in and make an offer (*Fisher* v. *Bell* (1960); likewise goods on a supermarket shelf are not an offer (*Pharmaceutical Society of G.B.* v. *Boots* (1953)).

Advertisements are not usually offers; they are normally invitations to treat (*Harris* v. *Nickerson* (1873)). However, in unusual cases an advertisement may be construed as a direct offer, e.g. in *Carlill* v. *Carbolic Smokeball Co.* (1893). A company advertised the efficacy of its products on a full page scale in various upmarket publications, such as the *Pall Mall Gazette* and the *Illustrated London News*. It is important to note that this was at a time when there was an influenza epidemic – at a time when flu was a serious death risk. Their smoke ball would prevent flu, it was claimed. The company were so confident that they said that they would pay £100 to anyone who, having used the product as prescribed, still managed to catch flu. The plaintiff did so, but remained unpaid. She sued. She won. The company defended themselves with arguments such as they were not able to make a contract with the 'whole world' (a rather exaggerated concept of the readership of the magazines!) defeated by the answer that the contract had only been made with those individuals in the world who had both read and acted upon their offer. It was then suggested that the remarks were nothing but advertising 'puff', and so not to be taken seriously. This was defeated on an examination of the artwork itself. It contained far too many details, far too many precise promises to be mere 'puff'; they had used the word 'reward' in the advertisement and stated that the company had deposited £1000 to meet claims.

These 'reward cases' are called, perhaps slightly illogically, 'unilateral' contracts. That is, the reader has to act and claim, rather than to communicate to the offeror, act and claim. A judge in the *Carlill* case, Bowen L.J., likened the facts to the case of a lost dog. The fretting owner does not wish to be told that you are off to look for the dog, he just wants to know that the dog has been found, and that the finder is claiming the reward.

The Trade Descriptions Act 1968 and the Consumer Protection Act 1987 both create criminal offences which may be committed by false or misleading advertisements. The offences usually do not require deliberate intention to mislead; the question is invariably what will the effect be on the consumer/customer? Further information is given in Chapter 6.

The Consumer Protection Act 1987 has introduced a general offence of applying a misleading price indication replacing earlier rather complicated and very detailed regulations. The Office of Fair Trading (OFT) has produced a Code of Practice which is not mandatory but certainly helpful to suggest to businesses what sort of price indications are likely to be regarded as misleading. The ASA provides a further public watchdog on the content and standard of advertisements; their public condemnation is generally unwelcome to businesses even if the costs are indirect rather than direct. Controls on broadcast advertising, familiar in the case of alcohol and cigarettes, are likely to increase as greater uniformity is sought within the EC and different member states seek to promote/protect their own interests. Such control may extend beyond content to frequency and duration in certain circumstances.

A business needs to be careful to distinguish between an offer and an invitation to treat because an offer can be accepted and by acceptance be translated into an enforceable obligation. Where the intention is to reserve discretion the plan must be not to make an offer but merely to invite others to offer which then may or may not be accepted.

By custom, certain rules have been developed concerning the validity of offers; no special form is required, an offer may be made orally, in writing, or even by conduct, e.g. placing goods in a basket on a supermarket till. It can only be accepted by the person to whom it is addressed, or by one of a group to whom it is addressed. Where a business is taken over, care should be taken with repeat orders. An order addressed to the original business cannot be 'accepted' by the new business since it was not made to it. Any such 'acceptance' will be interpreted as an offer which the original customer may or may not choose to accept. Clearly where goodwill is bought, it is the intention that customers shall continue to trade; where the company has itself been bought there is of course no new party.

An offer will lapse after the agreed time or a reasonable time – a marketing device less frequently used here than in the United States of America. A business may be well advised when quoting a fixed price for goods or services to stipulate clearly for how long the offer holds good; this not only protects against price variation but also induces the customer to make a decision. The alternative of quoting materials price as at date of invoice sometimes cannot be avoided, but is rarely attractive to a customer seeking a clear idea of cost and may contradict the purchaser's own terms

CASE STUDY 2.1

**THE CROSSED
LETTERS**

On October 1 sellers in Cardiff posted a letter to buyers in New York offering to sell tinplate.

On October 8 the sellers changed their mind and posted another letter to the buyers revoking their original offer.

On October 11 the buyers in New York having received the offer telegraphed acceptance.

On October 15 the buyers confirmed their acceptance by post.

On October 20 the sellers letter of revocation reached the plaintiffs.

It is clear that a contract is completed when an offer is made and accepted. Acceptance takes effect when posted even if it fails to reach its destination. In this case a straight application of these rules would mean a contract had come into force even though at no time the parties were in agreement because at the time the acceptance was sent the offer had already been revoked. So the question arose, when does a revocation take effect?

Logically there were two possible choices, when received or when sent. The judge in the case had no great difficulty in deciding that the moment of receipt was the only fair choice; for a business not to know whether an offer it had received was valid or not until way after they had accepted it would create uncertainty and injustice. Frequently when a deal is struck a buyer will want to sell on goods which he has just bought, especially in a rising market, the very situation where a seller might wish to retract his original offer. A seller wishing to retain some measure of control over the precise moment a deal is closed should perhaps make it a term of the contract that acceptance is received in writing. Unless and until it is so received there is no completed contract and until that moment the offer can be withdrawn; however, any withdrawal of an offer must itself be received. Happily telephone and electronic communication make contact much easier than it used to be and a combination of courtesy and business efficiency should achieve a fair result.

(*Byrne and Co.* v. *Van Tienhoven and Co.* (1880))

of order. The offer will cease on the death of either party; if rejected, including the making of a counter-offer; or if revoked, i.e. the offeror changes his or her mind.

NB   In this case the offer remains open until the offeree actually receives notice of the revocation. So if a business wants to change its terms of offer it should do it quickly and directly (The Crossed Letters: Case study 2.1).

In practice most businesses do not make individual offers but develop a standard form for their normal, routine transactions (Key concept 2.2). These should always be drafted with the assistance of a lawyer, either from within the organization, or brought in. Standard forms are normal in dealings with large undertakings, such as gas, electricity and telephone utilities, and anyone who has booked a package holiday is familiar with a standard form contract! Their use may reflect an inequality of bargaining power between the parties to a contract. One of them is in a position to say 'take it or leave it' to the other. There are certain protections afforded to the weaker party

A *Standard form contract* is a model contract which a firm habitually uses. It will invariably be written and contain a series of numbered clauses covering as many eventualities as the business has been able to identify, or has experienced, including exemption clauses (p. 51). By definition it is not tailored to any individual transaction. With experience a firm is able to refine its terms to its own advantage, leaving a small business or individual consumer with very little room to negotiate, offering a 'take it or leave it' service. Parliament has specifically restricted the effect of exemption clauses in standard form contracts to try to redress this balance in the Unfair Contract Terms Act 1977 (below).

KEY CONCEPT 2.2

STANDARD FORM CONTRACT

by the law independently of the contract, e.g., for the consumer dealing with a business the terms implied by the Sale of Goods Act 1979 concerning quality, fitness for purpose and correspondence with samples and descriptions, cannot be excluded in a consumer sale (Unfair Contract Terms Act 1977 below).

However, the small business entering into a contractual relationship with a large concern is not protected to anything like the same extent. The nineteenth century maxim *caveat emptor* (let the buyer beware) is still very much the rule. But where standard forms are used any exclusion clause is subject to the reasonableness test of the Unfair Contract Terms Act 1977 (below). The position may become rather complicated when both parties to a contract are using standard forms, and the forms are not compatible. This is known as the 'battle of the forms' (The Battle of the Forms: Case study 2.2).

Battle of forms A situation of conflict. Both parties to an agreement are using standard forms of contract – but the forms are different. The essence of the dispute between the parties is that the actions of one party are permitted by the terms of his or her standard form, but not by the other party's standard form.

What happens when the terms of the seller's offer are different from the terms of the buyer's acceptance? In theory there should be no contract because no agreement, but in fact how many businesses actually read the terms of an order closely before accepting it? If goods are delivered and accepted and there is then a dispute about terms, what happens?

Sellers offered to sell a machine to buyers for £75 535 on terms which included a condition that all orders were accepted only on their terms. These included a price escalation clause allowing them to increase the quoted price to that prevailing at the date of delivery. Buyers replied to the sellers offer ordering the machine at the quoted price but on their own terms and conditions which did not include a price variation clause! Instead it had a tear-off slip acknowledging acceptance of their order on their terms and conditions. This the sellers signed and returned endorsing the slip to the effect that the order had been accepted on their revised quotation effective at that date.

The problem now arose as to whether the sellers could claim the revised/increased price or were limited to the price originally quoted.

The Court of Appeal held that in the absence of real agreement so-called battle rules had to be applied; in this case it became clear that the

CASE STUDY 2.2

THE BATTLE OF THE FORMS

contract was on the buyer's terms not the seller's and their terms did not include a price escalation clause.

The moral seems to be, read carefully any terms you are using, or which are submitted to you, and do not fudge the issue of genuine disagreement. Where both parties are keen to forge a deal, mutually agreeable terms can probably be thrashed out; where this is not the case no satisfaction will be achieved from a lengthy court case, win or lose!

(*Butler Machine Tool Co. Ltd* v. *Ex-Cell-O-Corporation*
(England) Ltd (1979))

Acceptance

Offeror The party making the offer.

Offeree The party to whom an offer is made. (Similarly, *promisor* and *promisee*, *mortgagor* and *mortgagee*, and so on).

An acceptance is the unconditional assent of the person to whom the offer was made (called the 'offeree') to all the terms of the offer. Anything less cannot make a contract, it is a counter-offer. For example, the seller displays a price, the prospective buyer offers half of it, it is refused and three-quarters is suggested, and so on, offer and counter-offer, until the parties are settled upon a price. It may be that they do not, or cannot agree. The negotiations break down. There is no contract. A wise businessman or woman always concludes such negotiations, whether conducted face to face or through the post, with some kind of remark confirming the agreed details of the settled transaction. In this way the complications about who offered and who counter-offered and when they did so are avoided. There is an agreement, and it is confirmed.

By making a counter-offer the original offer is by definition rejected, however. If the counter-offer is itself rejected and the prospective purchaser unwillingly brings himself or herself to 'accept' the original price asked, he or she will find the goods or services no longer necessarily 'on offer' at that price. The seller has discovered the priceless information that he or she (the seller) has something that B (the buyer) wants. Therefore, the price may rise! In order to maintain the original offer while still seeking to strike a better bargain the purchaser should consider more subtle tactics such as 'Are you open to offer?' or 'Could you include some parts/service in your price?'. Such a request for further information is *not* a counter-offer and does not reject the original offer while increasing the scope for haggling.

In order to be effective the acceptance must correspond exactly to the terms of the offer. In a general way this means an offer made by Telex should be accepted by Telex, rather than for example by Post, and an offer made by Post may be accepted by Post. Where the offeror has inserted particular terms, e.g. acceptance by a particular date/time or in a certain format, in person, handwritten, typewritten, + deposit, sample, photograph, failure to comply will result in the acceptance being ineffective giving the offeror time to revoke his or her offer and failing to nail the bargain. Of course, it is open to the offeror to accept the counter-offer if he or she so wishes. It is worth being precise!

In the same way, a conditional offer – 'Yes, if . . . equals 'No'. This in part explains the problem frequently encountered in buying or selling houses, quite apart from the formal requirement of evidence in writing, a prospective purchaser usually agrees to buy only 'if the survey is acceptable' or 'if finance can be arranged'. Since his or her acceptance is not final, the vendor is not bound and the possibility of resale to a speedier purchaser becomes a possibility.

Consideration

A contract is essentially a *bargain*. Without some element of consideration (Key concept 2.3) there would be no contract at all, just a gratuitous promise – a promise for nothing (e.g. I will give you £100 because it is sunny today). Such promises are not legally binding. With few exceptions no promise is binding upon the promisor unless he or she has received something in return for it, some consideration. For example: 'I promise to pay if you promise to deliver' is a contract. We both stand to gain. We both stand to lose. It is this element of exchange that makes our arrangement a contract. If I pay and you fail to deliver, that amounts to a breach of contract. I have done my part, and now you must do yours, or pay me something for my trouble.

'Consideration' is a technical term used in contract law. Businessmen or women do not make contracts for the fun of it, they do so in order to obtain some benefit from the transaction. The benefit they are after is known as the consideration in the contract, or the quid pro quo.	KEY CONCEPT 2.3 ───────────── **CONSIDERATION**

In as much as there must be an element of exchange in a contract, it follows that merely to do that which you are already bound to do for the other party cannot support his or her promise to pay you more (*Stilk* v. *Myrick* (1809). However, if you do more than you are already bound to do, then you may well be supplying extra consideration with which you can support the promise of extra money (*Hartley* v. *Ponsonby* [1857]) p. 213.

In principle the parties make their own agreement and if extra money is promised it will usually be because market rates are rising and implicitly therefore the increase is earned, or because the promisor thereby gains some additional benefit, even the benefit of ensuring the original agreement is carried out as agreed as opposed to running the risk it is broken and having to sue for compensation. Where an agreement to pay extra is obtained by unfair pressure the agreement may be set aside on the grounds of duress and any extra paid recovered. For many years the degree of pressure thought necessary to avoid an agreement was direct physical force, or the threat of it, to the person or family of the promisor, but the common law has responded to business needs in extending relief to cases of un-justified economic duress (The Exhibition Stand: Case study 2.3) 'un-justified' because all bargains are ultimately struck as a result of pressure being brought to reach an equilibrium – I have it, you want it = a price – i.e. some degree of pressure is inevitable and acceptable.

In many cases where a fixed price is quoted and a request for additional

CASE STUDY 2.3

THE EXHIBITION STAND: NO ADDITIONAL PAYMENT FOR PERFORMING THE CONTRACT

A contractor undertook to erect an exhibition stand for a client, shortly before the exhibition was due to open. He asked the client for extra money to pay overtime to his carpenters and electricians or else the contract would not be fulfilled on time. In the circumstances and faced with the economic consequences of not having his stand available the client agreed to pay the extra. Subsequently the client sought to recover the money on the grounds that the agreement for the extra had been made under unjustified pressure. The court held the agreement voidable, i.e. allowed the client to set it aside, and gave judgment for the return of the additional money.

(*B and S Contracts and Design Ltd* v. *Victor Green Publications Ltd* (1984) 1 C.R. 419)

funds is then made it may be very difficult to resist the claim that something extra is being given in return because almost always a contract is framed with a clause permitting variations 'in the light of circumstances beyond X's control'. 'Variations' is a euphemism for increase and covers such things as delays in delivery of material, strikes, labour cost increases or site hitches in infinite variety.

Consideration in a business context will usually take the form of money on one side and some form of action on the other. Indeed, sometimes inaction on the other, since a forbearance to sue on an actionable matter would be a valuable consideration. The actual amount of the payment does not matter. The law of contract (in the absence of fraud) is not concerned with market prices. The basic principle is *caveat emptor* still. Provided that some value changes hands, then it is up to the parties how much value is involved. In *Thomas* v. *Thomas* (1842), for example, a house was let for £1 a year, and in *Chappell* v. *Nestle* (1957) the element of exchange included three empty chocolate bar wrappers which the recipients threw away.

The idea that the amount paid can be small or that consideration need not be adequate or equal on both sides does not extend to the payment of debts. If I owe you £100, and you agree to the settling of the debt for £50 I cannot hold you to your word should you change your mind and decide to come back for the rest of the money.

This has been settled since *Pinnel's Case* (1602) p. 213, and has quite recently been graphically re-emphasized in *D & C Builders* v. *Rees* (1965) p. 213. But if I owe you £100 at the end of the month, and you are short of money *now*, and you ask for *early settlement*, saying that £50 will do, then it will clear the debt. You have had something extra – early payment – and it does not matter how much this 'extra' is. The rule, at its most basic is: 'straight part payment will not do'. If the part payment is early, or to a different person, or in a different form, e.g. together with some property interest, or even in a different place, then this is not 'straight part payment', and, if the creditor agrees to the variation, then the debt is settled.

The use of a discount for prompt cash payment is frequently employed by businesses making use of this rule. Clearly if the customer were later liable for the full sum the incentive to pay promptly would be lost.

A note on the enforcement of judgment debts

The business enterprise will be in a constant state of cash flow. Money will be owed and owing. Some of the these debts may arise from actions successfully brought in the courts.

There are a number of ways in which such debts can be chased up, but the important point for the busy businessman or woman is that the court will not chase them for you. It is not as in the criminal courts, the Magistrates' and Crown Courts, where a prolonged unwillingness to pay a fine will see the court officers in pursuit; a civil judgment debt must be enforced by the judgment debtor. It may be that the business will write off the debt rather than spend time and money chasing it. If this seems the correct action, then was the action worth bringing in the first place? 'Never sue a man of straw'. If the business will have to spend time and money running around after small debtors then it may be worth writing the debt off. However, some businessmen or women feel that a reputation for inaction is a dangerous thing!

Should a judgment debt require enforcement the most common mechanism is called a 'warrant of execution' in the county courts (*fieri facias* in the High Court). It is what the lay-businessman or woman might refer to as 'sending in the bailiffs', and that is what is involved. However, if the judgment debtor does not have any property worth taking away and selling at public auction in order to clear the debt, an attachment of earnings could be sought. This would require a regular deduction from earnings paid into court to settle the debt. This may be inappropriate because the debtor is self-employed, unemployed or another business. (These orders were developed to assist in the collection of maintenance, but any debt could be recovered in this way.)

Fieri facias   The name given to the writ used to enforce a judgment debt in the High Court (sometimes shortened to *fi, fa*).

Additionally there is the garnishee order; if the creditor can find anyone who owes the debtor money, this payment can be diverted to settle the debt. Whatever the circumstances, a proper business system might have avoided the problem arising at all.

The contents of contracts

Having entered into a contract, the business should be aware of precisely what the extent of the contractual obligation is. Most businesses use standard forms (Key concept 2.2) of one kind or another when they enter regularly into the same kind of transaction. This is a good policy; it is clear and cheap and the business knows 'where it stands'. However, the contents of the contract may well extend beyond the words within the written document. For example, later in this book we discuss a variety of contractual terms which are implied into certain types of contract with which the business may well be concerned, such as those for the sale of goods and services (Chapter 6). There will be express and implied terms, and these implied terms might come from statutes, or they may arise from trade usages. These are matters which are well known within a particular trade, but not so well known generally. If both parties are within the trade, then the trade usages (or customs) may well be implied into the contract. Here the judges very clearly uphold and reflect business usage.

Express term   A term expressly agreed by the parties orally or in writing.

Implied term   Terms imported into the contract without deliberate act of parties by custom, statute or necessity.

British Crane Hire Corporation v. *Ipswich Plant Hire Ltd* (1974)

This contract was for the hire of a special crane. Both parties were in the business of hiring out heavy earth-moving equipment. It was accepted in the trade that if a machine became bogged down in marshy ground, then it was up to the hirer and not the owner to cover the cost of recovery. So when this happened in this case, sufficient notice of this liability had been given.

Furthermore, there may be terms implied into the contract by the courts simply because the deal would not make business sense without them ('terms implied to ensure 'business efficacy'', as some lawyers say).

The Moorcock (1889)

This case concerned a mooring at a jetty in the tidal part of the River Thames. The owners of a steamship, *The Moorcock*, hired the use of the jetty in order to discharge cargo. When the tide went out the ship grounded, as both parties must have known it would. This damaged the ship, because it grounded on a hard ridge on the river bed. The contract made no mention of the state of the river bed, and the owners of the jetty did not control it anyway. Nevertheless, unless the safety at mooring were held to be part of the contract, it would have made little business sense. The owners should have checked the state of the river bed, or at least warned hirers if they had not done so.

(a)   Terms of contract

The importance of the distinction between conditions and warranties is the different remedies for their breach (Key concept 2.4).

Broadly, for a breach of condition the innocent party can cancel, whereas for a breach of warranty he or she cannot: he or she is limited to damages. The business contract, particularly if it is a standard form contract, might specifically provide that breach of a particular term gives the right to cancel or might exclude the right to cancel where otherwise it would be available. Not all terms are so specific as condition or warranty. It may be that the particular term cannot be easily categorized. In these circumstances the rights of the innocent party will depend upon the consequences of the breach. That is, if the effect of the breach is such that the innocent party has been deprived of substantially all he or she contracted for, then he or

---

KEY CONCEPT 2.4	Whilst the contents of contracts are all contractual terms, these terms are not all of equal importance. The more important are called 'conditions' and the less important are called 'warranties'.
CONDITIONS AND WARRANTIES	This relative importance might reflect the attitudes of the parties to the contract or it might reflect the attitude of Parliament, in the sense that certain of the contractual terms which are implied into contracts by statute are conditions because the statute so provides. For example, most of the terms implied into contracts for the sale of goods by the Sale of Goods Act 1979 are conditions.

she can cancel. If the effect is not so serious, then he or she cannot: he or she can only sue for damages (*Hong Kong Fir Shipping Case* (1962)).

What makes a term a condition or a warranty is essentially the intention of the parties. Without understanding the difference or bringing the mind to bear on the problem it is unrealistic to suggest the parties intended anything. Nevertheless at a practical level the distinction in cost terms is crucial. If a party breaks a term which is a condition, the other party has the right to terminate the contract and claim compensation – either a fixed sum agreed in advance (liquidated damages) or the losses which have resulted from the breach. If the term were merely a warranty the right to damages could remain but the innocent party would continue bound to carry out his or her part of the bargain.

In the unhappy situation that a business cannot fulfil all its obligations to its customers, choices must be made about which customers are to be let down – the criteria for this may be manifold, e.g. whose order was received first? size of order, prospect of continuing business, past relationships, distance, method of payment, etc. but apart from moral obligation what about cost? Which customers are going to be the least expensive to let down, immediately and in future? Normally it will be more expensive (cause greater loss) to break a condition than a warranty. A business must therefore know, before it can make an essential decision, what exactly are the terms of the bargain it has made and what are their legal effects. Ignorance or disregard of potential liabilities and their cost is very foolish; careful construction and reading of contracts is essential.

It is very common to find exclusion clauses in business contracts (Key concept 2.5). They are not popular in the courts and will always be carefully construed against the party seeking to rely upon them. This reflects the clear object of such clauses, one party is seeking to maximize the benefit to be obtained from the deal whilst minimizing the obligation. This may seem to be sound business practice, but the ability to achieve it is circumscribed by law. Briefly, in order to be enforceable the exclusion clause must be part of the agreement at the time the agreement was made, it must cover the damage complained of, and be unaffected by statutory restrictions. We shall consider these requirements in turn.

There are only two ways in which an exclusion clause can enter a contract: by signature and by notice. The law takes a serious view of signed documents; you are bound by what you have signed whether you have read it or not. In order to give adequate notice, a sign or clause in an unsigned document must be effectively drawn to the other party's attention and this must be done precontractually. (*Thornton* v. *Shoe Lane Parking* (1971) and *Olley* v. *Marlborough Court Hotel* (1949)) (The Lost Slides: Case study 2.4).

The terms of a contract define both the rights and obligations of the parties to that contract, and might also purport to reduce those obligations which the law would otherwise impose. Such a term is called an exclusion or exemption clause.

KEY CONCEPT 2.5

EXCLUSION CLAUSE

CASE STUDY 2.4

THE LOST SLIDES: ADEQUATE NOTICE OF CONTRACTUAL TERMS

An advertising agency contacted a photographic picture library to enquire for some 1950s transparencies for possible use in an advertising promotion. The library sent 47 transparencies for consideration in a bag and a delivery note containing their terms of business to the agency. The agency telephoned to confirm receipt and to say that some of the pictures looked possible. Unfortunately, the pictures were then apparently forgotten and were not returned for 28 days. The terms of loan clearly printed on the delivery note, required all transparencies to be returned within 14 days and provided for a holding fee of £5.00 per day per picture plus VAT after that time. The agency received a bill of £3783.50 which they failed to pay and for which they were subsequently sued. The library relied on their terms of loan, deemed to have been accepted when the agency retained the transparencies.

At first instance the library succeeded but in the Court of Appeal the agency successfully pleaded that on analogy with exclusion clauses a harsh or unusual clause could not take effect unless adequate notice was given. In this case although the clause was clearly printed, the scale of the daily rate was so unusual and exorbitant and the likelihood of a hirer (particularly an advertising agency known for working at pressure) reading the terms was so slight that adequate notice was held *not* to have been given and therefore the clause was not effective and damages of a much more moderate sum were awarded.

(*Interfoto Picture Library Ltd* v. *Stiletto Visual Programmes Ltd* [1988] 1 All E.R. 348)

Even if adequate notice is given the clause will be construed strictly to cover only the kind of damage expressly excluded; for example, in most places where a cloakroom is provided for guests' or public use there will be a notice excluding liability for loss or theft of guest's belongings. If an item of clothing were soaked by a defective water sprinkler this would be damage not covered by the exclusion clause and for which the host would be liable.

The judges in applying the custom or common law wove a web of restrictive requirements to prevent the most offensive exclusion clauses taking effect but were powerless to do more than lay down specific requirements as to notice, interpretation of purpose and construction. It was left to Parliament in the Unfair Contract Terms Act 1977 to legislate comprehensively prohibiting the use of exclusion clauses altogether in certain cases, notably liability for personal injury or death caused by negligence, and in the case of consumer contracts prohibiting the exclusion of the consumer protection terms implied by statute (Chapter 6) and severely limiting the use of such clauses in certain other circumstances by subjecting them to the test of reasonableness.

Here is a clear illustration of the legal framework developing, becoming crystallized and expanding again as the judges tackle a problem; Parliament intervenes and the courts then interpret the statute by applying it to new situations.

For further detailed discussion of the rules and their application see a

It is common practice when a house is bought for the purchasers to obtain a loan from a building society, local authority or bank. Before such a loan is granted the lender usually requires the purchasers to pay for a survey/valuation. This survey is solely for the purpose of giving the lender an assurance on the value of the property as security, it is not intended to be a full structural report to the purchaser. However desirable it may be for a purchaser to have his own independent survey at additional cost the trend is increasingly for one stop shopping, and for the purchaser to rely on the valuation as proof that the property is basically sound. Noting this trend the courts have declared that a surveyor in this position does owe a duty of care to prospective purchasers.

The question then arises, can this duty of care be excluded? It galls many people that they should be billed a substantial fee for professional services and at the same time be told that any advice given is without liability. The question arose in a couple of cases which were heard together in the House of Lords under the name *Smith* v. *Eric S. Bush* [1989].

Their Lordships held that in principle this liability could be excluded but subject to the provisions of the Unfair Contract Terms Act 1977. This allows liability to be excluded provided the exclusion is fair and reasonable. Looking at the housing market, the high cost of houses and the high rates of interest charged to borrowers their Lordships held it would not be fair and reasonable for mortgagees and valuers to impose on purchasers the risk of loss arising as a result of incompetence or carelessness on the part of valuers.

Incidentally the court considered that in the case of commercial property, blocks of flats or very expensive property, where a purchaser could be expected to have his own survey, the exclusion might be reasonable.

Here is a useful illustration of the way a court will take into account changing social pressures in the very way Parliament presumably intended when they passed the legislation.

Smith v. *Bush* [1989]

CASE STUDY 2.5

THE DUTY OF CARE OF SURVEYORS

textbook on Contract, e.g. Cheshire, Fifoot and Furmston, *Law of Contract* (11th edn), Chapter 2 for background and Chapter 6 for detailed rules. The art of drafting clauses which give as much cover as possible is well developed – too wide an exclusion and the whole clause will be declared unreasonable and, therefore, void; too limited a clause and a business incurs unnecessary liability (The Duty of Care of Surveyors: Case study 2.5).

(b) Vitiating factors

These are elements or circumstances which can avoid the contract. Even where there is apparent agreement there may be a reason why the law will not enforce the contract. These reasons are collectively called 'vitiating factors'. Here is another example of the common law responding flexibly

Vitiate To spoil, or to deprive of efficacy.

through judicial decisions to social and economic pressure to ensure a just result. In this section we shall consider briefly some of the most common vitiating factors.

Lack of form

There are usually no formal requirements made of those who decide to make a contract. However, where there are, and the required formalities are not met, the contract is not properly made, and is not enforceable in the normal way.

Certain contracts must be made in the most formal of ways, using a deed, notably conveyances of land and gratuitous promises, e.g. covenants to charity. Some contracts must be made in writing. These include bills of exchange, transfers of shares in a company, consumer credit agreements, promissory notes, and most recently contracts for the sale of land (Law of Property (Miscellaneous Provisions) Act 1989). They do not require a formally executed document, but they must be made in writing. Guarantees require less than this, only written evidence that they have been made.

Of course, the careful business enterprise will often use writing, and keep written records of oral transactions with all relevant documentary evidence, but there are those occasions where formality of one kind or another is more than just good business practice, it is essential to validity.

Mistake

Since the basis of a contract is agreement, where the parties have made a mistake, it might be assumed there is no contract if there is no agreement. But in fact this is very rarely the case, for the agreement the law seeks is objective rather than subjective (a *consensus ad idem*). The only question to be asked is whether a valid offer was met by an unconditional acceptance. Where the terms of the offer and acceptance are unclear there is no agreement and, therefore, no contract. It is not a case of there having been an agreement but the agreement being set aside because of mistake, e.g. in *Raffles* v. *Wichelhaus* (1864) there was a contract for sale of a cargo of cotton on board *ss Peerless* in Bombay harbour. There were two ships of the same name both in Bombay harbour. The court held no binding contract had been made. One party thought one ship; one the other. It was impossible from the evidence to find an enforceable agreement.

As ever analysis of the problem creates the opportunity for a solution, the more precise the detail or the specification the less the possibility of misunderstanding of the parties. Too often in a hurried deal assumptions are made about quality, price, credit, delivery, etc. which when not met cause ill-feeling, argument and possible litigation. Time spent on clarifying and specifying detail is time generally well spent; even if the price to be charged reflects the time involved it will exclude the far greater time and cost of a later dispute.

Conveyance The document which has the effect of transferring the title to property from a seller to a buyer.

Guarantee A secondary liability, such that if X does not honour his or her obligations, then Y will.

Indemnity An indemnity is a primary obligation to repay a debt if the principal debtor defaults.

Consensus ad idem On the same wavelength. Agreement in the same terms, on the same subject matter.

KEY CONCEPT 2.6	You are bound by what you sign, whether or not you have read the document, and if you have read it, whether or not you understand it.
SIGNATURE	

The effect of a signature (Key concept 2.6) is of particular importance for the busy businessman or woman. There are many reported instances of documents signed in haste, monies paid on bogus invoices, and so on. A graphic illustration of the attitude of the law towards the binding effect of a signature can be seen in *Saunders* v. *Anglia Building Society* (1970).

Frequently, a signature is called for on a time-sheet, delivery note, receipt, etc. Given the knowledge that a signature cannot be rescinded on the grounds of mistake or misunderstanding the advice has to be 'do not sign without reading, marking and inwardly digesting' and if in any doubt calling for independent help! Such advice might bring a busy office to a standstill, perhaps the equivalent of a British Rail work to rule? More helpfully where a signature is needed its effect can be limited, e.g. rather than goods received + signature, goods received '*unexamined*' + signature. Where the signature acknowledges receipt of a specified quantity or weight of goods the signatory accepts the correct quantity unless again the signature is qualified by, e.g. 'goods not counted'. This will enable the carrier to go on his or her way while preserving the opportunity for the recipient to check the delivery carefully. Where the checking must be done before release of the carrier, costs will increase proportionately but release of carrier without checking may lose the purchaser the right to complain in the event of short delivery or damaged goods.

Where a signature is required as a witness there is no need to read the document concerned – this might well be considered an impertinence – but care should be taken to ensure that the witness actually *does* see the signature to be witnessed and qualifies his or her own signature by words such as 'witness to . . .' or 'signed as witness'.

Another mistake which is sometimes claimed as invalidating a contractual obligation arises from a fraud where one party to the contract pretends to be someone he or she is not. The businessman, thinking that he is contracting with a particular person, agrees to the deal. Often he or she takes a cheque in payment for goods; when the cheque bounces the fraud is revealed. The law here is fairly clear. Where negotiations take place between people face to face there is a presumption that the contract is made between them, and not any other character that one of the parties might be pretending to be *Lewis* v. *Averay* (1971). The contract may be set aside for fraud but unless and until it is, any innocent purchaser will obtain a good title (Key concept 2.7).

Where there is a shared or common mistake about the existence of goods, the contract will be void for mistake, e.g. in *Couturier* v. *Hastie* (1856) a contract for the sale of a cargo of corn which had already been disposed of at the date of the sale unbeknown to either party was held to be void. In this case the agreement was made on the tacit assumption that

| Behind most of common law contract, even in these days of supposedly increasing consumer protection, remains the basic principle *caveat emptor* (let the buyer beware). It follows that an error about the value of the goods involved in a contract cannot be pleaded so as to avoid the obligations. A mistake about value, in the absence of fraud, is not enough. | KEY CONCEPT 2.7

CAVEAT EMPTOR |

the goods did exist and it was possible to carry out the contract as made. Where this is not the case the agreement falls.

NB   It may be that one or other party guarantees to the other that the goods do or will exist. In this case their destruction or loss is held to be at the risk of the party holding them out as being available. Whether or not this is the intention of the parties could be crucial. Again very great care is needed.

Misrepresentation

During pre-contractual negotiations there may well be statements made which, although they lead to the contract, do not actually form part of it. This will be seen, for example, where the agreement is written down and certain of the pre-contractual statements are not included in the document.

It may be that one or more of these statements turns out to have been wrong. Thus one party may have been misled into making the contract and redress may be sought. Equity provides for the remedy of rescission, i.e. restoration to their original position to be available where this is possible. This differs markedly from the object of the award of common law damages for a breach of contract. Damages for breach are designed to put the parties into the positions they would have been in had the contract been performed.

Recission 'A giving and taking back on both sides', to restore the pre-contract position where possible. This is an equitable remedy. It is at the discretion of the court.

The remedy of rescission is given for an actionable misrepresentation, i.e. a false statement of fact which induced the contract. The statement must have been factual – not merely of opinion (*Bisset* v. *Wilkinson* [1927], but compare with *Smith* v. *Land and House Property Corporation* [1884]).

In the case of fraud, the property has usually moved into the hands of an innocent third party. Indeed, it is often the discovery of the goods there or the dishonouring of a cheque which reveals the trick. Nevertheless, the innocent party is not in a good position; he or she cannot recover his or her goods from an innocent third party (*Car and Universal Finance* v. *Caldwell* [1963]), but can only claim compensation if the 'rogue' is ever traced.

Sometimes silence itself can amount to misrepresentation. This is the case where something is said which is true but is only half the truth, e.g. 'The property is let at a good rent' but nothing is said of the fact that the tenants have given notice, or where there is a positive duty to disclose information and this is not done. A typical example in a business context is the contract for insurance cover. Such contracts as these are called *uberrimae fidei* (of the utmost good faith). A full and frank disclosure must be made upon an insurance proposal form. Failure to do so renders the contract voidable at the option of the party misled. That is, the insurers can refuse to pay out in the event of a claim because they were not given the accurate information they needed to assess the risk (e.g. *Locker* v. *Western Insurance* (1936) p. 215). (We deal in rather more detail with insurance law in Chapter 8.)

Further to the statement of fact having been made, it must have been relied upon by the other party. That is, it must have induced the contract (*Redgrave* v. *Hurd* (1881) p. 215, but compare with *Attwood* v. *Small* (1838) p. 215).

Of course, the grievance follows upon the statement relied upon having been false. It might have been made with the intention to deceive, or it could have been an innocent statement which was in fact wrong. Before the

Misrepresentation Act 1967 these were the only categories, and the early cases should be read in this light. However, since the 1967 Act there is a third category – negligent misrepresentation. Thus, if a reasonable man or woman would not have realized that the statement was false, it is an innocent misrepresentation, but if he or she should have realized it, then it is negligent.

This classification is important because the right to damages depends upon it. For fraudulent or negligent misrepresentation there is a right to damages. For non-negligent innocent misrepresentation the court *may* award damages in its discretion if rescission is not possible.

Illegal contracts

Certain contracts will not be enforced by the courts because of some illegality in the making or performance of the contract. 'Illegal' in this sense does not necessarily mean criminally unlawful, but that some rule of statute or common law has been broken either at the time, or in the way, the contract was made or in its performance. Such an illegal contract is normally void and unenforceable although there may be certain circumstances where one of the parties may be able to recover money paid or property transferred even if he or she cannot enforce the other side's promise.

Examples of contracts whose purpose is illegal by statute range from betting and wagering contracts under the Gaming Act 1945, agreements to restrict retail prices in most sectors (Resale Prices Act 1976) or to restrict competition (Restrictive Trade Practices Act 1976 and Articles 85 and 86 of the Treaty of Rome), to contracts for payment of surrogate mothers or the sale of human organs.

There is no criminal offence in the making of most of these contracts but the parties should know that the law will not help them to enforce their bargains should the other side default. In the case of breaches of Articles 85 and 86 the European Commission has power to levy substantial fines on any undertaking found to be in breach (British Leyland: Case study 2.6).

Some breach of regulation may occur in the performance of a contract, e.g. an unlicensed HGV may be used to transport goods. In *Archbolds* v. *Spanglett* [1961] the carrier of a cargo of whisky on a run from Leeds to London lost his load through negligence. Unknown to the plaintiffs the defendants did not have the necessary licence. The Court of Appeal allowed them to recover for the loss of the whisky despite the illegal way the contract had been performed on the grounds that the requirement of a licence was incidental to the main purpose, i.e. the carriage, and the plaintiffs being unaware were guilty of no illegality. *Had* the plaintiffs known, or ought to have known they could not have recovered for their loss and could probably have been found guilty of aiding and abetting the offence.

By contrast in *Anderson* v. *Daniel* [1924] the seller delivered ten tons of artificial manure. Statute then in force required an invoice stating the composition of the fertilizer to be delivered with the goods. The seller failed to deliver such invoice, and his subsequent action for the price failed since he could not rely on his own illegal performance.

Businesses should thus be very careful to ensure that they comply strictly with any licensing, tax, or statutory regulations applicable to their particular

CASE STUDY 2.6

THE BRITISH LEYLAND CASE: 'ABUSE OF DOMINANT POSITION' RULING BY THE EUROPEAN COMMISSION

In November 1986 British Leyland were held liable to pay a fine of 350 000 ECU in a judgment of the European Court upholding a ruling by the European Commission who had imposed the fine on BL for abuse of its dominant market position. 'According to the Commission BL had abused its dominant position contrary to article 86 of the Treaty of Rome in three ways:

☐ It had allowed the National Type Approval certificate needed to register a vehicle in Great Britain to expire in respect of left-hand drive Metros.
☐ In certain cases it refused to issue certificates of conformity for vehicles of that type which had been reimported from the Continent, although it was in a position to do so.
☐ In other cases it charged an excessive fee for the issue of a certificate of conformity.

trade since breach of such requirements may result not only in a fine, often of a fairly minimal variety, but in loss of ability to enforce any contract involved.

In addition to contracts illegal by statute the common law regards a wide group of agreements as illegal as contrary to public policy. The extent of this is to be divined from judicial decisions in previous cases. No one asked the public! There are many kinds of agreement broadly of an immoral or unethical variety in this group. Probably the most important for business purposes are agreements in restraint of trade. These include not only restraints on an employee leaving his or her employer (Chapter 7) but also those restraints which a buyer of a business might wish to impose upon the seller, so as to prevent him setting up next door in direct competition (The Nordenfelt Gun Case [1894]) and those contracts between big companies such as breweries or oil corporations and those who run pubs and garages. They are called 'solus ties'. Thus we refer sometimes to 'tied' houses and garages. In return for (usually) financial advantages the pub or garage undertakes to sell only the product of one company. Such a restraint of trade is void unless held to be reasonable in the circumstances. An interesting case, in that it shows both sides of this line, is *Esso Petroleum* v. *Harpers Garages* [1963]. The European Commission has provided specific guidelines for such agreements where they involve intra-community trade. It is equally important for a business to know what it *can* do to protect its affairs as what it cannot. Careful study needs to be made of previous decisions on what is 'reasonable'. Where only part of the agreement is contrary to these principles, that part will be removed and the rest, at least on the face of it, will remain enforceable (*Goldsoll* v. *Goldman* [1915] p. 216).

(c)   The discharge of contracts

A contractual relationship will not continue indefinitely. It will come to an end. When this happens the contract is said to have been discharged. There are a number of ways in which contracts can be discharged:

Discharge by agreement

All contracts are agreements, but, as we have seen, all agreements are not contracts. If a contract can be made by agreement, it can be unmade in the same way. Technically, the consideration from each side consists in a forbearance to sue. So that each party promises the other that he will not sue for non-performance. This exchange of promises makes their agreement a contract.

For example, X agrees to hire a car on a particular day from Y; later X changes his plans and agrees with Y to cancel his booking for the day. X releases Y from Y's obligation to provide the car and Y releases X from X's obligation to pay for the car. Probably X will wish to take the car another day and Y can re-let the car to Z so there is mutual satisfaction. There is no problem unless one party has partly performed his side of the deal; in this case he will require compensation for his efforts before he will release the other side from his obligations. So it might be that the parties will agree to end the deal by one making payment to the other to set matters even; such an agreement is called accord and satisfaction; for example, if Y had specially cleaned the car for X, Y might ask for part payment or retain a deposit made with the booking in return for the release.

Discharge by breach

We have observed that contracts are made up of contractual terms, and that these terms are not all of equal importance. The more important terms are called conditions, and the less important ones are called warranties (Key concept 2.4). We saw that the purpose of making this distinction was to establish which breaches entitled the innocent party to regard himself or herself as free of contractual obligations. We concluded that for a breach of condition the innocent party could cancel, but for a breach of warranty he or she could not. There are sometimes intermediate (or 'innominate') terms where the entitlement depends upon the seriousness of the breach (*Hong Kong Fir Shipping Case* (1962) p. 214). It follows from this that a contract is discharged by breach only if the breach is one of condition rather than warranty, for example non-delivery of goods or delivery of seriously defective goods. A breach of warranty, for example late payment by the buyer, will not usually entitle the supplier to cancel the contract unless prompt payment was made an express condition.

Discharge by frustration

Frustration, in this context, means 'supervening impossibility'. Often when a contract is formed it is performed very soon afterwards (Key concept 2.8). For example, an agreement in a retail outlet for goods is formed and performed within seconds, usually at the till. However, where there is a time lapse between formation and performance, there is a risk that something unforeseen might happen which might make performance impossible (*Re Shipton, Anderson and Co.* [1915] and *Condor* v. *Barron Knights* [1966], but compare with *Maritime National Fish* v. *Ocean Trawlers* [1935] where the frustration was self-induced). It is not enough that it is more difficult to perform the contract, or that any profit one party or the other was intent upon making out of the deal evaporates. Performance must be impossible before the contract can be said to have been discharged by

KEY CONCEPT 2.8	Frustration occurs where a contract possible when made subsequently becomes impossible owing to some supervening act or circumstance unforeseen by the parties and outside their control. The effect of frustration is to discharge the contractual obligations from the moment of the frustrating event. Where the parties have made their own provisions these apply. Where no arrangement has been made the Law Reform (Frustrated Contracts) Act (1943) applies.
FRUSTRATION	

frustration and the parties freed from their obligations under it (e.g. *Taylor* v. *Caldwell* (1863) but compare *Amalgamated Investments* v. *John Walker* [1976]).

It will be a question of commercial concern to what extent a party's purpose is made part of the contract. Clearly there will be occasions where I do not wish to reveal all my plans, but in this case if they become impossible it is I who am frustrated not the contract.

Most businesses include in their contracts a *force majeure* clause governing what is to happen in the event of contracted performance becoming impossible. Where frustration occurs the Law Reform (Frustrated Contracts) Act 1943 outlines what is to happen – where the loss falls is essentially a matter of chance. Far preferable for most businesses is to have an analysis of the possible risks that could occur and their apportionment. The identified risks can then be costed and where appropriate covered by insurance (Chapter 8), e.g. most transport contracts consider the possibility of delay due to strikes, weather or political action and make provision for alternative routes, times or even cancellation at the client's risk with the concurrent advice to insure! Where the carrier undertakes to deliver 'come hell or high water' he or she will no doubt charge accordingly.

Unfortunately, it is the business of lawyers to identify all the possible disasters, not to will them to happen but to evaluate their likelihood and their potential cost/risk factor. Precautions of a practical or financial nature can then be built in.

Discharge by performance

The contract will come to an end when each party has done what they said they would do; the contract is said to be discharged by performance. Provided that performance is complete on both sides that will be the end of the matter. Problems arise, however, when performance is incomplete. The basic rule is quite straightforward: 'part performance is no performance' (*Cutter* v. *Powell* (1795)). Strictly, any deviation from complete performance will be insufficient to bind the other party to his or her obligation. However, the harshness of this basic rule has been reduced over the years by various exceptions. It must be borne in mind, though, that if none of the exceptions applies, then the basic rule applies. The following are the main exceptions.

☐ Substantial performance – where most of the work has been done (*Hoenig* v. *Isaacs* [1952]) but compare with *Bolton* v. *Mahadeva* [1972].

The payment will reflect the worth of the work done, i.e. on a *quantum meruit* (as much as he has earned) basis. These kinds of dispute are very common and account for service companies, e.g. furniture fitters and double-glazing installers, sometimes seeking full payment in advance to avoid being held to ransom later.

☐ Where a contract can be seen as not an entire transaction, but a series of smaller deals, it is said to be severable. This means that the performance of one or more parts of the deal can bring the entitlement to payment even if the whole transaction is not completed. Stage payments are frequently employed; they not only aid cash flow but protect in the event of incomplete performance.

☐ Prevention of performance – fairly obviously, if the reason that performance is not complete is that the other party has prevented full performance, that will entitle the party who has partly performed to be paid for what he or she has done. For example, an author agreed to research and write a book. When he had completed about half the work the publishers cancelled the project. He was unable completely to perform, but he was held to be entitled to half the money he would have been paid if he had been allowed to complete the task on a *quantum meruit* basis (*Planché* v. *Colburn* [1831]).

Quantum meruit   *Quantum meruit* means simply 'as much as it is worth'.

☐ Acceptance of part performance – where one party has partly performed, and the other has accepted this, then he or she must pay at the contract rate for what he or she has accepted. That is, provided that he or she had a true choice about accepting it (e.g. *Sumpter* v. *Hedges* [1898]).

☐ Performance, time and standard form contracts. In a contract time can be made 'of the essence'. This is a very important principle in a business context. If time is of the essence of a contract, then late performance is a breach (*Rickards* v. *Oppenheim* [1950]). 'The well-prepared businessman or woman, particularly one who is contracting upon a repeating basis in the same line of business, will have a standard form of contract drawn up professionally. He or she will then 'know where he stands', as it were. Most businesses, and all utilities (gas, electricity, telephones, etc.), use standard forms. Within a standard form contract it is usual to find an expression about time for performance. For example, a contract for materials to be processed by the business enterprise will probably make delivery time 'of the essence'. It is no use if the materials arrive late. Late delivery will not discharge the contractual obligation to deliver (subject to any valid exclusion clause). The contract will be breached. The business will be able to refuse the late delivery, and recover as compensation the cost of obtaining materials elsewhere, or the lost profits sustained through not being able to minimize losses by obtaining materials elsewhere. If time is of the essence, and the performance is late, this will give the innocent party the choice of whether to accept the delivery or not. Once the choice has been made it cannot be re-made if late delivery is accepted. The right to earlier delivery has been waived. If a later time has been agreed, for example, delivery a week after the due date, this becomes the crucial time. Delivery after then will not do.

Remedies for breach of contract

(a) Damages

The innocent party to a breach of contract may seek compensation. The normal remedy is damages. The object of the award is to put the parties into the position they would have occupied had the contract been performed. The measure of damages is based upon the rules laid down in *Hadley* v. *Baxendale* (1854). The innocent party to a breach is entitled (1) to the measure of loss naturally and foreseeably arising from the breach, and (2) to extra, special, loss where the parties were aware of the extra loss which might be sustained were the contract to be breached (*Victoria Laundry* v. *Newman Industries Ltd* [1949]; *The Heron II* [1969] and *Parsons* v. *Uttley Ingham* [1978] p. 216).

Most business contracts try to anticipate what might happen and to make provision for it. This not only excludes the need to go to court, which is time consuming and expensive, but also identifies in advance the maximum financial liability to which the business could be exposed, thus allowing financial planning and insurance. In the case of breach it frequently happens that agreement is made in advance as to the sum which is to be payable (Key concept 2.9). The court's first job is to enforce the contract as made by the parties and this will therefore be the sum awarded unless it is seen to be gross or exorbitant and unrelated to the anticipated loss (Liquidated Damages: Case study 2.7). In The Lost Slides: Case study 2.4 in fact, almost certainly had the term been incorporated it would have been struck out under this rule.

KEY CONCEPT 2.9	Liquidated damages are a 'genuine pre-estimate of loss', i.e. a sum fixed in advance which will become payable in the event of breach. This will be the sum the court awards unless it is considered to be an *in terrorem* or penalty clause not related to the expected loss.
LIQUIDATED DAMAGES	

CASE STUDY 2.7	The essence of a contract is that it is an agreement; the court is there to enforce the parties agreement, not to impose their own. Where the parties have agreed in advance a sum to be payable in the event of breach, prima facie that is the sum payable.
LIQUIDATED DAMAGES	In every case, however, the court must be satisfied that the sum is a genuine pre-estimate of loss and not an attempt to impose a penalty. This is always a question of fact; the name the parties give a clause is not always conclusive. Many businesses happily use the term penalty clause expecting to be able to enforce it. In *Dunlop* v. *New Garage and Motor Co. Ltd* [1915] the House of Lords were faced with having to rule on the effect of a clause imposing a liability to pay a sum of £5 in respect of every tyre sold by the garage in breach of a retail price agreement they had made with the suppliers.

> On the facts of that case they found the sum was recoverable as liquidated damages and took the opportunity to outline the criteria for the distinction between penalties and liquidated damages: in principle a sum will be regarded as liquidated damages where it is a genuine pre-estimate of loss even if in the event the loss that has been suffered is more or less than anticipated or it is very difficult to estimate the loss in advance. The sum will be regarded as a penalty if it is extravagant or unreasonable; where a payment of a smaller sum is secured by payment of a larger sum; and where a single sum is payable for a range of breaches of differing degrees of severity – this being prima facie evidence that there was no genuine pre-estimate of loss.
>
> (*Dunlop* v. *New Garage and Motor Co.* (1915))

(b) Specific performance

It may be that the innocent party to a breach of contract would rather have the obligations undertaken in the contract specifically performed by the other party than to receive money in lieu. There are certain circumstances in which a court will be prepared to make such an order. It is called a 'decree of specific performance'. It will not be granted where damages would be sufficient, nor to enforce contracts for personal services (e.g. *Page One Records* v. *Britton* [1968] p. 216).

(c) Injunction

This is an order which might be granted in order to prevent a breach, or a repetition of a breach. Again, no injunction will lie where damages would suffice, although such an order could be used to prevent, say, a person who had promised exclusive services from working in the same capacity for another (*Warner Bros* v. *Nelson* [1937]).

(d) Other remedies

We have seen other remedies too, such as rescission within the material on misrepresentation, and *quantum meruit* within the discussion on the discharge of contractual liability. Further to these there is the possibility of having a written document rectified if it does not truly represent the contents of an oral agreement, and other remedies of lesser importance in a business context.

Impact of the common law: constraints of the law of tort

Introduction

In this section we shall briefly examine the relationship between the law of tort (Key concept 2.10) and the criminal law and review the general characteristics of a 'tort'. The main part of this section will concentrate in some detail on the law relating to negligence, which is important as far as the

KEY CONCEPT 2.10	Torts are civil wrongs. In contrast with contracts, torts impose obligations on individuals and businesses without agreement, in much the same way as the criminal law. These obligations cannot easily be avoided: indeed in most instances they cannot be avoided at all. Breach of obligation gives right to a remedy, normally damages by way of compensation.
TORT	

operation of a business is concerned. This will then provide the reader with the necessary understanding to study specific areas of the law of tort, such as vicarious liability, occupiers' liability, nuisance, etc. which are contained in other chapters of this book. There again the hand of the judges in gently moulding the law to reflect current social and economic trends, is clearly visible.

A given set of circumstances may give rise to proceedings involving both tort and cirminal law. For example, a factory occupier who fails to fence dangerous machinery commits a criminal offence under Section 14 of the Factories Act 1961 and Section 2(1) of the Health and Safety at Work Act 1974 for which he may be punished by a fine and if an employee is injured as a consequence, a tort is committed against that employee entitling him to compensation.

The criminal law is enforced by the agencies of the state (e.g. the Police, the Health and Safety Executive, Trading Standards Departments, etc.) and prosecutions take place in the criminal courts. In the example stated above the criminal prosecution under the Health and Safety at Work Act 1974 could take place in either the Magistrates' Court or the Crown Court, whilst the tort action would have to be pursued by the injured employee in the civil courts (County Court or High Court).

Not all criminal activity is necessarily also tortious; for example, dangerous driving where no injury has been inflicted. Likewise not all torts are also crimes; for example, trespass on land is a crime in exceptional circumstances, such as when the trespass is committed with intent to steal, commit rape, or murder.

The law of tort is concerned with compensation for damage suffered by the plaintiff. It is an instrument for shifting the balance of loss from where it fell on the victim (the plaintiff) to the party responsible (the defendant).

It is not in every case that a person who has suffered a loss can recover. He or she must first identify a legal right or duty owed to him or her. Over the years the judges of the common law have refined and extended the situations in which they will recognize such a right or duty.

In principle the victim must suffer some damage, for without damage there is no loss and no need for compensation but in the case of trespass (direct interference with a person, their goods or their land) or libel (an attack on a person's reputation in a permanent form) no proof of damage is required. The tort is said to be actionable *per se*, literally 'by itself'. The plaintiff's right not to suffer direct interference, and to an unsullied reputation, are recognized as sacrosanct.

To recover in tort the damage complained of must be caused by the defendant and not too remote a consequence of the defendant's conduct.

For example, in the old and famous case of *Scott* v. *Shepherd* (1773) the injury sustained when a firework exploded in a crowded, covered market was held not too remote a consequence of the defendant's act of throwing the lighted firework into the crowd. This was so despite the fact that it had been tossed around from stall to stall before it went off. This case is a graphic illustration of a 'chain of causation' where a series of events intervenes between the act of the defendant and the injury to the plaintiff. If one of these events was not reasonably foreseeable then the injury is said to be too remote, and the action will fail.

In *The Wagonmound* [1961] oil floating on sea water was ignited by sparks from a welding operation causing a great deal of damage. This was held to be not reasonably foreseeable because of the high flashpoint of oil on water and the chain of causation was thus broken by a *novus actus interveniens*.

Novus actus interveniens   A new act coming between the act of the defendant and the injury to the plaintiff.

Provided that the type of injury is reasonably foreseeable, the defendant will have to compensate the plaintiff for the whole extent of the injury. In *Stewart* v. *West African Terminals Ltd* [1964] Lord Denning said:

> It is not necessary that the precise concatenation of circumstances should be envisaged. If the consequence was one which was within the general range which any reasonable person might foresee (and was not of an entirely different kind which no-one would anticipate) then it is within the rule 'that a person who has been guilty of negligence is liable for the consequences'.

The chief source of the law of tort is the common law or judicial decisions reflecting changing environmental and social pressures. These cases provide that liability for damage in tort may arise:

☐ As a consequence of a wrongful act or omission, e.g. if X is under a legal duty to act in a certain way and fails to do so; or

☐ Because of the acts or omissions of another with whom the defendant is in a special relationship, e.g. an employer may be liable for the acts or omissions of his or her employee if the employee causes injury to a third party. This is known as 'vicarious liability' and is dealt with in Chapter 5.

Sometimes an intention to injure is required but in many cases negligence (p. 69) or fault is sufficient. Occasionally strict liability (Key concept 2.11) will be imposed irrespective of intention or negligence (*Rylands* v. *Fletcher* (1866)).

Motive is generally irrelevant in tort law, either a legal right is infringed or it is not. For example, in *Bradford Corporation* v. *Pickles* [1895] the defendant, in order to induce the corporation to buy his land at a high price, dug wells and extracted water that would otherwise have found its way into the town's water supply. Although the corporation had suffered loss, there had been no infringement of a legal right, for Pickles had only done what he was fully entitled to do on his own land, with water which was percolating underground and not in a defined stream. Lord Halsbury said:

> This is not a case in which the state of mind of the person doing the act can affect the right to do it. If it was a lawful act, however ill the motive

KEY CONCEPT 2.11 **STRICT LIABILITY**	Strict liability is liability without fault. The defendant will be liable for the injury because it has happened, neither intention nor fault is an element, e.g. Blackburn J. in *Rylands* v. *Fletcher* (1866) (a case involving the escape of water from a reservoir) held 'The person who for his own purposes brings on his land and collects and keeps there anything likely to do mischief if it escapes, must keep it at his peril, and, if he does not do so, is "prima facie" answerable for all the damage which is the natural consequence of its escape'.

might be, he had a right to do it. If it was an unlawful act, however good his motive might be, he would have no right to do it.

and Lord MacNaughten added:

It is the act not the motive for the act that must be regarded. If the act, apart from motive, gives rise merely to damage without legal injury, the motive, however reprehensible it may be, will not supply that element.

Being made to pay compensation for losses deliberately inflicted does not seem very radical but even here there is no general rule that all harm intentionally caused shall be recoverable.

But increasingly the defendant's *purpose* has been considered important as in recent years the doctrine of *laissez-faire* has subsided and the courts have striven hard to protect the economic interests of business. Rights for breach of which an action for compensation will lie have been extended in the areas of injurious falsehood or slander of title, where a trader falsely disparages the wares of a rival to potential customers, passing off, where one trade represents his or her goods as being those of another well-known business, interfering with contract, e.g. striking so that contracts made between the owner of goods and his or her suppliers/customers are necessarily disrupted; intimidation, or threatening an unlawful act unless harm is caused to X, and conspiracy, where two or more persons combine for an unlawful purpose.

A study of these developments demonstrates the judicial response to changing pressures and how the judges have complemented increasing statutory regulation with an extension of individual common law rights (Chapter 1).

Liability based on fault has also extended rapidly until negligence has become the single most important cause of action covering actions for loss ranging from personal injury caused in industrial or road accidents to compensation for purely economic loss caused through careless advice (see below). In this case social and economic considerations have played a large part both in the extension of the duty of care to new situations and the so-called 'policy' limitations of the duty.

The introduction of product liability, that is, liability without fault, under the terms of a European Community Directive in the Consumer Protection Act 1987 (see below) shows a further marked extension of the liability of a business to pay compensation, in this case in circumstances where it neither intended the loss nor was at fault. Social engineering has decreed business should carry yet more economic overheads. A knowledge of its legal obligations is thus increasingly important to management.

Parties

The general rule is that anyone may bring an action in tort, irrespective of their status: infants, aliens and convicted criminals are entitled therefore to bring an action in tort, and spouses may even sue each other.

Similarly it is the general rule that anyone can be sued in tort, though actions against corporations and trade unions have given rise to some difficulties in the past.

Corporations are regarded as the employer of their agents, from director to office boy, and employers may, as will be seen in Chapter 5, be held 'vicariously liable' for the torts of their employees acting within the course of their employment.

Joint tortfeasors

When a tort is committed by two or more persons acting together, e.g. when A and B combine to defraud C, then the liability of A and B is both 'joint' and 'several'. The plaintiff may, at his or her option, sue A and B together, or sue either of them alone.

Under the Civil Liability (Contribution) Act 1978 one tortfeasor who is jointly liable to a plaintiff with another, or others, may recover contribution from his or her fellow joint tortfeasors where the plaintiff has sued only one person. The amount of the contribution recoverable is such, as the Act says, '... as may be found by the court to be just and equitable having regard to the extent of 'the fellow tortfeasor's responsibility for the damage'.

General defences to tort actions

There are specific defences to particular claims: for example, justification as a defence to defamation; there are also a number of defences which are used in many torts, known as 'general' defences.

(a)   Volenti non fit injuria:

This is the most important of the general defences. It has long been established that a person who consents to run the risk of injury cannot maintain an action against the person who causes the injury. This consent might take the form of agreeing to be subjected to an act, e.g. an operation, where the wound would be successfully actionable were it not for the patient's consent, or the consent may be to run the risk of something that *might* happen, e.g. in taking part in some physical sport – if you engage in a boxing match you cannot sue your opponent for trespass when he hits you, because you have consented to the normal consequences of boxing.

There are two groups of people who are not generally taken to consent to run the risk of accidental harm: namely employees and rescuers. An employee frequently has no effective choice as to his or her working conditions and knowing does not equate with consenting as oil rig workers have found (*Smith* v. *Baker* [1981] p. 215 and *Haynes* v. *Harwood* [1953] p. 216).

Defamation Defamation is the publication of a false statement which tends to lower a person in the estimation of right-thinking members of society generally, or which tends to make them shun or avoid that person.

Volenti non fit injuria To he who consents, no harm is done.

(b)   Statutory authority

This general defence is available to those who are given the right to do certain things by Parliament in legislation, hence 'statutory authority'. Usually it will be limited authority conditional on the activity being conducted in a reasonable manner, so that in *Penny* v. *Wimbledon UDC* [1899] the authority to lay a road was not enough to avoid liability for leaving piles of earth unfenced and unlit at night.

(c)   Act of God and inevitable accident

These are very rarely seen in the reported cases. An Act of God has been defined as involving circumstances which no human foresight can provide against and of which human prudence is not bound to recognize the possibility. In *Nichols* v. *Marsland* [1876] a rainstorm, 'greater and more violent than any within the memory of witnesses . . .' caused damage when some ornamental lakes overflowed. The defence of 'Act of God' was successfully pleaded. This defence is virtually unknown today because increased knowledge limits the unpredictable.

Inevitable accident, on the other hand, does not involve blaming the Almighty. Sometimes things happen which simply could not have been avoided by reasonable precautions. An example occurred in *Stanley* v. *Powell* (1891) where an accident occurred during a hunt when a shot fired at a pheasant ricocheted off a tree and injured another party. The court held, in the absence of negligence, that the defendant, who fired the gun, was not liable.

Sir Frederick Pollock once said:

> People must guard against reasonable probabilities, but they are not bound to guard against fantastic possibilities.

(d)   Necessity

This is a dangerous defence because it involves an admission. The defendant agrees that he or she did the act complained of, they caused the injury, but that they did it to prevent a greater harm which they (reasonably) anticipatcd. A gamekeeper destroyed property to create a firebreak (*Cope* v. *Sharp* [1912]): the captain of a tanker discharged oil to save the lives of the crew (*Esso* v. *Southport Corporation* [1955]); and, more recently, a senior police officer ordered that a gas grenade be thrown into a gun shop occupied by a psychopath (*Rigby* v. *Chief Constable of Northamptonshire* [1985]). In this last case necessity was a good defence to every argument except negligence; it seems that the police had allowed the fire brigade to leave, through their roadblock, before they attacked the shop!

(e)   Contributory negligence

That is, that the plaintiff contributed to his or her own loss. At common law the rule was that a plaintiff who was in any part the cause of his or her own injury could not recover any damages at all. The Law Reform (Contributory Negligence) Act 1945 altered this. The Act provided that where a plaintiff suffered injury, '. . . as the result partly of his own fault and partly of the fault of any other person . . .', then he could recover damages, but the damages should be reduced, '. . . to such an extent as the court thinks just and equitable having regard to the claimant's share in the responsibility for the damage'.

In industrial accidents failure to wear safety equipment supplied or to follow safe working practices frequently contributes to the victim's injury. In *Froom* v. *Butcher* [1975] the plaintiff, who was thrown through the windscreen of a car in a collision, was found to have contributed to his injuries by failing to wear a seat belt. His damages were reduced by 20%. In *Sayers* v. *Harlow UDC* [1958], Mrs. Sayers had popped into a public convenience at the bus station. When she discovered she could not open the cubicle door she shouted and waved for fifteen minutes. She then tried to climb over the partition wall by putting her left foot on the toilet seat and her right foot on the toilet roll holder. The toilet roll holder began to rotate and she was injured when she fell to the floor. Her climbing attempt was unsuccessfully argued as a *novus actus interveniens* (p. 65) and so the defendants were held liable in negligence. Mrs. Sayers, however, was found to be 25% to blame and her damages were reduced accordingly.

Specific torts relevant to business

In this section we shall examine the tort of negligence, (Key concept 2.12), which is the most important of the torts as far as the business enterprise is concerned. Other specific torts, such as occupiers' liability, nuisance, breach of copyright and the tortious aspects of product liability, will be examined in more detail in the chapters relating to the functional aspects of business in this book. For purely economic torts referred to see Chapter 4 and Specific Tort textbooks.

Causing loss through carelessness – often equated with 'fault liability'. The plaintiff must prove that the defendant used less care than he or she ought and in so doing caused him or her harm. There is no apparent limit to the circumstances in which the duty to be careful will be judicially recognized and the tort has been expanded very rapidly in the last fifty years – it epitomizes judicial law-making.	KEY CONCEPT 2.12 **NEGLIGENCE**

(a) Negligence

The tort of negligence is committed when the defendant is in breach of a legal duty of care owed by him or her to the plaintiff, which results in injury to the plaintiff. In order to succeed in an action for negligence the plaintiff must prove:

☐ That the defendant owed him or her a duty of care; and
☐ That he or she broke that duty; and
☐ That as a result the plaintiff suffered damage.

In some recent cases the courts have added to this simplified analysis a 'policy consideration' such that if each of these three steps are taken the court then considers whether the plaintiff *ought* to succeed. This aspect is more detailed than space permits here, but the reader's attention is drawn to the specialist text books outlined at the end of this chapter.

At a basic level, therefore, the action can be regarded as something of a hurdle race; each hurdle must be successfully cleared before approaching the next: duty, breach and damage.

(b)   The duty of care

The first important point to note is that whether or not a duty situation exists is a question of law. In 1932 the House of Lords attempted to formulate the general principles in what is perhaps the most famous of all negligence cases, *Donoghue* v. *Stevenson* (1932).

On August 28 1928 in Vincenti Minella's ice cream parlour in Paisley, near Glasgow, Mrs. May Donoghue drank some ginger beer bought for her by a friend. On pouring the remaining beer from the now famous opaque bottle she discovered the remains of a decomposed snail. As a consequence she became ill and wished to claim compensation.

She had not bought the ginger beer herself, so a breach of contract action against the cafe owner was not possible, so she sued (successfully) the manufacturer for negligence.

The case reached the House of Lords on appeal from the Second Division of the Court of Session in Scotland, and thereafter became part of English law.

The importance of the *Donghue* v. *Stevenson* decision lies in the principles enunciated by Lord Atkin. His Lordship sought to show that at certain times the law recognizes that a duty exists to ensure that one does not injure other persons, whilst recognizing that practicality bars recovery for damages suffered in every situation. Unless the plaintiff can show that he or she had been owed such a duty of care by the defendant, then his or her action in negligence will fail, that is, it will fail at the first hurdle.

Lord Atkin attempted to define these situations by setting out his 'neighbour principle', stating as follows:

> The rule that you are to love your neighbour becomes in law, you must not injure your neighbour; and the lawyer's question, who is my neighbour? receives a restricted reply. You must take care to avoid acts or omissions which you can reasonably foresee would be likely to injure your neighbour. Who then, in law is my neighbour? The answer seems to be – persons who are so closely and directly affected by my acts that I ought reasonably to have them in contemplation as being so affected when I am directing my mind to the acts or omissions which are called in question.

The neighbour principle means that a duty of care exists where the parties concerned are placed in such a position that the defendant ought reasonably to have contemplated the damage suffered by the plaintiff, as being the likely consequence of his or her actions. In this case, therefore, the manufacturer, David Stevenson, clearly owed the ultimate consumer a duty to take care that his product was safe for human consumption.

One example of the courts following Lord Atkin's principle is *Haley* v.

LEB [1965] A.C. 778. Haley was a blind person who was walking carefully along the pavement, with the use of his stick, when he fell into a trench excavated by the defendants. The trench was adequately fenced for sighted persons but not for blind persons. The House of Lords held that Haley could recover compensation for his injuries as he was owed a duty of care by the defendants. Lord Reid pointed out that about 1 in 500 people are blind, and Lord Guest said:

> ... There is ... no authority ... which would compel one to take the view that the obligation of those responsible for the safety of foot pavements is restricted to those persons who have normal sight. They must have regard to all road users, which include the blind and other persons.

There are many other cases on the duty of care and reference should be made to the standard textbook or casebooks on tort. Obviously, however, there must be limits to this range of persons who can be included within the neighbour principle (*Hay (or Bourhill)* v. *Young* [1943]).

(c)   Breach of duty

The second hurdle to be cleared by the plaintiff is to prove that the defendant was in breach of the duty he or she owed. The test for deciding whether there has been a breach of duty was laid down by Alderson B. in *Blyth* v. *Birmingham Waterworks Co.* [1856]:

> Negligence is the omission to do something which a reasonable man, guided upon those considerations which ordinarily regulate the conduct of human affairs, would do, or doing something which a prudent and reasonable man would not do.

Thus the standard of conduct required by the defendant in any situation is judged by the 'reasonable man' test; obviously much is left to the intuition of the individual judge. Ordinary men will not be expected to act with the skill of a professional man; householders who do repair work in the home are not expected to reach the same standards as qualified carpenters (*Wells* v. *Cooper* [1958]).

The exact kind of injury need not be predictable, providing injury of some sort is foreseeable (*Hughes* v. *Lord Advocate* [1963] p. 216).

The court's approach is to assess the standard of care required by weighing the magnitude of the risk of injury against the measures required to prevent running the risk of the injury, i.e. a cost/benefit analysis. This can be clearly seen by reading two cases both heard in the House of Lords in 1951 – *Bolton* v. *Stone* [1951] and *Paris* v. *Stepney B.C.* [1951]. Much the same weighing up must guide commercial decisions with 'green' or environmental issues being given increasing weight.

The existence of a duty of care is basically a matter of law. The breach of that duty, where it is owed by the defendant to the plaintiff, is a matter of fact. From the cases mentioned above it can be seen that the courts examine the defendant's conduct to see whether he or she is blameworthy or not. Was he or she at fault? The general considerations are the likelihood of harm (*Bolton* v. *Stone*), the seriousness of the risk of injury (*Paris* v. *Stepney B.C.*), the social utility of the defendant's activity (*Watt* v. *Hertfordshire*

CASE STUDY 2.8

THE TEA URN: LIMIT OF THE DUTY OF CARE

The manageress of a tea room belonging to the appellant corporation, allowed some members of a picnic party to carry a tea urn full of boiling tea through one room and into another so that the picnic party could take refuge from the rain. One of the carriers lost his grip on the urn and as a consequence some children, who were buying sweets from the nearby counter, were scalded. In the action on behalf of the children against the corporation, it was conceded that there was a duty of care owed by the manageress towards the users of the tea rooms, including the scalded children. The next 'hurdle' to be tackled was to decide whether she was in breach of that duty via the use of the 'reasonable man' test.

Lord MacMillan said:

> . . . legal liability is limited to those consequences of our acts which a reasonable man of ordinary intelligence and experience so acting would have in contemplation.

It was held that this accident was not one which the manageress ought reasonably to have contemplated. She had done what the reasonable manageress in such a situation would have done; she was, therefore, not in breach of the duty of care owed to the children; their action therefore failed.

(*Glasgow Corporation* v. *Muir* (1943) A.C. 448)

C.C. (1954)), and the cost of avoiding the harm (*Bolton* v. *Stone* and *Paris* v. *Stepney B.C.*).

The question of breach of duty is a question of balance: on balance was the defendant's act or omission *blameworthy*? (The Tea Urn: Case study 2.8.)

(d) Resulting damage

The third hurdle is that the damage of which the plaintiff complains must have resulted from the breach of the duty owed to him or her by the defendant. This again is a matter of fact.

In *Barnet* v. *Chelsea and Kensington Hospital Management Committee* (1969), a nightwatchman came to the casualty department of the hospital complaining of stomach pains and vomiting after having drunk a cup of tea at work. The nurse on duty contacted the doctor, a Dr. Banerjee, by telephone, who recommended that he go home to bed and call his own doctor. A few hours later he died of arsenical poisoning. His widow sued the employers of the doctor. Clearly a duty of care was owed: and it had been breached by not examining the man, but on the evidence it appears that when he, i.e. the victim called at casualty he was already bound to die as he had taken a fatal dose. There was nothing which could have been done for him which would have saved his life, therefore, his widow's claim failed.

This sad case shows that if the damage does not, in fact, result from the breach of duty owed, then the plaintiff's case in negligence must fail and

Hedley Byrne and Co. Ltd were advertising agents who had placed substantial forward advertising orders for a client, Easipower Ltd, and were personally liable for the cost of the orders.

They wished to investigate the creditworthiness of Easipower Ltd so they sought assurance from their bankers, Heller and Partners Ltd. They were provided with a favourable reference but one which was headed by a disclaimer:

> . . . for your private use and without responsibility on the part of this bank or its officials.

The plaintiffs relied on this reference, and when Easipower Ltd went into liquidation, Hedley Byrne and Co. Ltd lost over £17 000. They alleged negligence on the part of Heller and Partners Ltd and failed to recover their loss only because of the disclaimer. The importance of the case lies in the discussion and the judgement of the House of Lords about what the position would have been without the disclaimer.

The House of Lords considered that careless misstatements which cause injury, whether in an economic or any other form would be actionable if the injury was foreseeable when the statement was made. This would apply if the circumstances were such that the defendant possessed or held himself out as possessing special skills, such as those of an accountant, lawyer, consultant, etc. and made the statement *in the course of his business*, knowing the plaintiff would rely on the statement made.

NB   The need for some form of special relationship between the parties. Casual information or advice given on a social occasion will not attract liability.

Hedley Byrne and Co. Ltd v. *Heller and Partners Ltd* (1964)

CASE STUDY 2.9

PROFESSIONAL ADVISERS: NEGLIGENT MISSTATEMENT

even where the damage does result it must be of a foreseeable kind or it will be treated as too remote (*The Wagonmound* No. 2 [1961]).

(e) *Negligent misstatement and professional liability*

Donoghue v. *Stevenson* [1932] extended the law by allowing, for the first time, a consumer to bring a tort action against a negligent manufacturer of a defective product (p. 138, Product liability, in Chapter 5).

In 1964 the House of Lords further widened the law in *Hedley Byrne and Co. Ltd* v. *Heller and Partners Ltd* (Case study 2.9), a negligence claim brought against professional advisers. All businesses need to be very aware of the principles involved here because of their increasingly wide implication.

The profession which has probably the most to fear in the business situation from the continually developing law of professional negligence is the accountancy profession. As per Dickson J. in *Haig* v. *Damford* (1972):

> . . . The increasing growth and changing role of corporations in modern society has been attended by a new perception of the societal role of the

profession of accounting. The day when the accountant served only the owner-manager of a company and was answerable to him alone has passed. The complexities of modern industry combined with the effects of specialisation, the impact of taxation . . . and the separation of owner-ship from management, the use of professional corporate management and a host of other factors have led to marked changes in the role and responsibilities of the accountant and in the reliance which the public must place on his work. The financial statements of the corporations upon which he reports can affect the economic interests of the general public, as well as of shareholders and potential shareholders. . . . With all the added prestige and value of his services has come . . . a con-comitant and commensurately increased responsibility to the public.

In *JEB Fasteners Ltd* v. *Marks, Bloom and Co.* (1983) it was held that a duty of care was owed by a firm of accountants to anyone who could be foreseen as likely to rely on their prepared accounts. However, this has since been qualified in *Caparo Industries Plc* v. *Dickman* (1989) where it was held that the duty extended only to existing members of the company and not to potential investors. No duty of care was held to arise to a lending bank with whom the auditors had no direct connection and to whom they had not sent copies of a company's accounts in *Al Saudi Banque* v. *Clarke Pixley* (1989). Here is another example of the courts trying to rec-oncile commercial practice with wide principle. Clearly any professional person should be very careful in giving any advice, though it is undesirable for liability to be extended too widely.

Given the possibility of liability arising from statements made by their servants or agents a business is well advised to protect itself in one or more of the following ways:

☐ Exclude liability where possible. Where a fee or other consideration has been given and a contract made the Unfair Contract Terms Act 1977 will apply rendering void, and therefore of no effect, any exclusion which is not 'fair and reasonable' (The Duty of Care of The Surveyors, *Smith* v. *Bush*: Case study 2.5).
☐ Where there is no contractual relationship the express use of a disclaimer may prevent the duty of care arising as in *Hedley Byrne* v. *Heller*. The use of 'without prejudice' or 'without responsibility' clauses may become widespread but not generate much customer satisfaction.
☐ In any event improve the quality control/care of the advice to be given. Whether successfully sued or not no business wants to be known for poor advice. Clearly in a speculative area some guesses are better than others but we are concerned with matters which should clearly be within the orbit of the business' control. Increased emphasis on training or supervision may be required.
☐ Take out insurance against potential liability. Unfortunately, in a chicken and egg situation the fact that potential defendants *have* insurance and therefore have substantial means may itself encourage litigation but no business can carry the threat of potential liability of an open-ended amount.

(f) Proof of negligence

The normal rule is that it is up to the plaintiff to prove negligence. However, this is not always easy. Sometimes he or she may be helped by the rule of evidence *Res Ipsa Loquitur* or 'the thing speaks for itself'. This applies where the facts are such that negligence can be presumed from the very occurrence of the event, i.e.

☐ The defendant was in control of the activity which caused the injury; and
☐ The injury was of such a kind as would not have occurred unless someone had been negligent.

In this case, the defendant is presumed to have been negligent and will be found so liable unless he or she can show a reasonable alternative explanation for the injury. For example, in *Scott* v. *London and St Katherine's Docks* (1865) a customs officer going about his business was hit on the head by six bags of sugar as he passed by the defendant's warehouse. They had no explanation to offer. Erie C.J. said:

> There must be reasonable evidence of negligence. But where the thing is shown to be under the management of the defendant or his servants, and the accident is such as in the ordinary course of things does not happen if those who have the management use proper care, it affords reasonable evidence, in the absence of explanation by the defendants, that the accident arose from want of care.

In *Richley* v. *Faull* (1965) the defendant's car skidded violently, turned round and collided with the plaintiff's car on the wrong side of the road. It was held that this, of itself, was sufficient evidence of negligent driving. Since the defendant was unable to give a satisfactory explanation of his skid, he was held liable.

On the other hand, in *Easson* v. *LNER* [1944] a four-year-old boy fell out of a train seven miles from the last station, Goddard L.J. said:

> It is impossible to say that the doors of an express corridor train travelling from Edinburgh to London are continuously under the sole control of the railway company.

Res Ipsa Loquitur did not apply and the plaintiff was left with the burden of proving there had been negligence.

The difficulty for a plaintiff in proving negligence was one reason for the introduction of product liability of a manufacturer (Chapter 5) and is behind the consideration of some form of 'no fault' accident compensation for medical injuries currently under discussion in Parliament.

Summary

In this chapter we have outlined some of the constraints on business provided by legislation and the common law. The part played by Parliament in introducing new legislation in response to European Community directives, party politics and social and economic pressure was illustrated particularly by reference to the growth in regulation in the field of employment and reference was made briefly to the increasing number of statutes concerned with competition, planning and the environment.

The continuous evolution of the common law by judicial decisions was outlined in the development of the basic rules of contract, focusing on the ways in which they both enable business to achieve its objectives and at the same time restrict its activities where these are deemed contrary to public policy or otherwise illegal. The circumstances in which the law of tort provides compensation for victims were seen to be fluid as the judges recognize new forms of liability and extend the boundaries of responsibility particularly for purely economic loss.

Further reading

Treitel, *The Law of Contract* (Sweet and Maxwell, latest edition) and Cheshire and Fifoot, *The Law of Contract* (Butterworths, latest edition) are the two established texts for contract law students and are very comprehensive, but also very long and detailed. Davies, *Contract* (Sweet and Maxwell, latest edition) is simpler, not so long but also a very good text. It is also very important to read the decided cases. However, where the student has no easy access to sets of Law Reports, case books are very useful, and two of the best are: Smith and Thomas, *A Casebook on Contract* (Sweet and Maxwell, latest edition) and Beale, Bishop and Furmston, *Contract Cases and Materials* (Butterworths, latest edition).

For Tort reading students should refer to Winfield and Jolowicz, *Tort* (Sweet and Maxwell, latest edition) or Street, *Street on Torts* (Butterworths) or Heuston and Buckley, *Salmond and Heuston on the Law of Torts* (Sweet and Maxwell), which are the leading texts. Baker, *Tort* (Sweet and Maxwell) is a shorter work, but nevertheless comprehensive and easy to read. For case books Weir, *A Casebook on Tort* (Sweet and Maxwell) and Hepple and Matthews, *Tort: Cases and Materials* (Butterworths) are well regarded.

Exercises

1. Draft a simple contract for the hire of a car. Identify which terms are: (a) conditions; (b) warranties. Include (a) an exemption/exclusion clause; ensure that it is 'fair and reasonable'; (b) a liquidated damage clause; (c) a *force majeure* clause. Would this contract be suitable to form the basis of a standard form contract? If there are several of you in the group compare your draft agreements and try to combine the best points of each contract. This is how businesses arrive at their model contracts – copying a model, improving and tailoring for their own use.

2. Draft a contract for the sale of a business to include the sale of the goodwill. Restrict the seller from competing with the vendor as you

think fit. Ensure that your constraint clause complies with all necessary legal requirements.

3. It is springtime – and Denzil, a travelling salesman, in ladies' clothing, is driving across the country. He is looking for a place to stay. He chooses Peter's Moorside Retreat.

This hotel has been recommended by the major motoring organizations. It has the approval of the county tourist board.

He is shown to his room. He noticed the 'overnight in-house laundry service'. He placed his two shirts in the plastic bag provided and he left it outside the door.

After a busy day he decided that a cup of coffee would be in order. He took the kettle he found in the room to the ensuite bathroom and filled it with water. He returned and plugged it in. He received a severe electric shock. He was thrown across the room. He knocked the television set off the shelf near the bed. It fell on his head. He was bruised. His expensive spectacles were shattered.

The following morning he woke to find the sunshine streaming into his room. He decided to take a half day off. He visited the hotel shop to buy a local guide book. He asked the young assistant for one which would enable him to explore the town in detail.

While in the shop he decided to buy gifts for his wife and two children. He chose a small container of bubble bath for his daughter, and a pack of picture cards featuring a famous tank engine for his son. For his wife he decided to buy perfume. The assistant sprayed from a 'tester' some fragrance called 'Midnight in Penzance'.

When he wandered out to 'see the sights' he found that the guide book contained only the vaguest material about the town, although it did contain plenty of pictures of the district, and general information about holiday attractions in the area.

Disappointed, he returned at lunchtime to find that his shirts had been returned. They looked as if the local military band had marched across them. He noticed that the bag had a note attached which included a statement to the effect that no responsibility was accepted by the hotel proprietors for the quality of the laundry service because it was provided by another local company.

When he returned home his daughter could not get the bubble bath to make bubbles, the picture cards were all the same and the perfume smelt like rotten fish.

Discuss the legal position.

(Consideration of the common law principles which we have outlined and the statutory interventions by such legislation as the Sale of Goods Act 1979, the Supply of Goods and Services Act 1982 and the Unfair Contract Terms Act 1977 will be necessary before this exercise can be fully answered.)

4. ABC Ltd is a car hire firm. Every two years it sells off the fleet and buys new cars for the business. Usually it employs the services of the local car auction, but for some reasons, which are not clear, the auction failed to sell a Ford Escort car when the fleet was last sold off, so the company advertised it for sale in the local evening newspaper, thus:

Ford Escort car, ex-hire, two years old, average mileage, £4000

Fred, a private individual, replied to the advertisement: 'I accept your offer to sell. I enclose my cheque for £4000. If I hear nothing more by Thursday I will assume that the car is mine and I will collect it at the weekend'.

Bert also replied to the advertisement: 'I accept your offer to sell the Escort, but I can only afford £3500'. ABC received Bert's reply last Monday, and sent a note back by return: 'We cannot agree to £3500. In fact on reflection we think we want £4500 for the car'. When Bert received this he immediately replied: 'OK, £4500 it is. Here is the first payment of £1000 and I will pay the rest in monthly instalments of £500'.

Elsie also replied to the advertisement: 'I will give you the £4000'. ABC posted a reply to Elsie's letter last Monday stating 'I am now looking for £4500' and it reached her on Wednesday. Elsie replied accepting the new price.

However (just to complicate things), last Thursday morning Charles visited ABC's premises to hire a car, and, seeing the Escort with a price ticket of £4500 on it, he agreed to buy it. He completed a form supplied to ABC Ltd by Fleecem Finance Ltd with a view to setting up a hire purchase contract for the car.

Discuss this complicated legal situation. Will your discussion be affected by the knowledge that the car was not sold at auction because it was in a very poor mechanical condition, having been driven poorly for the two years it was out on hire from ABC Ltd?

5. ABC Ltd, still a car hire business, intend to have their premises redecorated, and several firms have tendered for the work. Slapdash Ltd's tender is accepted, in the face of close competetition. However, within a few days of having started the jab, Slapdash Ltd cease trading, and their workforce is removed from the site.

Having tendered a similar price for the work, Splashit Ltd are employed to complete the task. They are promised free access to the entire premises for the period of redecoration, and their estimate of the cost is based upon this. However, a special fleet hire contract is placed with Wellings and Co. and Splashit are denied access to part of the premises for the first week of the contract period.

Furthermore, there has been a series of arson attacks in the area of ABC's premises, and one night during the early part of the redecoration period, the premises are damaged by fire. This incident results in one of the buildings on the site being so badly damaged that it requires a great deal of work to redecorate it.

Eventually, Splashit Ltd complete the job, but their invoice is far in excess of the price they had tendered. They attributed this to the lack of access when available to work, and fire damage. However, ABC Ltd suspect that Splashit Ltd deliberately under-estimated in order to obtain the contract, and that they are now charging the true rate for the job.

Discuss the legal position.

6. In what circumstances will a mistake avoid a contract at common law?

7. Explain what a plaintiff must do in order to succeed in an action for the tort of negligence.

8. Denzil was roller skating along a street in Plymouth. He was using a 'personal stereo system' with headphones. As he passed a factory entrance a heavy trolley rolled out into the street. Oblivious to his surroundings, Denzil collided with the trolley and sustained a broken leg. Advise Denzil and the factory owners.

 **3** # The organizational context of business

Introduction

This chapter deals with the organizational level of the Business in Context model. In it we shall be considering the nature of the business organization itself, the different forms of business enterprise which the law recognizes and how these may be established and brought to an end. Some of the criteria for choosing one form over another will also be examined.

Types of business organization

A business enterprise in the United Kingdom will usually be one of three types: the sole trader, the corporation or the partnership (firm).

Sole traders

The law has nothing special to say about sole traders. They consist of individuals trading, perhaps employing a number of others to assist in the business, but essentially alone and for themselves. There are no additional legal requirements about disclosure of internal matters, such as accounts and membership details, but any necessary licences must be obtained and if VAT is payable the trader should be registered.

Corporations

The separate identity of a corporation (Key concept 3.1) was clearly identified in the famous case of *Salomon* v. *Salomon and Co. Ltd*.

Mr. Salomon was a leather merchant and bootmaker. In 1892 he decided to form a limited company as a means of carrying on trade. The company thus 'took over' the business. He signed the Memorandum of Association, as did his wife and each of their four sons. They all subscribed for one share each. The company then bought the business. Mr. Salomon received

KEY CONCEPT 3.1	A corporation is a person in the eyes of the law. Such a fictitious person has an identity which is quite distinct from that of the people who are involved with the operation.
A CORPORATION	

about £1000 in cash, £10000 in debentures and half the nominal capital in issued shares. The business failed. The creditors were owed nearly £8000. The assets of the business amounted to something like £6000. The creditors argued that they should have the assets on the basis that the enterprise was very little more than a one-man operation. However, it was held that the company was a separate entity distinct from that one man. The debentures were perfectly valid, and as a debenture holder Salomon was entitled to have first call on the assets (*Lee* v. *Lee's Air Farming Ltd* (1960) and *Multinational Gas and Petrochemical Co.* v. *Multinational Gas and Petrochemical Services Ltd* (1983) p. 217).

This principle of separate identity is very rarely broken. When it is, when the 'veil of incorporation is pierced', it is usually where the company has been used in connection with fraudulent or otherwise improper conduct, for example *Jones v. Lipman* (1962) p. 217. A man who was the controlling shareholder in a company had a house which he owned personally conveyed to the company in order to avoid certain obligations.

Strict adherence to this principle is also relaxed in the case of large companies which set up subsidiaries (consider *Smith, Stone and Knight Ltd* v. *Birmingham Corporation* [1939] and *DHN Food Distributors Ltd* v. *Tower Hamlets* [1976] p. 217). It follows from this principle of separate identity that a company can make contracts in its own name, own property, and enjoy 'perpetual succession', in that, until it is formally wound up, it continues to exist no matter what may befall the people who gave rise to its creation.

Corporations can be classified in a number of ways. For example, corporations sole and corporations aggregate. Corporations sole are rare. They comprise an official position or job which changes hands from time to time and in which property of one kind or another is vested – such as the monarch or the Archbishop of Canterbury. New corporations sole are not easily created. It must be done by statute. For example, the Office of Public Trustee was created by the Public Trustee Act 1906.

A corporation aggregate, on the other hand, is the kind of business organization which would be most readily recognized by a layman as a company. There are a number of people involved with it – indeed, the number may be huge! It has a Board of Directors, and, perhaps, a substantial share capital. These are the corporations with which this book is mainly concerned.

Corporations can be classified in another way: by the manner in which they are created.

□ A corporation can be created by Royal Charter – this would follow a 'request' by the promoters to the Privy Council. Whilst this was the manner in which the East India Co. and the Hudson Bay Co. were set up, there are few recent examples in common. The BBC, the Institute of Chartered Accountants and Robinson College, Cambridge were set up in this way.

□ A corporation can be created by its own statute. This is not uncommon, in the case of the 'utility' industries such as coal and electricity (e.g. Coal Industry Nationalisation Act 1946 and more recently British Telecom and Eurotunnel Co.).

Debenture   A debenture is a document which creates or acknowledges a debt. The issue of debentures is the most usual form of borrowing by a company. Debenture holders are not members of the company, they are creditors. They are provided with a fairly safe but limited income.

KEY CONCEPT 3.2

A PUBLIC COMPANY

A public company (plc) is one which is limited by shares or by guarantee and that has an issued share capital of at least £50 000. It may sell its shares to the public.

☐ A corporation can be created by registration under the Companies Act 1985. This is by far the most common method, and the most important from a business point of view. Such registered companies can be sub-divided, into public and private companies.

A public company (Key concept 3.2) is defined by law. Any company which does not meet the definition is a private company. Well over 90% of registered companies are private. A public company's memorandum of association (the company's charter, as it were) must be in the form prescribed by the Companies Act 1985, and it must state that the company is public. Its name must end with 'public limited company' – or the abbreviations which are permitted, which are 'plc' (and 'ccc' in Welsh). It must have a minimum authorized share capital of £50 000, of which at least one-quarter must have been paid up. There are many differences between public and private companies, as we will see, but the key feature for the business enterprise must be that a private company cannot offer securities to the public at large. If the operation requires this input of funds, then those operating it must submit themselves to the formalities and publicity required by the legislation, mostly because the public needs a certain degree of protection from those who offer investment opportunities.

Clearly one of the primary reasons for incorporation is the ability to raise money, therefore most businesses with a high capital requirement opt to be public companies with the additional controls imposed on them. Money may be raised initially at the launch of the company or during the company's life with the issue of new shares (Eurotunnel: Case Study 3.1).

Partnerships

A partnership (Key concept 3.3) is a creature of agreement. Subject to their own agreement, which may provide whatever terms are mutually acceptable, all partners share equally in the profits and losses made by the business and are wholly liable as individuals for all the debts of the business. This means that if the firm were unable to pay its debts from the partnership property the partners individually could be called upon to make good the shortfall. Clearly this open ended liability may limit the attraction of this form of business enterprise. Businesses which choose the partnership form frequently do not require very large amounts of capital or have no choice because they are professionally barred from incorporation, e.g. doctors and solicitors. In the case of certain professions it is customary or required by law that practitioners are covered by professional liability insurance.

It is possible for a partner to have limited liability. Under the Limited

International banks are putting increasing pressure on Mr. Alastair Morton, chairman of the British side of Eurotunnel, to raise extra funds from shareholders to complete the project.

This week, Mr. Morton will deliver an interim report widely expected to confirm that the costs of building the Channel Tunnel have soared to about £6.5 billion, almost £2 billion more than originally forecast.

The big banks, including Midland, National Westminster and many leading foreign institutions, will provide a large proportion of the extra money if Eurotunnel itself raises a quarter of what is needed in the form of new equity. This is likely to involve selling new shares by way of a rights issue to raise about £300 million.

Mr. Morton, and M. André Bénard, his co-chairman, did not want to consider raising extra funds until 1991 at the earliest on the grounds that shareholders would not be prepared to take part in a cash raising exercise more than once before the tunnel opens in June 1993.

But in view of the pressure from the banks, they are likely to agree to go back to shareholders early next year. The banks could pull the rug from under Eurotunnel if the cost estimates run away with the funds available, but this is considered highly unlikely.

The job of predicting costs in a project the size of the Channel Tunnel was always expected to be highly risky. Eurotunnel was initially thrown off course by early delays in the construction timetable while first forecasts about the rates of inflation and interest rates have also proved inadequate.

However, Mr. Morton will hope to be able to accompany any rights issue with some encouraging news for shareholders in terms of revenue projections. Some reports suggest that cross-Channel traffic will double in the next 15 years.

The tunnel is being built by 10 French and British construction companies grouped in the Transmanche Link consortium.

Over the past 12 months, the estimated construction costs have risen from an initial forecast of £4.7 billion to £6.5 billion. It seems likely that before agreeing to any further loans, the banks will demand assurances that building costs will not escalate any further.

(*Source:* Cliff Feltham, 'Banks press Eurotunnel to seek extra funding from investors', *The Times*, 2 October 1989)

CASE STUDY 3.1

EUROTUNNEL: A RIGHTS ISSUE BY A PUBLIC COMPANY

Partnerships Act 1907 such a firm must register with the Registrar of Companies. There must be at least one general partner, who, as is usual in all other firms, carries unlimited liability, but other members of the firm can have their liability limited to their capital contribution. However, such partners are not entitled to participate in the management of the enterprise. This, together with the ease of setting up registered companies, and indeed buying them 'off the shelf' – ready assembled – has meant that there are very few of these limited partnerships.

KEY CONCEPT 3.3	Partnerships are unincorporated associations with no separate identity apart from their members. They are often called 'firms'. Farwell L.J. explained in *Sadler* v. *Whiteman* (1910): 'In English law a firm as such has no existence; partners carry on business both as principals and as agents for each other within the scope of the partnership business; the firm name is a mere expression, not a legal entity'. Firms are trading organizations formed by two or more people, who usually share the workload and the profits (if any). The basis of the law here is to be found in the Partnership Act 1890: S.1. 'Partnership is the relation which subsists between persons carrying on a business in common with a view of profit'.
PARTNERSHIP	

Setting up a business enterprise

All businesses must have the necessary planning permission for the use of their premises, the appropriate licences, and must register with the local tax office if employing staff, and for VAT if applicable. In addition there are the following particular rules:

Sole traders

There are virtually no additional formalities, just buy some business stationery and some insurance and get on with it! If you are not trading in your own name, then the Business Names Act 1985 requires that the names of the proprietors appear on the business stationery.

Corporations

Of the three methods of creating corporations we discussed above, by far the most common is registration under the Companies Act. Setting up a registered company involves the drafting and submission to the Registrar of companies in Cardiff (or Edinburgh for Scottish companies) of several formal documents. Before considering them it is worth noting that in reality many registered companies are bought 'off the shelf'. For a hundred pounds or so the whole process of registration can be avoided. There are businesses that make their money out of setting up businesses.

Creating a corporation is a formal process of incorporation. That is of creating what will be a person, in the eyes of the law. So it follows that until the process is complete no person exists. This will be important for those who are anxious to get the operation up and running. Any contract made before incorporation is complete, even if made in the name of the company in the process of formation, probably involves personal liability for the individual. It is unwise to 'jump the gun'. As an illustration of how this principle entered into the delicate world of the pop music industry, see *Phonogram* v. *Lane* (1981). A contract was made 'for and on behalf of' a company, Fragile Management Ltd, which in fact was never formed. An advance paid under the contract had to be repaid.

This process of incorporation involves the following documents:

(a)   The Memorandum of Association

This is the charter of the company. It regulates external affairs. It is available as a source of information to those who propose to deal with the company. (Consider here *Ashbury Railway Carriage and Iron Co.* v. *Riche* (1875) and *Rolled Steel Products (Holdings) Ltd* v. *British Steel Corporation* (1875).) The memorandum includes the company name, the address of the registered office, the objects (the purposes for which it was created), a statement of how liability is limited – by shares or guarantee, the amount of share capital, the division of that amount into shares, and the association clause, which is a statement by the named subscribers to the effect that they wish to be associated as a company. If this is to be a public company, then this must also be stated here.

Memorandum of Association This formal document amounts to the charter of a registered company. It must contain the details of the way in which the company is constituted. It presents the company to the outside world.

(b)   The Articles of Association

These are the regulations for the internal affairs and management of the company. A model set of articles known as Table A was provided in the 1948 Companies Act; a revised set was produced in 1986. Most companies choose to use these as the basis of their own articles.

Indeed, if no articles are submitted those in Table A will apply anyway. The articles will deal with the issue and transfer of shares and dividends, general meetings, voting rights, accounts, audits, the appointment and powers of directors, the managing director and the company secretary.

Articles of Association This formal document sets out the internal regulations for the company. The articles will deal with such matters as the issue and transfer of shares, the procedure at meetings, the powers and duties of the directors, the payment of dividends, and so on.

(c)   A statement of names

This will contain the names of the proposed first directors and the secretary, signed by or on behalf of the subscribers and containing the directors' consent to act as such.

(d)   A statement of nominal capital

For example, £60 000.

(e)   A statutory declaration

This is usually made by the solicitor who has acted for the subscribers in setting up the company. It states that the formalities have been complied with. The Registrar may accept this declaration as sufficient evidence of compliance. When the Registrar is satisfied that the requirements have been met, he or she will issue a certificate of incorporation, and will publish a notice that he or she has done so in the *London Gazette*.

Once this has been done the company exists as a legal entity, bearing the name in the memorandum.

(f)   Partnerships

Partnerships are formed by agreement, no formality is required. The agreement could be oral, in writing or in the form of a deed under seal. To avoid uncertainty over the split of rights and obligations some form of written record is certainly desirable. Most professional partnerships use a deed which is then known as Articles of Partnership. Under the provisions of the Business Names Act 1985 it is necessary to give publicity to the names of all the partners where the firm does not use their names as its own name, e.g. Freshfields. All business stationery should include the names of all partners, thus allowing clients and customers to know with whom they are dealing and underlining the personal responsibility of the partners. However, the firm may be known by its firm or trade name; clearly this is a useful marketing device where the firm name is itself a brand image.

Deciding which form of enterprise to operate

It may not be easy for the aspiring businessman or woman to choose between the relative advantages and disadvantages of registered companies and partnerships. Here we tabulate the major distinguishing features in Table 3.1:

Table 3.1 Comparison of a company and a partnership

Company	*Partnership*
1. Separate legal personality	None
2. Strict formality required in formation	None
3. A company needs at least two members	There is a general upper limit of twenty partners – except for a number of professional firms, including solicitors, accountants and patent agents
4. Shares transferable, in accordance with the articles	Unless all the partners agree, a partner can only assign his or her right to profits from the firm not his or her capital share
5. Differing classes of share possible – with differing rights	Unless agreed otherwise, all partners share equally, in management, profits and losses
6. There are legal restrictions placed upon the increase and/or maintenance of share capital	None. The amount of capital can be altered by the firm by simple agreement
7. Companies can borrow on debentures and create floating charges over company assets	Firms cannot do either of these things
8. The company directors handle the management of the company. Ordinary members cannot contract for the company, although they can make contracts with the company	Each general partner is entitled to participate in the management of the firm, and the firm can be bound by his or her actions. A partner cannot contract with the firm
9. The members of a company benefit from limited liability – either by shares or by guarantee (this would encourage investment)	General partners have unlimited liability (i.e. they carry *personal responsibility* for the debts of the firm). It is possible, although complicated and unpopular, to limit a partner's liability. However, a limited partner cannot participate in management
10. The company's activity is limited by the objects clause in its	A firm can do anything lawful. It can change activity by simple agreement

Table 3.1 (Con't)

Company	Partnership
memorandum and by legislation governing companies	
11. Company property is vested in the company. It remains there despite the movement of members	The firm's property belongs to the partners
12. Where a company is insolvent and therefore wound up, no member is liable for its debts	The opposite applies! Every partner may be bankrupted unless he or she is a limited partner
13. A company's accounts are generally open to public inspection. (This does not apply to unlimited and certain small companies)	Accounts are private. This is often regarded as a key advantage of partnerships
14. The death or bankruptcy of a member has no effect on the company. This is called 'perpetual succession'	Unless they have agreed to the contrary, the death or bankruptcy of a partner will automatically dissolve the firm

15. Taxation – the advantages and disadvantages with regard to taxation are not so readily tabulated. A company will be subjected to the rules relating to corporation tax, whereas a partnership – being a collection of individual partners, each subjected to personal taxation – is taxed in a different manner. There will be a point at which it would be cheaper for the business to be taxed in accordance with the corporation tax rules rather than for the individuals to pay at personal rates. At this point the business organization should consider incorporation. It follows that the size and turnover of the enterprise will become critical considerations. For a detailed treatment of the principles involved, reference should be made to the specialist texts – bearing in mind that very little in law changes faster than the laws of taxation!

Apart from the technical distinctions between the two major forms of business organisation it may be important to appreciate some of the more intangible differences. A partnership is essentially a personal relationship, although the size of some of the major accounting and law firms in London and elsewhere rather belies this in practice. All partners are agents of the firm and of each other while acting on partnership business – so every partner is acutely dependent on his or her peers. While the precise terms of each partnership agreement may vary, there is usually a provision requiring unanimity before major changes – including the introduction of a new partner – can be made. In practice it may be very difficult to dissent from the majority view without doing the decent thing and resigning but there is no external mechanism other than dissolution and reformation of a new partnership to avoid such limitation. Of course the agreement may not require unanimity, only an expressed majority to cover this difficulty.

The unlimited personal liability which partners carry for their firms debts may be terrifying more in prospect than in reality. Most professional partnerships certainly carry professional liability insurance (Chapter 8) and any partnership would be well advised to consider this, although it will form a substantial part of their overhead costs. It may be attractive to customers to feel they are dealing with a business where the buck stops here.

The major attractions of incorporation are not simply the ability to obtain limited liability, i.e. the investors or shareholders are separate from the

Member Member = shareholder.

Floating charge A loan to a company could be secured on a particular item within the company assets. Alternatively, it could be 'secured on assets' generally. This is called a floating charge. The lender will have priority in the queue to be paid if the company is liquidated.

Guarantee A promise by the guarantor to pay the debt if the debtor fails to repay.

legal persona of the company and are not as such liable for its debts – anyone going into business and basing his or her decisions on anticipation of failure deserves to fail – but much more importantly the ability to raise capital, to allow investors liquidity, to separate management from capital and to capitalize your own skill or other assets by creating in the shares of the company a saleable product.

Many modern operations require enormous capital investment, and an appeal to the market by offering shares to the public in the venture is much more attractive commercially than taking on loans at exorbitant rates of interest (e.g. Eurotunnel: Case study 3.1).

Partners, of course, invest in their own firm but such investment is not generally recoverable until death or retirement or the partnership is otherwise dissolved. When this occurs, with or without notice according to circumstance, the firm faces an immediate withdrawal of capital to the retired partner or his widow for which provision must be made since no firm can maintain unlimited funds in its contingency reserve. This is usually done through appropriate insurance cover. Investors in a company may sell as much or as little of their holdings at any time as they wish according to need and market forces without impinging in any way on the running of the company.

Whereas it may be seen as an attraction that all partners are legally entitled to participate in the management of a business there are many shareholders who are very happy to invest their capital in the hope of a gain and interim dividends who have neither the time nor the skill to devote to the running of a business. The ability to buy shares and take prospective profit without the obligation to participate in management is a major attraction.

It can be seen that incorporation is very much associated with raising money (Eurotunnel: Case study 3.1) and with capital intensive enterprises. Partnerships are more commonly found in the service industries where capital is less essential. To the extent that partners cannot generate a separate identity which they can take to the market and sell they lose the opportunity to capitalize their skills. To the extent they may be taxed more highly as individuals than a company subject to corporation tax, where they, as individual directors, would receive a salary and dividends and the prospect of capital appreciation, their decision not to incorporate may be hard to understand. Some professions do not permit incorporation by their members, including the medical and legal professions at present. As the Royal Institute of British Architects has recently lifted its prohibition, it might be interesting to see how many architects have taken advantage of their new-found freedom.

To some the privacy and lack of requirement to present public accounts annually, coupled with immunity from a hostile take-over, still makes the partnership the ideal format with its close personal ties and personal responsibility. For a small business just starting up the combination of skills and capital which it can represent often make a partnership the ideal form. Incorporation can always follow when the commercial risks become too big to carry individually or the business is sufficiently established to have a track record which will induce investors to participate in it.

Terminating the enterprise

Corporations

We will concentrate here on registered companies. Others can be ended by repeal of statute, or the revocation of a charter, whichever is appropriate. A registered company's operations are brought to an end by a process called 'winding up' (Key concept 3.4).

Corporations do not die or fade away. They are created by operation of law, and they must be legally terminated.	**KEY CONCEPT 3.4**
	WINDING UP A COMPANY

The winding up of a company is a process prescribed by statute which has the effect of terminating its existence. Winding up discontinues the operation, collects in whatever assets exist, and distributes them in a set order until they are exhausted. There are, broadly, two methods of winding up: compulsory winding up by a court and voluntary winding up, either by members or by creditors.

Creditors Those who are owed money by the business organization.

(a)   Compulsory winding up by a court

Under the Insolvency Act 1986, a company can be wound up by the court if:

☐ A special resolution has been passed by the company to request it (extremely rare, it is much easier voluntarily to wind up).
☐ It has not satisfied the Registrar that the minimum share capital has been subscribed, and a year has elapsed since registration, (this only applies to public companies).
☐ The company has not commenced business within a year since registration, or it has not traded for a year, (the court will need to be satisfied that the company does not intend to trade – *Re Metropolitan Railway Warehousing Co Ltd* (1867), *Re Capital Fire Insurance Association* (1883) and *Re Middlesborough Assembly Rooms Co.* [1880]).
☐ There are less than two members, (very rare, the company will probably voluntarily wind up).
☐ The company is unable to pay its debts (this is the usual ground and it will probably involve either:
   (a) a creditor who is owed at least £750 having formally demanded payment and been left waiting for at least 21 days, or
   (b) a court order to pay remains unsatisfied, or
   (c) it has been shown that debts exceed assets. (These grounds are dealt with in S.123 of the 1986 Act).
☐ The court is satisfied that winding up would be just and equitable in all the circumstances. In *Loch* v. *John Blackwood* (1924), for example, in order to keep shareholders unaware of the value of the company assets

CASE STUDY 3.2

KENTISH HOMES: THE LIQUIDATOR'S ROLE

Kentish Homes, the principal trading subsidiary of Kentish Property, the collapsed Docklands housebuilder, has an £18.8 million deficiency of assets, creditors were told at a packed meeting in London.

However, several creditors expressed scepticism about the account given by Mr. Roger Powdrill, one of the joint liquidators of Kentish Homes, and Mr. Keith Preston, chairman of Kentish Property, about the speed of the company's demise.

According to Kentish, the board did not become aware of the company's financial difficulties until April and May, when it was able to sell only 14 out of 23 units at the second phase of Burrell's Wharf, a development of 343 flats on the Isle of Dogs. It examined the possibility of new marketing initiatives to promote sales during June, but it was only on 14 July, on the advice of its auditors, that it consulted Mr David Freeman, a leading insolvency solicitor.

However, in questioning Mr. Preston and Mr. Powdrill, accountants acting on behalf of trade creditors and would-be housebuyers established that management accounts for the first quarter of 1989 had been available earlier than mid-July. These showed Kentish Homes had made a loss of £404 000 before capitalized interest in the three months to March on turnover of just £855 000. Those sales compared with £25.9 million for 1988, budgeted to rise to £60 million this year.

Several speakers questioned whether it was plausible to have expected the remaining £59 million of turnover to be achieved in the remaining nine months, but Mr. Preston explained that substantial sales had been contracted to take place in the second half.

Kentish Homes' largest creditors, after the parent company, are the 258 people who put up £2.58 million in deposits on flats at Burrell's Wharf and the Bow Quarter, a development of 638 flats and 19 houses in Bow, East London. J.A. Elliott, the company building Burrell's Wharf, is owed £2.28 million. Further down the list come 13 housebuyers who are owed an average of £22 000 each in mortgage subsidies. One creditor at the meeting said she bought her flat on 11 July, a week before the company asked the Stock Exchange for its shares to be suspended.

Those present did, however, confirm Mr. Powdrill and Mr. Nick Lyle, both partners of Spicer and Oppenheim, the accountant, as liquidators of Kentish Homes. At earlier meetings the pair had been confirmed as liquidators of Kentish Residential and Island Club Leisure.

The Island Club had been set up to operate a health club at Burrell's Wharf but now has a deficiency of £67 000. Mr. Powdrill said that creditors could expect to receive about 20p in the pound.

(*Source:* Jeremy Andrews, 'Kentish Homes' £19m shortfall', *The Times*, 16 August 1989)

and thus to buy shares at a low price, the directors failed to call meetings, submit accounts or recommend dividends. Winding up was ordered (*Re Factage Parisien Ltd* (1855) and *Re A and BC Chewing Gum Ltd* (1975) p. 217).

Where a winding up order is made, the court will appoint a liquidator to collect in the assets and, as far as possible, pay out the debts (Kentish Homes: Case study 3.2).

(b)   Voluntary winding up

A company can be wound up voluntarily if:

☐ It was created for a fixed term or a set purpose, and the term has expired or the purpose been achieved, the articles provide for winding up, and a resolution has been passed to this effect; or
☐ A special resolution has been passed voluntarily to wind up; or
☐ An extraordinary resolution has been passed that liabilities exceed assets, and winding up would be appropriate.

Such resolutions as these must be advertised in the *London Gazette* within fifteen days.

The effects of voluntarily winding up are that the company ceases trading, except as benefits the winding up; a liquidator must be appointed (one of the advantages of voluntarily winding up is that the members can choose their liquidator, who must be an insolvency practitioner); when he is appointed the directors' powers generally cease; no variation of members' status is permitted; and no transfer of shares can be made, unless the liquidator agrees.

When the general meeting of the company agrees voluntarily to wind up, if the directors are prepared to make a formal statement that the company is in a position to pay its debts within a year, the voluntary winding up is said to be a members' winding up. However, if no such statement can be made, then it will be a creditors' winding up. A creditors' meeting must be called within fourteen days of the general meeting, and at that meeting the liquidator will be nominated. If there is a disagreement, then the creditors' nominee wins.

Once the liquidator has collected in all he or she can, he or she must then distribute the assets. There is a rigid priority in the manner in which he or she must do this. Those creditors who have security in fixed charges will rely on that and avoid having to share in the distribution. Otherwise the order of priority is:

☐ Winding-up costs, charges and expenses (such as the liquidator's fees!)
☐ Preferential debts – in the main these consist of twelve months PAYE deductions which are due from the company, six months VAT, twelve months national insurance contributions, any outstanding amounts of occupational or state pensions and six months employees' remuneration (subject to a maximum under Insolvency Act 1986). Incidentally, these are all of equal status, so that if there is not enough left to pay them all, then they all abate equally.
☐ Creditors whose security is by floating charge
☐ Unsecured creditors
☐ Unpaid sums due to members, such as dividends declared before the winding up began.

A company that is really struggling is not likely to have enough left to pay the preferential creditors, let alone the unsecured ones. So that many

Liquidator An official who supervises the winding up of a company, taking over control of the company assets and generally doing whatever is necessary to facilitate winding up.

London Gazette Certain matters are required by law to be 'Gazetted', or published in the *London Gazette*. These include details of winding up orders, bankruptcies, creditors' meetings, the change of company names and the constitution of partnerships. Publication of information constitutes notice to the nation.

of the ordinary customers who, perhaps, paid for goods in advance and have not received them, will find their chances of repayment rather slim.

In fairly recent years an alternative to winding up a company which has fallen upon hard times has been developed, which is called 'administration', and there has emerged a new profession – the insolvency practitioner. An administrator must be such a professional practitioner. An administration order can be made by a court when it seems that such an order would achieve either the survival of the company as a going concern, or the approval by the creditors of the company of what is called a 'composition in satisfaction of debts' (that is, they agree to take, say, 50p in the £1), or the approval of the company members of a 'scheme of arrangement' for handling the debts, or at the least, the better realization of the company assets than would be achieved on a winding up. An application can be made by the company itself, the directors, the creditors, or a combination of these. Notice must be given to anyone who has appointed a receiver or who could do so. The effects of the application are to prevent the winding up of the company, and to stay any enforcement of rights (e.g. hire purchase and other property claims) against the company, without the consent of the court. If the order is granted, the company's affairs are managed by the administrator, and the company cannot be wound up immediately.

This new procedure is governed by the provisions of the Insolvency Act 1986. It is only of use to a company which retains some chance of genuine recovery. Otherwise, winding up is the only alternative.

Partnerships

The dissolution of a partnership can be done with or without the aid of the court. The Partnership Act 1890 provides that, subject to contrary agreement, and without the assistance of a court, a firm will be dissolved if it was formed for a fixed time or purpose, and this has expired or been achieved, or on notice of the desire to dissolve it having been given by one or more of the partners. Furthermore, the death or bankruptcy of any partner will dissolve the firm, as will the happening of any event which makes the business of the firm illegal – such as war breaking out with the home nation of the firm's trading businesses.

The court can order dissolution of the firm if one partner becomes too mentally ill, or in any other way incapable of managing his or her affairs, or if a partner's conduct is seen to be prejudicial to the firm's business affairs. This is not a matter of moral censorship. In *Snow* v. *Milford* (1868) a banking firm was not dissolved by the court simply because of the widespread adultery of a partner in Exeter. It meant the end of his marriage, but it was held not to have discredited nor injured the credit of the firm.

The court can order dissolution if one or more of the partners persistently acts in breach of the partnership agreement, or in some other manner as makes it impossible to continue with the enterprise, as in *Cheesman* v. *Price* (1865) and *De Berenger* v. *Hamel* (1829). The court can order dissolution if the business can only be run at a loss and where, on other grounds of fairness and justice in all the circumstances it sees fit to do so. This might follow persistent quarrelling or deadlock between the partners,

Receiver   A person who is appointed to take over the property of a debtor (a sole trader, firm or a corporation) to supervise the collection of assets and, as far as possible, the payment of debts.

Bankruptcy   This is a process whereby a person who is unable to pay his or her debts (i.e. insolvent) may be adjudicated bankrupt and thus be subjected to all that this entails. For example, another person (a trustee in bankruptcy) will 'step into his or her shoes' with regard to the collection of his or her assets and the payment, as far as possible, of his or her debts.

or some other basis upon which it is seen to have become impossible for the business to carry on in a proper manner.

Summary

In this chapter we have discussed the nature of the business enterprise. We have examined the manner in which such organizations are created, how their operations can be terminated, and considered some of the characteristics of each.

Further reading

The law relating to business organizations is well provided for in legal literature. The books vary from the very expensive to the rather expensive and finally to the less expensive. As you may by now have realized – there is no such thing as a cheap law book!

At the top end: Gore Brown (and others), *Companies* (Jordans); Magnus and Estrin, *Companies Law and Practice* (Butterworths); Lindley and Scamell, *The Law of Partnership* (Sweet and Maxwell); in the mid-range: Gower, *Modern Company Law* (Sweet and Maxwell); Pennington, *Company Law* (Butterworths); Milman and Flanagan, *Modern Partnership Law* (Croom Helm); and less expensively: Thomas, *Company Law for Accountants* (Butterworths); Smith and Keenan, *Company Law* (Pitman); Morse, *Introduction to Partnership Law* (Financial Training); Underhill, *Principles of the Law of Partnership* (Butterworths).

Exercises

1. George is the senior buyer for Depeche Modes Ltd, an extensive chain of fashion stores across the south-east of England. His contract of employment contains a clause which purports to restrict him, should he leave the company, from working for any other business enterprise in the United Kingdom which is concerned with retailing clothing, for a period of ten years from the date he leaves Depeche Modes Ltd, and furthermore, that he will not take with him any client or customer lists which he may have obtained in connection with his employment with Depeche Modes Ltd.

   Late last year, after a disagreement concerning the spring collection, George left Depeche Modes Ltd, and he set up a in business with his friend Maxwell. Maxwell is a clothes designer. Together they have taken the fashion world by storm. Maxwell is designing for the rich and famous. George is seeing to it, using old friends in the fashion business, that the high street stores stock slightly modified versions of the key items in their joint collection.

   Discuss the legal position.

2. The pair are making such an impact in their chosen field that they are considering formalizing their business relationship, especially with a view to raising enough money to open a retailing outlet of their own.

   Advise George and Maxwell.

3. Company law contains a great deal of specialized terminology. From the material in this chapter, and the recommended reading, explain the following terms as used in this area of the law: (a) a contributory; (b) wrongful trading; (c) administrative receiver; (d) petitioners; (e) minorities; (f) declaration of solvency; (g) scheme of arrangement; (h) auditors; (i) annual return; (j) insider dealing.

Innovation, research and development 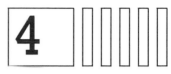 4

Introduction

The great majority of business enterprises exist by selling some product, be it goods or services. As a general rule it is in the best interests of the business, and also its employees, to secure as large a share of the potential market as possible, whilst at the same time keeping costs to a minimum. This aim can be aided by the elimination of competition, preferably lawfully. One way to achieve this is for the business to protect those products which are lawfully theirs to exploit.

The development of new 'products', and their subsequent protection from unfair competition is examined in this chapter. Firstly we briefly explore the obligations imposed on a designer or manufacturer by statute law when developing a new product.

Then we examine some of the legal devices open to a business or individual to prevent their product from being copied or unfairly exploited by others.

Finally we examine the right to ownership of inventions made by employees, the right to exploit those inventions, and the methods by which a business can prevent an ex-employee from setting up in competition, or leaving and taking the company's secrets with them.

Environmental aspects

A business has to operate within external constraints as well as internal limitations. The law is responsible for a number of controls affecting the ability of a business to conduct its research and development usually related to health, safety, pollution, planning or the environment generally. We shall examine some of them here.

Some legal duties are imposed on a business or an individual without their choice, notably those duties creating criminal or tortious liability. The criteria in both cases usually involve harm, or the risk of harm, to others. In the case of criminal liability the harm may be merely threatened and there need be no specific victim, the purpose of the criminal law is the protection of the public. In the case of tortious liability there is usually a victim who has been individually affected by the defendant and whose rights have been so infringed that the law recognizes a claim for compensation.

In the case of innovation, research and development the major environmental constraints and controls arise from a concern for the safety, both of the public at large and the individuals involved in the development. At micro level the Health and Safety at Work Act 1974 provides a specific legislative framework governing both the production process (Chapter 5) and the research and development phase. At a more macro level pollution controls and planning legislation govern very tightly a business's ability to use its premises, restricting its ability to threaten or cause actual damage by, for example, noise, vibration, waste disposal, effluent or smoke.

The Health and Safety at Work Act 1974

This provides purely criminal liability, i.e. breach of its terms will not automatically give an injured individual any right to claim, although proof of breach may be evidence of breach of a civil duty of care owed to the victim. Its provisions are like preventive medicine, they are designed to educate, help and publicize problems that may be encountered with a view to eliminating potential difficulties. Breach of the Act may result in a criminal prosecution, and in a serious case, an order to stop a process or improve the manner of working. Although the size of the fines may not be an enormous deterrent, no business wishes to present itself to the public, its markets or its workforce as slapdash and uncaring so close attention to the statutory controls is needed.

Most of the Health and Safety at Work Act 1974 is concerned with safety in the work place, but Section 6 provides four major duties applicable to research and development which will be covered here (Key concept 4.1).

It shall be the duty of any person who designs, manufactures, imports or supplies any article for use at work, or any article of fairground equipment –

(a) to ensure, so far as is reasonably practicable, that the article is so designed and constructed as to be safe and without risks to health at all times when it is being set, used, cleaned or maintained by a person at work;

(b) to carry out or arrange for the carrying out of such testing and examination as may be necessary for the performance of the duty imposed on him by the preceding paragraph;

(c) to take such steps as are necessary to secure that persons supplied by that person with the article are provided with adequate information

KEY CONCEPT 4.1	There are four obligations on companies or businesses who are in any way concerned in the design or manufacture of any new (or existing) article or substance for use in a work situation. These statutory obligations are set out in section 6 of the Health and Safety at Work Act 1974.
OBLIGATIONS ON EMPLOYERS FOR THE USE OF ARTICLES AT WORK UNDER THE HEALTH AND SAFETY AT WORK ACT 1974	

about the use for which the article is designed or has been tested and about any conditions necessary to ensure that it will be safe and without risks to health at all such times as are mentioned in paragraph (a) above and when it is being dismantled or disposed of; and

(d) to take such steps as are necessary to secure, so far as is reasonably practicable, that persons so supplied are provided with all such revisions of information provided to them by virtue of the preceding paragraph as are necessary by reason of its becoming known that anything gives rise to a serious risk to health or safety.

S.6(2)   It shall be the duty of any person who undertakes the design or manufacture of any article for use at work or of any article of fairground equipment to carry out or arrange for the carrying out of any necessary research with a view to the discovery and, so far as is reasonably practicable, the elimination or minimisation of any risks to health or safety to which the design or article may give rise.

S.6(4) and (5) extends the above obligations to designers or manufacturers of 'substances' used in a work situation.

S.53 is the definition section of the Act (students should always research the definition section to discover the limits of the obligations imposed by any statute). For example, in the Health and Safety at Work Act 1974, an 'article for use at work' is defined as being 'any plant designed for use or operation (whether exclusively or not) by persons at work, and any article designed for use as a component in any such plant'. Thus a sale to a DIY enthusiast is not covered by the Health and Safety at Work Act because he or she will not be using the article whilst 'at work', albeit that he or she is working with it at home. The Consumer Protection Act 1987, however, now extends liability for defective products to all producers, suppliers, importers, etc. of all consumer products, whether used in a work situation or at home.

The word 'plant' includes 'any machinery, equipment or appliance'. A 'substance' is 'any natural or artificial substance, whether in solid or liquid form, or in the form of gas or vapour', and 'substance for use at work' means any substance intended for use (whether exclusively or not) by persons at work. 'Persons at work' covers both employees and self-employed persons.

In more detail the four duties imposed by S.6 are:

(i) To ensure, so far as is reasonably practicable, that the article is so designed and constructed as to be safe, or the substance is safe, and without risks to health when being set, used, cleaned or maintained.

In the Health and Safety Executive's Guidance Note on Section 6 it states,

If the user makes an unusual or unexpected use of the product, or chooses to disregard the information (otherwise than in some small and/or irrelevant particular), by deliberately overloading a machine, failing to install a machine correctly for noise control purposes, or failing to maintain equipment, for example, then it will be considered that there has not been a proper use and the manufacturer, etc., will not, under those circumstances, be held responsible under S.6.

In a Scottish case, the supplier of a mincing machine was prosecuted for supplying a machine which had an unguarded opening into which the meat was fed, and which permitted the operator to insert his hands. The machine came complete with a wooden plunger, and providing this was used there was no danger. The sheriff accepted that though the machine was intrinsically unsafe, it was 'safe . . . when properly used', and the summons was dismissed.

(ii) To carry out or arrange for the carrying out of such testing and examination as may be necessary for the performance of the duty imposed on him by the preceding paragraph.

Most testing and examination will take place at the design stage (e.g. by using a prototype) and at the manufacturing stage. The Act states that a person (e.g. an importer, supplier, erector or installer) is not required to repeat any testing or examination which has been carried out by some other person, in so far as it is reasonable for him or her to rely on those results.

(iii) To take such steps as are necessary to ensure that there will be available in connection with the use of the article or substance at work, adequate information (and any subsequent revisions of information) about the use for which the article (substance) has been designed and tested, and about any conditions necessary to ensure that it will be safe and without risks to health when used.

This information may be given in the form of an instruction manual or data sheet, or the user may be referred to a standard in a Code or other authoritative source, including British Standards. This obligation on the designer and manufacturer is the first step in the 'chain', whereby relevant information on the safe use of an article or substance, passes from them, through the supplier to the employer, and on to the employee using the article or substance. Chapter 5 discusses this 'chain' from the employers' point of view in a little more detail.

(iv) A designer or manufacturer of an article or substance is under a duty to carry out, or to arrange for the carrying out, of any necessary research, with a view to the discovery and, so far as is reasonably practicable, the elimination or minimisation of any risks to health or safety to which the design of the article, or the substance, may give rise.

Again there is no need to repeat research already carried out by some other relevant person, so far as it is reasonable to rely on those results. The Health and Safety Commission devotes a considerable proportion of its budget to research, the results of which, together with the reports of Joint Standing and Advisory Committees, are available to designers and manufacturers. This is the first time in English law that there has been a legal obligation to carry out research.

A new practice is for purchasers of the article or substance to be used by a person at work to make the contract conditional upon compliance with S.6 (Key concept 4.2) of the Act. We must now await the first case where a purchaser rejects a product on the grounds that a failure to comply with the

KEY CONCEPT 4.2

THE SCOPE OF S.6 OF THE HEALTH AND SAFETY AT WORK ACT 1974

The exact scope and meaning of S.6 has still to receive authoritative judicial interpretation, because although there have been some prosecutions, there have yet been no appeals to the High Court. The purpose of this section is, however, to try to ensure that acceptable levels of health and safety are built into articles and substances at the design and manufacture stage, whether by compliance with recognized standards (e.g. British Standards), or Health and Safety Executive Guidance Notes, or by other acceptable tests.

requirements of S.6 renders the product not of merchantable quality, as required by the Sale of Goods Act 1979 (Chapter 7).

Consumer goods

The Consumer Protection Act 1987 extends similar duties to those described above to all producers, suppliers, importers, etc. of consumer products. S.2 of the Act states that '... where any damage is caused wholly or partly by a defect in a product ...' then the producer of the product, or any person who (via use of name, trade mark or other distinguishing mark) holds himself or herself out as being the producer, and the importer, shall be liable for the damage caused. Damage means death or personal injury or any loss of or damage to any property (including land).

S.4 lists the accepted defences to any action under the Consumer Protection Act 1987 as:

☐ The defect is attributable to compliance with any EEC obligation or enactment; or
☐ The company did not supply the product; or
☐ The product was not supplied in the course of a business; or
☐ The defect did not exist at the time the product was supplied; or
☐ The state of scientific and technical knowledge at the relevant time was such that it was not reasonable that the company should have discovered the defect.

(The Consumer Protection Act 1987 is fully explained in Chapter 5 of this book.)

Strategic aspects

In addition to imposing certain involuntary constraints the law provides a number of significant ways in which a business can choose, as a matter of policy choice, to take advantage of the rules laid down to improve its position; for example to protect its inventions or innovations from exploitation by others, or to create the grant of a monopoly which the law will then protect, or to claim damages where the original work of one is copied or passed off as his by another.

The circumstances in which the law may grant a right and the steps which a business can or should take to protect itself will be discussed in this section. The most important statutory rights are patents, copyright, design right and trade marks. The common law also recognizes some further rights of action, such as passing-off which will be briefly mentioned. One of the advantages of the common law system is that it is not finite and the judges are able to adapt existing principles to meet new situations.

Statutory protection

(a) Patents

The rationale of the patent (Key concept 4.3) system is to encourage technological development, whereby inventors are granted a monopoly over exploitation of the invention during which time they can, in theory, recoup their investment in research and development. Patenting is not compulsory, and some companies would prefer to rely on trade secrecy to protect their innovations.

For this purpose a patent is the exclusive right to make use of a new process or invention for the life of the grant. This may be done by the holder of the patent himself or herself manufacturing and exploiting it exclusively, or by licensing its use to others on suitably restricted and lucrative terms, or by outright sale of the patent rights.

Not every invention can be patented, however. The Patents Act 1977 says:

S.1(1)   A patent may be granted only for an invention in respect of which the following conditions are satisfied, that is to say –
(a) the invention is new;
(b) it involves an inventive step;
(c) it is capable of industrial application;
(d) the grant of a patent for it is not excluded by subsections (2) and (3) below; and references in this Act to a patentable invention shall be construed accordingly.

(2)   It is hereby declared that the following (among other things) are not inventions for the purposes of this Act, that is to say, anything which consists of –
(a) a discovery, scientific theory or mathematical method;
(b) a literary, dramatic, musical or artistic work or any other aesthetic creation whatsoever;
(c) a scheme, rule or method for performing a mental act, playing a game or doing business, or a program for a computer;
(d) the presentation of information . . .

(3)   A patent shall not be granted –

KEY CONCEPT 4.3	A patent is an arrangement between the state and an inventor whereby the inventor is granted a monopoly of exploitation of the invention for a limited time period in return for full disclosure of his or her new machinery, industrial process or product. The patent is a right to stop others exploiting an invention belonging to the patentee.
PATENTS	

(a) for an invention the publication or exploitation of which would be generally expected to encourage offensive, immoral or anti-social behaviour;

(b) for any variety of animal, or plant or any essentially biological process for the production of animals or plants, not being a microbiological process or the product of such a process . . .

Thus the product will need to be new to be patentable, and, at least from a business person's point of view (not as a matter of law) important enough to warrant the time, trouble and considerable cost of obtaining the patent, and in need of protection.

There are many different systems for patents. Every major country has its own (including the USSR and China), and there is an international application system (the Patent Co-operation Treaty). The procedure involved is basically the same for each. Firstly a specification is drafted, usually by a patent agent in consultation with the inventor. The filing secures initial protection pending further investigation and effectively secures a priority over other inventors who may developing products of a similar nature.

The second step is a preliminary examination of the specification, including a search among existing patents to ensure novelty. The search results are normally available within two to three months of the initial request and a search can be requested any time within the first twelve months from the data of application. The specification will then be published. Thirdly a full examination will take place to ensure that the requirements of the relevant legislation have been compiled with. Examination often amounts to a negotiation process between (e.g. in the UK) the Patents Office and the applicant. Eventually (but not inevitably) the patent is granted and will last for twenty years from the date of filing (not the date of grant).

The patentee pays an annual renewal fee and the patent is his or her property in law. It can be sold, assigned, licensed, etc. to another person or company. Difficulty may arise if the inventor is an employee. This will be examined in detail later in this chapter (p. 111).

Assign Assign means to 'transfer'

If the invention can be developed further, then each improvement can be patented, provided that each improvement itself satisfies the conditions for the award of a patent. This will effectively extend the life of the principal patent. Successful action taken against an infringer of the patent will usually result in an injunction to stop further infringement and compensation, based on the patentee's loss of notional royalties.

The Patent Co-operation Treaty, operated under the auspices of the World International Property Organisation (WIPO) in Geneva, and signed by over 30 countries, including the United States, the Soviet Union, the UK and most European states, provides for a single application designating the countries for which the applicant seeks protection. A single search is carried out and the application is then sent to each of the designated countries for separate examination as a national application according to their local laws. Within Europe the European Patent system provides a similar single application procedure, through which many UK patents are now granted.

CASE STUDY 4.1

UNITED BISCUITS:
ENFORCING PATENT
PROTECTION

United Biscuits will have to pay out part of a $125 million (£81 million) settlement to Procter and Gamble for violating P and G's patent on 'crisp and chewy' cookies in the United States.

P and G sued Nabisco, FritoLay (owned by Pepsico) and Keebler (owned by United) for patent violation after the Cincinnati company introduced Duncan Hines 'crisp and chewy' cookies in 1983. The three defendants launched similar products shortly afterwards.

The settlement, the biggest ever in a patent case, was signed by Judge Joseph Longobardi of the Delaware District Court. It will also prevent the three companies from illegally infringing P and G's patent in the future.

Mr John Pepper, president of P and G, said: 'We've worked hard to prove we're right, and we won. We believe this judgement is a complete vindication of our rights'.

He added: 'It was very frustrating to see our competitors beating us to market in most of the country with the very product we had developed and patented'.

United, which reports interim results today, said last night in London that Keebler would pay a total settlement of $52.9 million in five equal annual installments of $10.6 million.

(*Source:* Mike Graham, New York, 'UB must pay for patent violation', *The Times*, 15 September 1989)

It is commonly thought that filing a patent is laborious, time-consuming and expensive; the brief explanation given above may indicate that although time is needed to ensure the invention is genuinely original, and money must be spent to buy the necessary legal skill to draft the patent application in the best way, the rewards of a successful application can be enormous (United Biscuits: Case study 4.1).

Recent advances in bio-technology and drug manufacture bear testimony to some of the most public discoveries but there are many, many, quite minor inventions or processes which are regularly patented which do not necessarily capture a world-wide or even a national market, but which nevertheless net their inventors a tidy sum which would not have been the case had the discovery been otherwise available without compensation in the free market. From a dog in the manger point of view, if company A patents a process it may fail to induce company B to license it from them but it may involve company B in substantial time and expense in trying to develop a parallel product, valuable market time for company A to establish its brand. Of course Company A may not have the slightest wish to license its product to competitors, preferring to enjoy the exclusive fruits of its invention, as Xerox did with photo copiers and Polaroid with instant cameras for 20 years.

(b) Copyright

What copyright (Key concept 4.4) gives its owner is the right to prevent others copying the product of his or her effort, skill and judgment. It

> The law protects the expression of ideas where the finished work is literary, dramatic, musical or artistic. Ideas are not protected but the law prohibits the copying of their fruition without permission. A huge array of business documents thus acquire protection.

prevents others from taking the benefit of the intellectual effort which has been expended, from saving themselves the labour and effort of creating an independent work by relying on the skill of the copyright owner.

In a leading case *Ladbroke (Football) Ltd* v. *William Hill (Football) Ltd* (1964) I.V.L.R. 273, 291, Lord Pearce states:

> the protection given by copyright is in no sense a monopoly, for it is open to a rival to produce the same result if he chooses to evolve it by his own labours.

The law has been restated and amended by the Copyright, Designs and Patents Act 1988. The general effect of this reworking is that copyright protection will no longer be available for industrial designs, except in relation to works of artistic craftsmanship, and even there, where such works are exploited industrially, protection will be limited to a maximum of 25 years (rather than the life of the author plus 50 years, as under the previous legislation). Most industrially produced products will be protected under the new 'design right', or may be registered designs (except where a patentable invention is concerned).

As a rule copyright belongs initially to the author or creator of the work, but if the work is a commissioned photograph, engraving, portrait or sound recording (subject to an agreement to the contrary), the copyright will belong to the person commissioning the work and not to its author. Also, if the author is an employee, and the work is produced in the course of his or her employment then copyright will belong to the employer.

Infringement of copyright will only be upheld if there has been a substantial copying of the work. In this case the copyright owner may sue for damages, and/or seek an injunction to prevent further abuses. Any unlawful copies, plates, stencils, recordings, etc. will be regarded as the copyright owner's own property.

A copyright is property in law, and may, therefore, be assigned or transferred to someone else provided it is so assigned in writing and signed by the owner or his or her agent. A copyright owner can issue licences to copy, which again must be in writing, and a copyright can be bequeathed in a will and transferred upon a bankruptcy.

There is no requirement of literary merit in order for a work to be protected. Such diverse works as street directories, logarithm tables, examination papers, advertising brochures, test reports, information bulletins, etc. are entitled to copyright. A computer software program (undefined in the Act) is included as a literary work and thus itself attracts copyright. In the business context copyright prevents company A from copying, for example, the plans, designs, or sales and promotional literature produced by their more successful rival company B (British Leyland: Case study 4.2).

CASE STUDY 4.2

BRITISH LEYLAND: THE MARINA EXHAUSTS

As most motorists know car exhausts have a limited life and may need to be replaced every couple of years. A novel attempt to use the law of copyright to gain a competitive advantage was tried by British Leyland, manufacturers of mass market family cars. BL claimed that their copyright in the design drawings for the exhausts for the Marina model entitled them to prevent any unlicensed manufacturer from making replacement exhausts to fit the Marina whether with the aid of their drawings or not. It was BL's practice to license a number of component manufacturers with the right to make spare parts for their cars and to take a royalty by way of fee. The market in BL spare parts amounted to £800 million a year, a not inconsiderable sum! When an unlicensed manufacturer began to make exhausts without the appropriate licence BL took them to court seeking an injunction to stop further production in breach of their copyright and damages for loss of income. The trial judge and the Court of Appeal upheld the plaintiffs claim but the defendants appealed to the House of Lords. After an exhaustive résumé of the law their Lordships found that BL had the copyright in the design drawings and that this had indeed been infringed by the reproduction by the defendants of the exhaust in three-dimensional form; however, in a fascinating example of judicial ingenuity, their Lordships held that as a matter of public policy the owner of copyright could not exercise his right in such a way as unduly to restrict the right of a purchaser of goods to keep those goods in repair. In the case of a car exhaust, therefore, the manufacture by anybody of a replacement part which had to be made in a certain way to fit could not be held to breach copyright.

In reaching their decision their Lordships considered the purpose of copyright protection and the way in which the protection it afforded differed from the protection given by patent and design rights. The 1988 Copyright, Designs and Patents Act has clearly limited the application of copyright protection or design right to must fit or must match articles.

(*BL* v. *Armstrong Patents* [1986])

(c) Designs

Registered designs (Key concept 4.5) are governed by the Registered Designs Act 1949 as amended by the Copyright, Designs and Patents Act 1988.

A design is something artistic added to something practical, e.g. the motif on a sweat shirt, the pattern on a wallpaper, or a pattern of lace, or the design of the item itself, for example a chair, car, shoe or spade. Designs are concerned with the appearance of products (Lego Bricks: A Design?: Case study 4.3).

Registered designs

Registration under the 1988 Act gives the registered proprietor exclusive rights in the design for an initial period of five years from the date of registration, renewable for five year periods on application and payment to the registrar up to a maximum of 25 years. The design must be new, so an

KEY CONCEPT 4.5

A DESIGN

A design is defined by the Copyright, Designs and Patents Act 1988 s. 265 to mean: 'features of shape, configuration, pattern or ornament applied to an article by any industrial process being features which in the finished article appeal to and are judged by the eye, but does not include a method or principle of construction, or features of shape or configuration which are dictated solely by the function which the article has to perform, or are dependent upon the appearance of another article of which the article is intended by the author of the design to form an integral part'.

CASE STUDY 4.3

LEGO BRICKS: A DESIGN?

Most people are familiar with the LEGO brick-building system beloved of children and their constructive parents. To what extent the owners of the original drawings could restrict the copying of their product by so-called reverse engineering was the subject of a recent dispute with a Hong Kong based company. The law to be applied was that of Hong Kong which in this case is substantially the same as that of the UK. Under the relevant legislation, copyright could not subsist in any artistic work which, at the time when the work was made, could have been registered under the Registered Designs Act 1949. LEGO had registered their brick and acquired 15 years' protection, which had since expired. They now sought to argue that the brick should not have been registered as it was not capable of qualifying as a design. In this case it would qualify for the longer 50-year term of copyright protection. Could a child's building brick be registered as a design? Yes, the court held, as long as the article had 'eye appeal'; it did not matter that some of its features were dictated purely by functional requirements. Since the design of the bricks was registered it was outside the protection of the law of copyright.

(*Interlego AG* v. *Tyco Industries* [1988])

application should be made before there is any disclosure. Exact copying of the registered design is not necessary before action can be taken, resemblance is enough.

Unregistered designs
The Copyright, Designs and Patents Act 1988 creates a new Design Right which does not require registration for original (not 'commonplace') designs created or recorded after the Act came into force. It stands in addition to other rights and methods of protection, but where copyright exists the design right may be suppressed. It does not apply to design features which *must* be a certain shape – such as component parts which obviously *must* fit. So spare parts for engines, exhausts and so on will not attract the design right as far as the 'match and fit' features are concerned. This is part of the policy intended to prevent monopoly abuse (BL: Case study 4.3).

Where the design right does arise it protects the design of the product itself, not the design drawings; it arises when the design is first put into a design document or first manufactured, and it lasts for 15 years, although if the article is made available for sale or hire within five years of its design the duration is ten years from that date. In effect, then, the duration is ten years from first marketing. The right is subject to a licence which is available on payment of royalty to anyone in the last five years of the period.

(d) Trade marks

For goods

Trade marks (Key concept 4.6) are protected both under the common law of passing off (p. 109) and under the Trade Marks Act 1938. A trade mark is essentially any word or symbol, or combination of both, which is used 'so as to indicate, a connection in the course of trade between the goods and some person having the right either as proprietor or as registered user to use the mark . . .' (S.68 Trade Marks Act 1938) (Kline: Case study 4.4).

KEY CONCEPT 4.6 **TRADE MARK**	The primary purpose of the trade mark is to identify a particular source of goods or services for the convenience of the customer, and the ultimate profit of the manufacturer. Modern examples include logos such as storks on margarine packets, and lions on syrup tins, and word marks such as: Oxo, Michelin, Kodak, Esso, Hoover and Hotpoint.

CASE STUDY 4.4 **COLOUR-CODED DRUG CAPSULES: A 'TRADE MARK'?**	SKF were manufacturers of medicinal drugs. Among their products were certain 'sustained release' drugs consisting of small spherical pellets enclosed in soluble capsules. In order to distinguish their drug from those of other manufacturers, SKF coloured half of each capsule. SKF sought a Class A registration for their colour combinations, and this was opposed by one of their rivals. The rival company claimed that the mere external appearance of the product was not a 'mark', and alternatively, that if the product was a 'mark' it was not 'distinctive' so as to render it registrable.

The House of Lords held:

☐ The definition of 'trade mark' did not exclude a mark which covered the whole of the visible surface of the goods to which it was applied. It followed therefore that the external appearance of SKF's product was a 'mark' within the meaning of the Act.
☐ The mark was 'distinctive' because the colour combinations were used to distinguish SKF's products from those of other manufacturers.

This decision reversed the Court of Appeal decision, [1974] 2 All E.R. 826, that a 'mark' had to be something which could be represented or described separately from the goods in relation to which it was to be used in the sense that it was not merely a description of the goods as they appeared to the eye. Here, the Court said the capsule was recognizable by its whole appearance rather than by the fact that it bore an indicative mark.

Another, more recent but unsuccessful application, was for the registration of the famous Coca Cola bottle (1985 F.S.R. 315). This was refused, despite the fact that a drawing of the bottle would have been registrable – this case has been perceptively analysed by Mr. Pratt: 'Can a bottle be a trade mark?' (1985 E.I.P.R. 180).

(Smith Kline and French Laboratories Ltd v. Sterling-Winthrop Group Ltd (1975) 2 All E.R. 578)

Registration of a trade mark is not compulsory, but again, as with patents, the effect of registration is to confer a monopoly in the use of that particular mark in relation to certain goods. The Trade Marks Register is divided into Part A and Part B. Class A trade marks must be sufficiently distinctive, and the mark must consist of or contain at least one of the following:

(a) the name of a company, individual or firm, represented in a special or particular manner (S.9(1)(a));
(b) the signature of the applicant for registration or some predecessor of his in business (S.9(1)(b));
(c) an invented word or words S.9(1)(c));
(d) a word or words having no direct reference to the character or quality of the goods, and not being according to its ordinary meaning, a geographical name or surname (S.9(1)(d));
(e) any other distinctive mark, but a name, signature or word, other than those covered by (a) to (d) above, is not registrable except on evidence of distinctiveness (S.9(1)(e)).

Sometimes registered trade marks become almost synonymous with the articles themselves – typical examples are 'Thermos' and 'Yale': vacuum flasks are commonly called thermos flasks, and 'Yale' locks may not have been actually made by Yale at all! However, if the marks actually did become synonymous with the articles, then they would become invalid. This, of course, is why the owners of these two marks police them assiduously.

The limitations set out in section 9(1)(d) are to ensure that no one trader can monopolize, through his or her trade mark, words which other traders may legitimately want to use in connection with their products, such as descriptive words, or the name of the area in which they trade, etc.

The effect of a Class A registration is the right to exclusive use of the trade mark, and after seven years it is presumed to be valid unless it was obtained by fraud, or the mark is scandalous, deceptive or contrary to law.

A Class B trade mark may be registered where it is capable of distinguishing the goods of its owner from those of other manufacturers, but is not sufficiently distinctive to merit inclusion in Class A. A Class B mark which is not distinctive when first used may become distinctive with use: here it can be re-registered as Class A though this is rarely done. The protection afforded to Class B owners is not so complete as that offered to

Class A, and in particular, infringement will not be recognized where the infringer can show that the public is not likely to be confused: *Taw* v. *Notek* (1951) p. 219.

The defences commonly available to *infringement actions* are:

- [ ] That the mark is invalid, e.g. for non use for a period of five years (S.26), or that registration contravened Ss.9–12.
- [ ] That there is no infringement, e.g. because the marks or goods are different.
- [ ] That the defendant used his mark prior to the first use by the proprietor of the registered mark, or prior to its registration (S.7).
- [ ] That the defendant is bona fide using his own name or that of his place of business (S.8(a)).
- [ ] That the defendant is using a bona fide description of the character or quality of his goods (S.8(b)).
- [ ] That the defendant is himself the registered proprietor of the mark complained of (S.4(4)).
- [ ] That the plaintiff has no title.
- [ ] Other general defences, such as acquiesence, estoppel or that the plaintiff's use of the mark is fraudulent or deceptive.

For services

Prior to October 1986 a curious anomaly existed in that only trade marks for goods were capable of registration. However, many businesses are concerned with the provision of services and they may have a distinctive name or symbol, for example, hotels (e.g. Trust House Forte), major banks, travel agents, insurance companies, etc.

Until 1 October 1986 when the Trade Marks Act 1984 came into force it was only possible to take a common law passing-off action in the High Court if another company misappropriated a business name or symbol. Under the Trade Marks Act 1984 it is now possible to register trade marks for services ('service marks') and to obtain the same protection as for trade marks for goods, subject to similar limitations as apply to trade marks for goods (see above). The owners of such service marks are thus now better protected and will normally not need recourse to passing off.

Remedies for infringement

A successful plaintiff is entitled to an injunction and to damages based either on his or her loss, or on the infringer's profits, and an order for the destruction or modification of the offending material. Once a person or company has a trade mark registered, he or she is also in a position to defend themselves against potential trade competitors, by making use of the 'passing off' and 'trade libel' laws.

The Copyright, Designs and Patents Act 1988, S.300 amended the legislation concerning trade marks. There is now a criminal offence of fraudulent use of a registered trade mark with which comes a maximum of ten years imprisonment – higher than the Trade Description Act and equivalent to the penalty for theft. This is another step against the increasingly significant practices of counterfeiting goods.

The tort of passing off is committed where one trader sells or attempts to sell goods by pretending that they are made by another (usually better known) company, when in fact they are not. One obvious way in which 'passing off' might occur would be via the unlawful use of a trademark (whether registered or not). If the trademark was registered the injured party could also bring an 'infringement' action, as outlined above in the section on trade marks.

KEY CONCEPT 4.7

PASSING OFF

Common law protection

(a) Passing off

In a passing-off action (Key concept 4.7) it is essential for the plaintiff to prove:

☐ That because of the reputation attached to his or her goods or his or her business, there . . . is a goodwill attached to the marks or names he or she uses in connection with those goods or that business.

☐ That the defendant is misrepresenting that the goods he or she sells or that his or her business is, or are connected with, the goods or business of the plaintiff.

☐ That he or she has suffered, or there is a real likelihood that he or she will suffer damage to his or her business or goodwill.

A successful plaintiff is entitled to an injunction and to damages based on his or her loss, or the profits made by the defendant, and to an order for obliteration, or modification of the mark, name or set-up complained of.

Examples of passing off include the following.

In *Bollinger* v. *Costa Brava Wine Co.* [1960] 3 All E.R. 800 it was held that a sparkling Spanish wine sold as 'Spanish Champagne' was a misrepresentation, as the name 'champagne' denoted the sparkling white wine produced in the Champagne region of France, and not just any sparkling white wine. (In 1974 the English company of H.P. Bulmer were similarly restrained from using the word in connection with cider or perry.)

In *Annabel's (Berkeley Square) Ltd* v. *Shock* [1972] R.P.C. 838 the plaintiffs ran an exclusive club in Mayfair under the name 'Annabel's'. The defendant started an escort agency called 'Annabel's Escort Agency'. It was held that there was a sufficient likelihood that a significant number of members or potential members of the Annabel's Club would assume that the escort service was connected with or approved by the Club, and an injunction was issued against the defendant.

In *Parker-Knoll* v. *Knoll International Ltd* [1962] R.P.C. 265 both parties were manufacturers of furniture, the plaintiff in the UK and the defendant in the United States. The defendant had recently begun to trade in the UK, and even though it was using its own lawful name, the House of Lords granted an injunction to restrain them from using their name without distinguishing its goods from those of the plaintiff. It was said that the central question in each case is whether the name or description given by the defendant to his or her goods is such as to create a likelihood that a substantial section of the purchasing public will be misled into believing that his or her goods are the goods of the plaintiff.

(b) Injurious falsehood (trade libel)

Any scurrilous abuse or derogatory statement directed at the product of a trade rival, once communicated to a third party, is actionable by the maligned manufacturer without proof of actual loss. Where it is falsely and maliciously stated that a particular trader has ceased to carry on business, the latter will receive damages if he or she can show that his or her business was damaged as a result.

There is a very thin line between trade libel (Key concept 4.8) and the sort of advertising which suggests that 'in exhaustive tests', product A consistently performed better than product B.

KEY CONCEPT 4.8 **INJURIOUS FALSEHOOD (TRADE LIBEL)**	The tort of injurious falsehood, also known as 'trade libel', is committed when a defendant makes a false and malicious representation to a third party disparaging the plaintiff's property or business, but not necessarily defaming the plaintiff's personal character. If the words are in some permanent form, e.g. written in an advertising brochure, then there is no need to prove actual damage before the injured party can claim compensation. The same is true of any statement which is calculated to injure the plaintiff's trade or business.

Examples of trade libel include the following: *Wilts United Dairies* v. *Thomas Robinson* [1958] R.P.C. 94 – knowingly selling defective goods made by the plaintiff as if they were normal; *Barrett* v. *Associated Newspapers* (1907) 23 T.L.R. 666 – stating that a house the plaintiff was selling was haunted; *Lyne* v. *Nicholls* (1906) 23 T.L.R. 86 – stating specifically that the defendant's business was more successful than the plaintiff's.

Organizational aspects

What staff are employed, on what terms and with what incentives are key questions for a business. The relationship between an employer and his or her employees is essentially personal; in the absence of express contractual terms detailing rights and obligations on both sides, the common law or custom has regularly implied terms to produce a result giving a fair balance to both sides.

Most common law implied terms can be varied or excluded by express agreement so it is important for a business to know whether what the law implies accurately reflects its wishes or whether express terms are needed. The very fact that certain duties have been judicially recognized helps to crystallize rather loose understandings and may be used by an organization in drafting its own amended or express terms.

A business needs to have regard to two possible problems, both of which we shall consider in this section. Firstly the balance between the firm and an employee who invents or creates a valuable product, design, copy, etc. and secondly the balance between the firm's need to protect its own business secrets and an ex-employee who needs to sell his or her skills on the open market. In each case the law has guidelines and there are many judicial precedents which can assist a business to achieve its objectives as painlessly as possible.

Employee inventions

Over 10 000 UK patents are granted each year to UK companies, most as a result of an invention by an individual whilst at work. As a matter of practice, the common law area of breach of confidence can often be used against employees who leak confidential information but where the issues centre upon patent law, the question arises: who owns the invention – the employee inventor or his or her employer who is paying his wages?

(a)   Individual contracts

In the past it was left to the contract of employment and the settled principles of 'master and servant' to determine the question of ownership of the invention. Most contracts of employment stated that all employee inventions belonged to the employer. For example, the standard Civil Service contract stated; '... ownership of an invention made by a servant of the Crown vests in the Crown'. At GEC the standard employment contract stipulated that 'all inventions and registered designs, connected with the company's business made by an employee while in the company's service shall be the property of the company'.

Here is a typical example of a complicated clause in an employment contract offered recently to an ex-business studies graduate:

> I hereby agree, for myself, my heirs and representatives, to assign, transfer and convey, and I do hereby assign, transfer and convey to [Name of Company] its successors and assigns all my rights, title and interest in and to any and all creations which are or may become legally protectible or recognised as forms of property including all designs, ideas, inventions, improvements, writings and other works of authorship, theses, books, computer programs, lectures, illustrations, photographs, motion pictures, scientific and mathematical models, prints and any other subject matter which is or may become legally protectible or recognised as a form of property which I, either solely or jointly with others, have conceived, made or suggested, or may hereafter conceive, make or suggest, during my employment by [Name of Company] or its successors and the six-month period next following the termination of such employment, and which in any way relate directly or indirectly to its business, procedural, technical or commercial needs, problems, developments or projects or to its production, research or experimental developments and projects of every name and nature under consideration and/or being carried on by or for [Name of Company] prior to termination of my employment.

In the absence of clear contractual provision, the Courts determined the question of ownership essentially by reference to the nature and scope of the employee's duties. It was held in *Patchett* v. *Sterling Engineering Co. Ltd* [1955] A.C. 534 that where an employee makes an invention which falls within his duty to make, then the invention belongs to the employer.

For many years arguments raged because of the inequity of the law as regards the rights of employee inventors. Eventually a working party was set up which included representatives from the TUC and CBI, as well as patents experts, and its proposals, after lengthy deliberations, resulted in the Patents Act 1977, which now makes the ownership of employees' inventions a matter of statutory, rather than common law.

S.39 provides:

(1)   Notwithstanding anything in any rule of law, an invention made by an employee shall, as between him and his employer, be taken to belong to his employer for the purposes of this Act and all other purposes if –

(a) it was made in the course of the normal duties of the employee or in the course of duties falling outside his normal duties, but specifically assigned to him, and the circumstances in either case were such that an invention might reasonably be expected to result from the carrying out of his duties; or

(b) the invention was made in the course of the duties of the employee and, at the time of making the invention, because of the nature of his duties and the particular responsibilities arising from the nature of his duties he had a special obligation to further the interests of the employer's undertaking.

(2)   Any other invention made by an employee shall, as between him and his employer, be taken for those purposes to belong to the employee.

Even if the invention does belong to the employer, the employee may obtain a 'fair share' of the benefit to be derived by his employer, if he can show the invention is of outstanding benefit to the employer and he deserves some compensation for his efforts (S.40). In effect there are two circumstances in which an employee can be paid. First if the employer is the owner but the invention is of outstanding benefit, or second, if the employee is the owner but he assigns the invention to his employer for an inadequate amount.

The Act (S.41) sets the amount of compensation payable to the employee as a 'fair share (having regard to all the circumstances) of the benefit which the employer has or may reasonably be expected to derive from the patent'. In addition S.41(4) sets out criteria which, among other things, should be taken into account when determining what is a fair share. These are as follows:

(a) the nature of the employee's duties, his remuneration and other advantages he derives or has derived from his employment, or has derived in relation to the invention under this Act;

(b) the effort and skill (if any) which he has devoted to making the invention;

(c) the effort and skill which any other person has devoted to making the invention jointly with the employee concerned, and the advice and other assistance contributed by any other employee who is not a joint inventor of the invention; and

(d) the contribution made by the employer to the making, developing and working of the invention by the provision of advice, facilities and other assistance, by the provision of opportunities and by his managerial and commercial skill and activities.

Where, according to S.39, the invention belongs to the employee, he can dispose of it as he wishes. He can sell it to his employer, or to anyone else. Usually, however, the employee will not have the finance or resources to develop and exploit the invention himself, although individuals do develop their inventions, and they assign or license them, to third parties. It might be that he will grant an exclusive licence under the patent to his employer.

S.39 of the 1977 Act was amended by the Copyright, Designs and Patents Act 1988 in order to deal with an anomaly. This was that whereas copyright in works produced in the course of employment would normally vest in the employer, this would not necessarily cover ownership of any associated patent. The 1988 Act has inserted a new subsection (3) into S.39 of the 1977 Act which has the effect of protecting an employee who is entitled to a patent under S.39 from liability for infringement of any design right or copyright belonging to his employer 'in any model or document relating to the invention'. It is the policy of S.39 to enable an employee to exploit his patent rights. Without the amendment his employer could use copyright or design rights to prevent this exploitation.

The 1977 Patents Act also provides that any terms in the contract of employment which are inconsistent with the Act are void and therefore unenforceable.

(b)   Collective agreements

The provisions of the Patents Act do not apply to an employee who works under a collective agreement that entitles him or her to compensation for inventions made at work. In such a case, the provisions of the collective agreement prevail over the Act's system for assessing compensation, so he or she will not be entitled to the statutory compensation. Usually, of course, the union will have negotiated terms in the collective agreement that are more generous than those under the Act. But this applies only if the employee concerned is a member of that trade union. If he or she is not, they will be subject to the usually less advantageous provisions of the Act, and it could be that they will receive no compensation at all!

Restraint clauses

The common law implies a duty of fidelity and confidentiality into every contract of employment (Chapter 7). These implied terms, however, will not carry on beyond the life of the employment contract; so an employer who wishes to protect himself or herself and/or the company after the employee leaves must include a written restraint clause (Key concept 4.9) in each of the contracts of employment of employees party to such company secrets.

A restraint clause (i.e. one which restricts the future activities of an

KEY CONCEPT 4.9

COVENANTS IN RESTRAINT OF TRADE

Certain employees will be party to very confidential company information. In some cases, if one of these employees leaves his or her job and decides to set up in competition with his or her former employer, or to work for a competitor, he or she could do a great deal of damage by using this information. Therefore a clause restraining them from working for competitors after leaving employment is frequently inserted into their contracts.

employee after the termination of his current contract of employment) is construed by the courts *contra proferentem*, i.e. strictly against the person seeking to rely on it (the employer). These clauses are 'prima facie' void and will only be upheld if the employer has a 'genuine interest to protect' and the clause itself is 'reasonable' as between the parties, and not contrary to public policy (Chapter 2).

Restraint clauses must be in writing to be enforceable (*Faccienda Chicken Ltd* v. *Fowler* (1986) p. 219, *U.S.C. Ltd* v. *Felton* (1974) p. 219). The employer must have a genuine interest to protect (*Commercial Plastics Ltd* v. *Vincent* (1965)) and he or she cannot stop an ex-employee using any personal skill or experience even if this has been acquired in the service of the employer (*Stenhouse Ltd* v. *Phillips* (1974) p. 219).

The restraint clause itself must be reasonable as between the parties, and since the case of *Herbert Morris Ltd* v. *Saxelby* (1916) this has been assessed according to the stated restrictions on the scope of employment, the geographical area covered by the restraint and the duration for which the clause will live on after the contract has been terminated must be reasonable. Each case must be judged on its own particular facts, and the consequence of a clause being too wide in geographical area, or too long in time, for example, is that the clause will be void in law, and therefore unenforceable.

Restrictive covenants (restraint clauses) are normally enforced by injunction, as the employer wishes to prevent the ex-employee from continuing to damage his or her business. As it is a breach of an express term of a contract, however, the employer could, as an alternative to the injunction, sue for compensation for breach of contract.

Novel points concerning 'restrictive' clauses in employment contracts arose recently in *Strathclyde Regional Council* v. *Neil* [1984] I.R.L.R. 11 where an employee objected to returning to her former position after completing a period of paid training leave. She had agreed to return to the employer for at least two years after a paid training leave. If she did not do so she would have to 'refund . . . an amount proportionate to the unexpired portion of the contracted minimum period of service'. The Scottish Court rejected each of her objections to the clause in turn:

(a) This was not an unlawful restrictive clause since the employee was not restrained from using her skills after leaving the Council;
(b) There was no restraint on her liberty beyond that normally involved in a contract of service;
(c) There was no evidence of such compulsion as would invalidate her contractual consent;

(d) The terms of repayment were not a penalty.

((c) and (d) above are explained more fully in Chapter 2 of this book.)

With the European Social Equality Action Programme suggesting that paid time off for educational purposes should become the norm for all employees, this case could be of great importance in the future, and such clauses may become the norm for employment contracts.

Summary

In this chapter we have considered some of the legal constraints faced by a business involved in innovation and research. These were environmental constraints – principally safety, pollution and planning, of which only a brief mention could be given here and remember that regard should be had to local bye-laws or controls in force and regulations governing particular industries; some strategic considerations were identified where the law makes available protection for original work and inventions, a business must decide what tactics are appropriate to take maximum advantage; and lastly, organisational matters balancing the interests of past and present members of the organisation and the business itself.

In each of these areas the rules derive from a combination of custom and practice, judicial decision and parliamentary legislation. Where the rules provide an enabling mechanism, the registration of a patent, the drafting of an enforceable restraint clause, the protection of original material, etc. good legal advice is both essential and valuable. There is very little point in a firm spending large sums on innovation and development if it then fails adequately to protect its investment.

Further reading

An excellent general work in this area is: Jeremy Phillips, *Introduction to Intellectual Property Law* (Butterworths). Other useful works include: Dworkin and Taylor *Copyright, Designs and Patents Act 1988* (Blackstone); Cornish, *Intellectual Property* (Sweet and Maxwell); White and Jacob, *Patents, Trade Marks, Copyright and Industrial Designs* (Sweet and Maxwell) – and, of course, there are a large number of texts which specialize in particular aspects of this wide and complicated field, plus others which purport to take a 'practical' approach for the busy businessman or woman.

Exercises

1. Examine the following case study carefully, read the listed relevant cases, then consider the likely attitude of the court to the problem involved.

    Claire was assistant research manager at the ABC Drug Company's research laboratories in Plymouth. Her employer was a leading manufacturer in the pharmaceutical field and also owned a chain of chemists across the south of England. Claire had agreed in her contract of employment that she would not, within 2 years after her employment had ceased, 'carry on or assist in carrying on either as principal or as manager, agent or servant, or in any capacity whatsoever, or be in any way engaged or concerned or interested in the pharmaceutical industry, within the United Kingdom or western Europe'. After a row with her manager, Claire took employment in Scotland as a research manager with XYZ plc, a leading competitor of her former employer. The ABC Drug Co. obviously wish to enforce the contract against Claire and thus prevent her from continuing in her new job.

(a) Is the restraint clause in writing? *Faccenda Chicken Ltd* v. *Fowler* (1986) All E.R. 617.

(b) Does the employer have a 'genuine' interest to protect? *Commercial Plastics Ltd* v. *Vincent* (1965) 1 Q.B. 623; *Spafax Ltd* v. *Harrison* (1980) I.R.L.R. 442.

(c) Is the clause 'reasonable' in relation to content, area and duration? *Attwood* v. *Lamont* (1920) 3 K.B. 571; *Fitch* v. *Dewes* (1912) 1 All E.R. 13; *Home Counties Dairies Ltd* v. *Skilton* (1970) 1 All E.R. 1227; *T. Lucas & Co. Ltd* v. *Mitchell* (1972) 3 All E.R. 689 *Marion White Ltd* v. *Francis* [1972] 3 All E.R. 857; *Littlewoods Organisation Ltd* v. *Harris* [1978] 1 All E.R. 1026; *Greer* v. *Sketchleg Ltd* [1979] I.R.L.R. 445; *Marley Tite Co. Ltd* v. *Johnson* [1982] I.R.L.R. 75.

2. Peter likes to draw. A couple of years ago he drew a cartoon matchstick figure to amuse his children. He called it 'Tom'. Soon he had to begin inventing stories about 'Tom', and gradually 'Tom's' reputation spread. Soon he was featuring in the local press. More recently, he has been taken up by a national newspaper. There are proposals for worldwide syndication. Peter has made his career in fabric design. He owns his own small company, producing a limited renge of curtain and dress fabrics for the UK market. He has incorporated 'Tom' into his latest designs for children's fabrics.

Bill is a manufacturer of toys and children's games. Without Peter's consent he has incorporated 'Tom' pictorially into a board game for the Christmas market in the UK, and in the USA. In addition, he has developed an existing board game by marking on the box 'Tom's favourite game!' He has plans to adapt the character for use in conjunction with a 'dress-up' doll called 'Bandy' which he has promoted successfully for several years. He plans to give 'Bandy' a selection of gifts, including flowers, jewellery and clothing and to print 'with love from Tom' on each.

Discuss the legal position.

The production process: health, safety and liability 5 |||||

Introduction

The production function is a 'transformation process which takes a variety of inputs such as materials and labour and turns them into goods and services' (Needle, Business in Context). The production function of a business exists in a much wider context than the pure manufacturing of goods; it exists, for example, in department stores, restaurants, banks, local government, schools, hospitals, etc.

The law has always influenced and constrained the production function of business. The siting of a factory, or warehouse, or office is closely controlled by local and national planning laws. The construction and maintenance of the building is subject to local and national building laws and regulations. The environment of the unit is controlled by the Factories Act 1961, the Offices, Shops and Railway Premises Act 1963, the Health and Safety at Work etc. Act 1974, and so on. The 'product' itself is subject to restrictions imposed by the Health and Safety at Work etc. Act 1974, the Patents Act 1977, the Copyright etc. Act 1988, etc.

In civil law the producer has to contend with the laws relating to negligence, nuisance, manufacturer's and employer's liability, the responsibilities imposed by the Occupier's Liability Act 1957, and the Consumer Protection Act 1987, and so forth. The producer, as an employer, is restrained by the myriad of employment legislation, including protective legislation designed to outlaw the exploitation of women, young persons and children.

Chapter 6 of the Business in Context book by David Needle in this series outlines the main reasons for the recent decline in manufacturing industry in Britain and the government's attempts to regenerate it. This decline and attempted regeneration has been accompanied by more and more legal regulation within the government of the day's regional policy.

The designation of areas in need of special assistance, development grants to offset the cost of buildings and equipment, rate and rent reductions on special sites and the discouragement of business expansion outside of these areas are today all functions of legislation. Government policy in the 1980s has attempted to redress the balance between the prosperous south and the poorer north and to halt inner city decay through the creation of special enterprise zones and development coporations, by measures requiring legislation.

The purpose of this chapter is to examine briefly the legal environment within which the production process has to function. It is not possible in a book of this size to examine all the areas of relevant law, so a fairly close examination of a few of the more important areas of the law will be given. Court and tribunal decisions will be used to illustrate the legal attitudes towards production, with judges, who do not normally have experience in industry, interpreting statutory and common law in various ways, some helpful and some very unhelpful to the company which has to produce to survive. We shall examine in detail the Health and Safety at Work etc. Act 1974 because it is of central importance to the production of any business, but only brief mention will be made of other employment legislation. People are obviously very important in all aspects of business, including production, but full discussion of employment law will be confined to Chapter 7; The Personnel Function.

We shall also examine the liability of the producer in civil law to his or her employees, to third parties and to the public in general for 'injuries' caused to them by his or her production process. Finally we shall examine the law relating to product liability: having produced his or her 'product' the producer may still be liable in law for 'injuries' caused to the ultimate consumer.

The production process

The Health and Safety at Work etc. Act 1974

First we examine in detail sections of the Health and Safety at Work etc. Act 1974 covering the duties imposed on employers, employees, designers, manufacturers, importers and suppliers of goods and services, to ensure the health and safety of employees, persons other than employees and the general public. The Act was based mainly on the recommendations of the Robens Committee on Safety and Health at Work, which reported in 1972. The Committee were appointed to review safety and health of persons in the course of their employment, to consider whether any changes were necessary in existing legislation, and to consider the further protection of the public from hazards arising from industrial and commercial activities.

The Committee reported that every year more than 1000 people were killed, a half-million were injured and 23 million working days were lost through industrial injury and disease. These figures did not include the 1000 people dying each year from prescribed industrial diseases, those persons absent from work due to injury or illness for just one or two days only, and any statistics relating to approximately 20% of the workforce who were not within the scope of any existing occupational safety and health legislation.

The Health and Safety at Work Act 1974, a direct result of the Robens Report, was drafted against the background of numerous existing Acts and Regulations, some dating back nearly one hundred years. The accelerating rate of technological change, plus the slow, cumbersome Parliamentary procedure for amending, revoking or introducing legislation (Chapter 1), meant a new framework was essential.

One of the aims of the Act was, therefore, to repeal all existing safety legislation and replace it gradually with more up to date regulations and codes of practice. So far this exercise has not been very successful and we still have to refer to the earlier legislation, e.g. Factories Act 1961, Offices, Shops and Railway Premises Act 1963, the Chemical Works Regulations 1922, etc. The old legislation is written in a difficult legalistic style, largely unintelligible to those persons who are supposed to understand and implement the detail. Line managers, supervisors and shopfloor operatives are not lawyers and Robens said all new legislation should be easily understood by all workers.

The Health and Safety at Work Act is intended to provide for reasonable safety and health for all persons at work, including the self-employed, and for the general public as well. The only excluded category of worker is that of domestic servants.

(a) General duties of employers to their employees

Under S.2(1) of the Act it shall be the duty (Key concept 5.1) of every employer to ensure, so far as is reasonably practicable, the health, safety and welfare at work of all his employees.

A duty is a legal obligation imposed on a specified person in specified situations. S.2(1) Health and Safety at Work Act says it is the duty of every employer to ensure, so far as is reasonably practicable, the health, safety and welfare at work of all his employees. Thus the duty only extends to employees whilst they are in the course of their employment; there is no obligation on employers to concern themselves with health, safety or welfare matters which arise outside work (although many companies do so concern themselves).

Lord Reid (in *Nimmo* v. *Alexander Cowan and Sons Ltd* [1968] A.C. 107, 113): '. . . Sometimes the duty imposed is absolute; certain things must be done and it is no defence that it was impossible to prevent an accident because it was caused by a latent defect which could not have been discovered – still less it is a defence to prove that it was impracticable to carry out the statutory requirement. But in many cases the statutory duty is qualified in one way or another so that no offence is committed if it is impracticable or not reasonably practicable to comply with the duty. Unfortunately there is great variety in the drafting of such provisions. Sometimes the duty is expressed in absolute terms in one section and in another section it is provided that it shall be a defence to prove that it was impracticable or not reasonably practicable to comply with the duty. Sometimes the form adopted is that the occupier shall, so far as reasonably practicable, do certain things. Sometimes it is that the occupier shall take all practicable steps to achieve or prevent a certain result. And there are other provisions which do not exactly fit into any classes. Often it is difficult to find any reason for these differences'.

KEY CONCEPT 5.1

THE DUTY OF THE EMPLOYER TO ENSURE THE HEALTH AND SAFETY OF WORKERS

What does ' . . . so far as is reasonably practicable . . . ' mean? Asquith
L.J. (in *Edwards* v. *N.C.B.* (1947)) said:

> . . . Reasonably practicable is a narrower term than 'physically possible',
> and seems to me to imply that a computation must be made by the owner
> in which the quantum of risk is placed on one scale and the sacrifice
> involved in the measures necessary for averting the risk (whether in
> money, time or trouble) is placed in the other, and that, if it be shown
> that there is a gross disproportion between them – the risk being
> insignificant in relation to the sacrifice – the defendants discharge the
> onus on them. Moreover, this computation falls to be made by the owner
> at a point of time anterior to the accident . . .

The standard seems to be the common sense standard applied by the
judges in the common law cases on negligence. The following examples
will provide useful illustrations.

In *Paris* v. *Stepney B.C.* [1951] A.C. 367; P. was employed to scrape
away rust and other accumulated rubbish from underneath the Council's
buses. It was not customary to provide protective goggles for this kind of
work. However, P. had only one good eye, a fact known to the employer,
so the risk of serious injury was greater for P. than for a two-eyed worker.
Inevitably an accident happened and P. was blinded.

The court held that the duty of care is owed to the plaintiff himself and
therefore, if he suffers from some disability which increases the magnitude
of the risk, greater care is owed by the employer towards him. Here a
serious risk of injury could have been averted by a low-cost pair of
protective goggles. The employer had not done all that was reasonably
practicable and was therefore liable to the plaintiff.

In *Bolton* v. *Stone* [1951] A.C. 850 the plaintiff was standing on the highway in a road adjoining a cricket ground when she was struck by a ball
which a batsman had hit out of the ground. Such an event was foreseeable
and, indeed, balls had occasionally been hit out of the ground before.
Nevertheless, taking into account such factors as the distance from the
pitch to the edge of the ground, the presence of a seven foot perimeter
fence, and the upward slope of the ground towards the perimeter fence,
the House of Lords considered that the likelihood of injury to a person in
the plaintiff's position was so slight that the cricket club was not negligent
in not taking other precautions. Here the cost of averting a very low risk
of injury would have amounted to many thousands of pounds – a gross
disproportion.

The following recent cases were appeals against enforcement notices
issued by Health and Safety Inspectors under the Act, but they illustrate
the current industrial tribunal attitude to ' . . . reasonably practicable . . . '.

In *Associated Dairies Ltd* v. *Hartley* [1979] I.R.L.R. 171 the company
used 'roller trucks' (hydraulic trolley jacks) for the handling and transport
of articles in their warehouse at Grimsby. They provided a facility whereby
employees could purchase safety shoes at cost price via weekly payments.
When an employee suffered a fractured toe as a result of a roller truck
running over his foot, an inspector issued an Improvement Notice (see
later for definition) requiring the company to provide safety shoes, free of

charge, to all employees. The company appealed successfully to the tribunal for cancellation of the Notice:

> ... The absolute obligation upon an employer under S.2 (of the Act) to make arrangements for securing the safety at work of his employees is subject to the words 'so far as is reasonably practicable'.

The Inspector's requirement was practicable but not reasonable! The tribunal said it was proper to take into account the time, trouble and expense of the requirement, and to see if it was disproportionate to the risks involved. It would have cost the company £20 000 in the first year, and £10 000 per year thereafter, yet the likelihood of an accident occurring was 'fairly remote', and there was no evidence that the employees would use the boots even if they were provided.

Also relevant are the following: *Otterburn Mill Ltd* v. *Bulman* [1975] I.R.L.R. 223; *Bellhaven Brewery Co. Ltd* v. *McLean* [1975] I.R.L.R. 370. The general 'umbrella' duty contained in S.2(1) is particularized by five specific duties placed on the employer by S.2(2) as follows.

(i) The provision and maintenance of plant and systems of work that are, so far as is reasonably practicable, safe and without risks to health.
The case of *R.* v. *Swan Hunter Shipbuilders Ltd* (1981) illustrates that this duty covers employees and persons other than employees who may be affected by the system of work (S.3(1)).

(ii) The arrangements for ensuring, so far as is reasonably practicable, safety and absence of risks to health in connection with the use, handling, storage and transport of articles and substances.
Thus in appropriate cases, protective clothing, proper equipment and tools, etc. must be provided. Handling must be considered: is the weight too excessive ?; are dangerous parts covered or guarded ?; are storage facilities adequate and safe?; have fork lift drivers been instructed in safe stacking? The transportation must also be carried out in a safe manner, e.g. loads must be secure and weight evenly distributed.

Page v. *Freight Hire (Tank Haulage) Ltd* (1981) illustrates how this section means that employers must have regard to the health of specific employees as well as employees generally. Ms Page was rejected for the full-time position of a HGV driver (she already worked on a casual basis) because she was 23 years old and the tanker would be carrying dimethylformamide (DMF), which presented a danger to women of child-bearing age if they came into contact with the chemical. The refusal was held not to be sex discrimination because the interests of safety clearly required that she should not be exposed to the handling of a substance which was potentially hazardous, and which had a possible embryotoxic effect.

(iii) The maintenance, so far as is reasonably practicable, of any place of work under the employer's control in a condition that is safe and without risks to health, and the provision and maintenance of means of access to and egress from it that are safe and without such risks.
Premises must be safely maintained, obstacles removed, dangerous wiring replaced, defective floors and stairs repaired, pavements, pathways, car parks, etc. kept in a good state of repair. The duty applies to places under

the employer's 'control', which is of course a wider concept than that of 'ownership'. The other existing legislation, e.g. Factories Act 1961, contains much detail on what is considered to be 'safe and without risks to health' in those places of work.

(iv) The provision and maintenance of a working environment for his employees that is, so far as is reasonably practicable, safe, and without risks to health, and adequate as regards facilities and arrangements for their welfare at work.

The employer has to pay proper attention to systems of noise control; eliminate noxious fumes and dust; lighting must not be excessive or inadequate; toilet accommodation, washing facilities, cloakroom arrangements, etc. must be appropriate.

(v) The provision of such information, instruction, training and supervision as is necessary to ensure, so far as is reasonably practicable, the health and safety of his employees.

This fourfold duty is part of a battery of requirements which are all aimed at a well-informed workforce and others who may be involved in or by work related activities.

The detailed requirements include:

☐ The employer must provide a written safety policy statement (e.g. figure 5.1), including accident procedure, fire regulations, details of required safety training, employees' responsibilities, etc.

> S.2(3): except in such cases as may be prescribed, it shall be the duty of every employer to prepare and as often as may be appropriate revise a written statement of his general policy with respect to health and safety at work of his employees and the organisation and arrangements for the time being in force for carrying out that policy, and to bring the statement and any revision of it to the notice of all his employees.

An employer who carries on an 'undertaking' with fewer than five employees is exempt from this provision, (Employers' Health and Safety Policy Statements (Exceptions) Regulations 1975); but see *Osborne* v. *Bill Taylor of Huyton Ltd* [1982] I.R.L.R. 17, where employers operated 31 betting shops, these were held to be 'an undertaking' for the purposes of the Act, and although each shop employed less than five employees, since there was central control, all the shops together represented a single 'undertaking'.

XYZ Ltd Safety Policy Statement (as required by S.2(3) Health and Safety at Work Act 1974)

1. The Company will take all reasonable measures to ensure the safety, health and welfare at work of all employees in fulfilment of its moral, legal and economic responsibilities. These measures will also be aimed at protecting others who may be affected by our day to day working activity.

2. The Managing Director of the Company, or his nominee, will be responsible for the overall safety function. He will report to the Board of Directors on company safety and health matters at regular intervals.

3. The Managing Director is responsible for safety at Head Office.
   The Production Director and Senior Supervisors are generally responsible for safety at the various company sites.
   Each Supervisor is responsible for implementing company safety procedures and for complying with all legal requirements in the areas under their supervision.

4. The management undertakes to provide the appropriate circumstances under which work may be carried out safely and without risks to health. However all employees must be aware that they have a legal duty, not only to work in a safe manner, but also to co-operate in efforts made to create safe and health working conditions.

5. The management will make suitable arrangements for the training of employees on how to recognise and guard against foreseeable hazards, and how to meet the responsibilities placed upon them. Employees for their part must agree to take part in any and all appropriate safety training.

6. Employees are expected to involve themselves fully in all safety matters and to report immediately any unsafe equipment or dangerous situations to their respective supervisor.

7. The Company will co-operate with other employers' safety arrangements when working within their orbit and we will accordingly expect co-operation on safety matters by other employers working on our sites or within our control.

8. This Company has a good health and safety record. The co-operation of every employee is necessary in order that standards may be maintained and improved wherever possible

> W.J. Cole,
> Managing Director,
> 1st January 1987

☐ In companies where trade unions are recognized for collective bargaining purposes the union(s) have the right to appoint safety representatives and safety committees must be formed if requested (SS.2(4),(6), (7)). The Safety Representatives and Safety Committees Regulations 1977 detail the functions, rights and obligations of safety representatives and employers in these situations. The employer must consult any such representatives with a view to the making and maintenance of arrangements for enabling their effective co-operation in promoting, developing and monitoring measures to ensure health and safety at work of employees.

☐ There is a duty on the Health and Safety Commission (Key concept 5.2) to provide information (S.11(2)(b) and (c)).

☐ There is a duty on a Health and Safety Inspector to provide information to workforce representatives in certain circumstances (S.28(8)).

☐ Regulations may be made requiring information on health and safety to be included in directors' reports (S.79). It was said in Parliament when

KEY CONCEPT 5.2

HEALTH AND SAFETY COMMISSION

The Commission consists of nine members plus a Chairman appointed by the Secretary of State for Employment. Three members represent employers' organizations, three represent employees' organizations, and the other three are appointed after consultation with all interested parties. Its duties are to assist and encourage persons concerned with health and safety to further the purposes of the Act, to arrange for the carrying out of research, publication of results, and the provision of training, to provide an advisory service, and submit proposals for change and the making of regulations. The Commission also issues Codes of Practice and Guidance Notes on health and safety matters.

debating this provision that it ' . . . would concentrate the minds of chairmen and directors most wonderfully if the company's health and safety performance had to be accounted for in public'.

☐ There is a duty on manufacturers (and designers, suppliers and importers) of articles and substances for use at work to make available adequate information about their products, about relevant tests and about conditions under which they can be safely used (S.6).

☐ The Employment Medical Advisory Service (EMAS) has the function of keeping everyone concerned with the health of employed persons informed of matters about which they ought to know in order to safeguard and improve health (S.55).

(b) Duties to persons other than employees (S.3)

An employer and a self-employed person shall conduct their undertaking in such a manner that persons other than employees are not exposed to risks to their health and safety. They also have a duty to give information to persons other than employees about aspects of the business which may affect their health and safety.

The concern expressed by the Robens Committee over the possibilities of a large-scale disaster arising from the storage or production of dangerous gases and liquids was soon shown not to be misplaced (Case studies 5.1 and 5.2).

CASE STUDY 5.1

THE FLIXBOROUGH DISASTER (1974)

Britain's biggest explosion at Flixborough, near Scunthorpe happened in 1974, at the chemical works of Nypro (UK) Ltd, a company jointly owned by Dutch State Mines, the National Coal Board and Fisons Ltd. A temporary by-pass pipe failed resulting in the release of cyclohexane, a chemical having similar properties to petrol above its boiling point, at a rate faster than one ton per second from the two pipe stubs. After 45 seconds the vapour cloud ignited producing rapid deflagration and a powerful pressure wave as the remaining one thousand tons of cyclohexane caught fire.

The explosion killed 28 people and injured a further 105 and over 2000 buildings were damaged; the cost of damages were over £40 million.

CASE STUDY 5.2

THE SEVESO DISASTER (1976)

This disaster, with serious lasting consequences, occurred in Seveso, in northern Italy near Milan in 1976, when a runaway reaction during the production of triphenol resulted in the discharge of products containing tetrachlorodibenzodioxin (TCCD) over an area of 28 sq. km (700 acres). Four per cent of the domestic animals living in the contaminated zones died spontaneously and the remaining 77 716 animals were slaughtered as a preventive measure to protect the food chain. Some 736 people were exposed to relatively high doses of TCCD and it is too early to estimate the damage caused except to say that an unusually high incidence of chloracne was detected in the area of the contaminated townships. Seveso itself is still fenced off and out of bounds to everyone today.

(c) Duties of persons in control of premises (Ss. 4 and 5)

The Act provides that a person who has control of any work premises owes a general duty of care to persons other than his employees who are working there, or using those premises in any way. This means he shall ensure, as far as is reasonably practicable, that the premises and the means of access to and egress from, and any plant or substance in the premises, are safe and without risks to health (*Northampton B.C.* v. *Farthingstone Silos Ltd* (1981)).

(NB   similar provisions are contained in the Occupiers Liability Act 1957 (p. 134 of this chapter) infringement of which may lead to civil claims for compensation. Under S.47 Health and Safety at Work etc. Act, however, no civil claims can be brought for infringement of the Act, only criminal prosecutions by the state.

S.5(1) states that it is the duty of the person who has control of a business where noxious or offensive fumes are involved, to use the best practicable means to prevent these fumes from entering the atmosphere. The Control of Pollution Act 1974 is also very important in this context, and in S.72(2) provides that 'practicable' means reasonably practicable, having regard among other things to local conditions and circumstances, to the current stage of technical knowledge and to the financial implications.

(d) Duties of designers, manufacturers, importers and suppliers (S.6)

The Act requires anyone who designs, manufactures, imports or supplies an article or substance for use at work to ensure, so far as is reasonably practicable:

(a) That it is so designed and constructed as to be safe when properly used.
The H.S.E. Guidance Note on S.6 says:
...If the user makes an unusual or unexpected use of the product, or chooses to disregard the information (otherwise than in some small and/or irrelevant particular), by deliberately overloading a machine, failing to install a machine correctly for noise control purposes, or failing

to maintain equipment, for example, then it will be considered that there has not been a proper use and the manufacturer, etc. will not, under those circumstances, be held responsible under S.6.

(b) That such testing and examination as may be necessary have been carried out, to ensure compliance with the above duty.
Thus, a supplier of machinery (for example) who buys from a reputable manufacturer and relies on that manufacturer's undertaking that proper testing at design, prototype and production stages have been carried out, will not normally be required to carry out further tests.

(c) That adequate information about the safe use of the article [or substance] is provided.
The difficulty here is that the information provided by the designer and manufacturer must pass through the supplier to the employer. The employer's duties under Ss.2(1) and 2(2)(c) then place the obligation on him to ensure that employees are in receipt of such relevant information and are adequately trained and supervised in the correct and safe use of the article or substance. There is, of course, further potential for both civil and criminal liability for the supplier – if his product is intended for consumer use. This will be considered in more detail later.

(d) That all necessary research has taken place to eliminate or minimise any risks to health or safety which the design of the article or substance may give rise.
(Further detail on the duties imposed by law on designers and manufacturers is given in Chapter 4).

(e) Duties of erectors and installers (S.6(3))

A person who erects or instals any article for use at work in any premises where that article is to be used by persons at work shall ensure, so far as is reasonably practicable, that nothing about the way in which it has been erected or installed makes it unsafe or a risk to health when properly used.

(f) Duties of employees (S.7)

Under S.7 employees have a duty whilst at work to:

(a) take reasonable care for the health and safety of himself;
(b) take reasonable care for the health and safety of others who may be affected by his acts or omissions at work; and
(c) co-operate with his employer to enable compliance with the requirements of the legislation.

Thus an employee who refuses to wear safety equipment or use safety precautions is liable to be prosecuted, as is the employee who indulges in horseplay and thereby causes injury to another (Case study 5.3).

(g) Enforcement

The HSE Inspectors and local authority safety inspectors have been given wide ranging powers by the Act, including the right of entry to premises;

CASE STUDY 5.3

**HORSEPLAY: THE
EMPLOYEE'S DUTY OF
CARE**

In the December 1982 issue of the EETPU journal it was described how two workmates took a 62-year-old fellow employee and put him in a lift which was designed to carry goods only. The lift jammed and when the instigators attempted to free it, it plunged to the bottom of the lift shaft. Its occupant sustained a broken back, and has since been permanently crippled. Each of the men responsible was charged under S.7 and convicted. In their defence they claimed it was only 'good fun' and that the victim did not complain about the treatment meted out to him. If this really was the case, it is arguable that he failed to ensure his own health and safety as far as reasonably practicable, and could therefore also have been prosecuted.

KEY CONCEPT 5.3

**HEALTH AND SAFETY
EXECUTIVE**

The responsibility for the day-to-day enforcement of the Health and Safety at Work etc. Act falls upon the Health and Safety Executive (HSE), consisting of a Director and two Assistant Directors.

the right of making examinations and investigations; the taking of measurements, photographs and samples; the production and inspection of books and documents; the provision of facilities and assistance; the questioning of people; the seizing and rendering harmless of articles and substances, etc.

In addition to the above powers inspectors are also able to issue Improvement and Prohibition Notices. Appeals against the issue of Prohibition and Improvement Notices (Key concept 5.4) are heard by the Industrial Tribunal, but application for such an appeal must be made within 21 days of the notice being issued. The effect of an appeal is that an Improvement Notice will not come into effect until the appeal has been heard, but a Prohibition Notice will continue to operate until the appeal is heard. The tribunal has the power to confirm or cancel a notice, or to amend it as it thinks fit.

Premises Premises are defined by S.53 of the Act as including '. . . any place and, in particular, includes –

☐ any vehicle, vessel, aircraft or hovercraft,
☐ any installation on land (including foreshore and other land intermittently covered by water), any offshore installation, and any other installation (whether floating or resting on the seabed or the subsoil thereof, or resting on other land covered with water or the subsoil thereof), and
☐ any tent or moveable structure.'

KEY CONCEPT 5.4

**IMPROVEMENT AND
PROHIBITION NOTICES**

An *Improvement Notice* can be served on a person where an inspector is of the opinion that the person is contravening one or more relevant statutory provisions, and the notice must specify a date by which it must be complied with, giving a period of at least three weeks for the necessary improvements to be made. A *Prohibition Notice* can be served if the inspector is of the opinion that an activity involves or will involve risks of serious personal injury. A Prohibition Notice can be served whether or not there has been or will be a contravention of legal rules. The notice may be issued with immediate effect, or, at the discretion of the inspector, deferred to a specific time.

Any employer who fails to comply with the legal requirements of the Health and Safety at Work etc. Act can also be prosecuted by the Health and Safety Executive in either the Magistrates' Court, where the maximum penalty is a £2000 fine, or in the Crown Court, where the maximum penalty is an unlimited fine and/or up to two years imprisonment. Unfortunately the level of fines imposed by the courts is generally so low that it often pays the company to ignore safety and pay the occasional fine, if and when prosecuted. Health and Safety Inspectors should, according to the International Labour Organization, inspect every workplace twice per year. In the UK there are so many workplaces and so few inspectors that each workplace is visited, on average, once every seven years!

The future role of the HSE Inspectorate gives some cause for concern. Economic and political policy results in many companies seeing safety as an additional burden, and a costly burden to bear. The number of inspectors employed by the HSE has fallen in the past few years, and they have tried to concentrate on persuasion as the best method of enforcing safe standards of working. In 1983 the HSE launched the 'Site Safe '83' campaign to improve conditions in the construction industry, which has a very bad safety record. Persuasion was the order of the day. Since 1983 there have been more fatalities on construction sites than before the campaign!

In the 1975 Redgrave Memorial Lecture, Mr Bill Simpson, the first Chairman of the Health and Safety Commission, attacked the low level of fines imposed by the courts:

> The fines for safety misdemeanors should show some relationship to fines for other misdemeanors in our society. Equity alone should demand that the gravity or potential gravity of the offence should be suitably punished. Being tough in this way fires a broadside at all those who are being negligent in their statutory duties. It devalues the work of inspectors, trade unions, researchers, policy makers and Parliament if, on conviction, safety miscreants are fined piddling amounts, that have more in common with a dog fouling the pavement than with the breaking of the law of the land by employers, which can result in the killing or maiming of workers. Preventing future accidents does need a vigorous enforcement of the law. Heavier fines do not prevent accidents that have happened, they do, however, have some deterrent effect and would certainly show that the law was serious in seeing that the provisions (of the Act) were observed.

The average fine today is still under £500 for infringements of the Act, and in 1987 a director of three companies was sentenced to 18 months imprisonment for allowing his employees to work removing asbestos without having a licence issued under the Asbestos (Licensing) Regulations 1983 and being in contravention of a prohibition notice. Yet the sentence was suspended for two years!

Case study 5.4 gives an example of the court's attitude to safety. This case clearly illustrates the dilemma for the inspectorate – why waste time taking prosecutions when the courts impose such derisory fines, yet advice, such as 'Site Safe '83', appears to have no effect in improving safety

CMS Ltd, a small cleaning company, entered into a contract with International Stores plc (IS) to clean their premises. The work involved the use of certain bulky electrical cleaning equipment, including a polisher/scrubber. CMS employees cleaned IS premises during the early mornings, but at this time the loading bay was in constant use and could not be cleaned. It was agreed therefore between the two companies that IS employees would clean the loading bag at the end of each day, using the CMS machine.

On November 10th 1984 an employee of IS was electrocuted whilst using the CMS machine because its main cable was defective. During the case, tried on indictment at the Warwick crown court, the legal arguments revealed that CMS were in breach of many duties imposed by the Health and Safety at Work etc. Act 1974. They had certainly infringed sections 2(1), 2(2)(a), 2(2)(b), 2(2)(c), 3(1), and probably S.6 and possibly S.2(3) as well.

The HSE inspectors thought strongly enough about the case to bring a prosecution before the Crown Court, where the maximum penalty was an unlimited fine, and/or up to two years imprisonment. The result, confirmed by the Court of Appeal in November 1986, was a fine of £200!

Comment: Many questions must be asked about this case, including:

☐ Why did the case take so long to get to court? The worker was killed on November 10th 1984; the Crown Court convicted on February 27th 1986; the Court of Appeal confirmed the decision on November 12th 1986 – a period of two years between death and ultimate conviction!

☐ How much did the case cost? The true cost of the case must run into hundreds of thousands of pounds. It took two years, involved solicitors, barristers (for both sides), a crown court judge and a jury of 12 persons many crown court personnel, the Health and Safety Executive, three Appeal Court judges, many Appeal Court personnel, employees and witnesses for both CMS and IS, and expert witnesses – yet the fine imposed was only £200!

☐ How much is a life worth? £200?

CASE STUDY 5.4

SMALL FINES FOR BREACHES OF HSW ACT

standards. Perhaps we should now consider giving health and safety inspectors the power to impose instant fines on companies and individuals, up to an agreed level. This power would surely have had a greater impact on CMS, given more satisfaction to the family and workmates of the dead employee, and certainly have saved the taxpayer a great deal of money.

In the introductory section to this chapter we mentioned that the legal environment within which the production function has to operate includes elements of civil law as well as the criminal law. Whilst the Health and Safety at Work etc. Act 1974 imposes duties in criminal law on the employer, manufacturer, etc., the civil law also acts as a constraint on the way a business operates. We shall now examine some of the areas of civil law which are relevant to the production function of any business.

Vicarious liability

A business enterprise employs people. It is consequently subject to the possibility of incurring vicarious liability (Key concept 5.5), that is, the employer can, in certain defined circumstances, be held responsible for injuries caused to others, by those who work for him or her. Particularly in the service sector, customers or clients may be injured or damaged in the course of the contract's performance. It is not necessary that the employer should have directly participated in the action which caused the injury, nor is it necessary that the employer should have breached a duty of some kind which he or she owed to the injured party. The crucial relationship here is that between the employer and whomever directly caused the injury. The conduct which gave rise to the injury must be referable to that relationship.

KEY CONCEPT 5.5 **VICARIOUS LIABILITY**	Vicarious Liability means liability for the tort of another. It arises in a number of situations, in particular employers will be held liable for the torts of their employees committed in the course of their employment. This liability is in addition to, not instead of, that of the wrongdoer.

In this section we will be concerned with the vicarious liability of an employer for torts committed by his or her employees, but the principle of vicarious liability is wider than this – partners can be liable for each others' torts, principals for their agents, and even parents for children.

An employer will not, however, be answerable for the tortious activities of everybody he or she employs – vicarious liability only follows where it can be shown that:

Tortfeasor The person who commits a 'tort' against another party.

☐ The tortfeasor was his 'servant' (as opposed to his 'independent contractor'); and
☐ The servant commited the tort within 'the course of his employment'.

(a) Servant or independent contractor?

It is essential, then, to be able to distinguish between 'servants' and 'independent contractors': servants are said to be employed under 'contracts of service', whereas independent contractors are said to be employed under 'contracts for services'.

This rather archaic use of 'master and servant' terminology will be dropped straightaway. Nobody (other than the most stuffy of lawyers) uses it nowadays. We will use the generally used term 'employee' instead of 'servant', bearing in mind, however, that independent contractors are also employed and paid for what they do.

This crucial distinction between 'servants' and 'independent contractors' is not easily made. Various tests or guidelines have been invented and developed by the judges over the years. For example, the 'control test' was outlined in *Yewens* v. *Noakes* (1880) – 'a servant is a person subject to the command of his master as to the manner in which he shall do his work' –

that is, a servant can be told what to do and how to do it, whereas an independent contractor can only be told what to do. This test is not of much use nowadays. It was all very well in an age when a servant could realistically be regarded as an extension of the employer, doing what the employer would do if only he or she had the time. But now, in an age of increasing technological knowhow and specialization, such theories have little about them that resembles reality.

An alternative was suggested by Lord Denning (in *Stevenson* v. *MacDonald* (1952)):

> ... one feature which seems to run through the instances is that, under a contract of service a man is employed as part of the business – whereas under a contract for services his work, although done for the business, is not integrated into it but is only accessory to it.

These two, and other 'tests', have now been run together, and the latest version used by the courts is called the 'multiple' test. It comprises two parts:

☐ Is there control?
☐ If so, are the other provisions of the contract also consistent with it being a contract for service?

This 'multiple' test was first used in *Ready Mixed Concrete (S.E.) Ltd* v. *Minister of Pensions and Social Security* (1968).

These tests are still referred to by High Court judges, but in reality the question 'who is an employee?' is most commonly asked in Industrial Tribunals in relation to the 'new' employment rights (Chapter 7). Tribunals do not have jurisdiction to deal with cases involving vicarious liability, however, so the development of principle, which is so common in the English law, using the delicate threads of the doctrine of precedent, have not been seen in this instance. No new definition of what amounts to a 'servant' has emerged, despite the fact that the modern-day occupant of such a job differs markedly from his prototype, the manual or domestic worker. Hospital authorities have been held vicariously liable for the torts of nurses, doctors and radiographers – as have companies for their executives.

(b) Course of employment?

The business organization, as an employer, will not be made vicariously liable for every tort committed by its employees – only those committed whilst 'within the course of their employment'. The scope of this course of employment has been tested in many cases.

On basic principles of agency law, the employer will be answerable for those acts which he or she actually (expressly) or impliedly authorizes, and for those which are normal and incidental to the employee's normal duties (Case study 5.5). The mention of the 'first' and 'second' defendants in this case is an important reminder that what we are concerned with here, vicarious liability, is not an alternative but an additional liability. The injured party can sue both the employee and his or her boss. Naturally he or she will rarely exclude the employer.

CASE STUDY 5.5

IN THE COURSE OF EMFLOYMENT?

Some demolition contractors had permission to use their employer's van during the day. They decided to take it nine miles away, to a cafe, for tea. On the way back the negligence of the driver resulted in the death of one of the men, His widow sued, arguing the vicarious liability of the employer. The claim was resisted by the employer's insurers, arguing that the incident occurred outside the course of the driver's employment. Diplock J. (as he then was) said:

'I think that the true test can be best expressed in these words: was the defendant doing something that he was employed to do? If so, however improper the manner in which he was doing it, whether negligently or fraudulently, or contrary to express orders. I have got to look at the realities of the situation. What were the circumstances, and what was the purpose for which this journey to the cafe and back was taken. Looking at the realities of the situation, it seems to me to be clear beyond a peradventure that what happened was this: the four men having taken the view that they had done enough work to pass muster, were filling in the rest of their time until their hours of work had come to an end. They decided to go to the cafe after sitting and chatting on the job for some time, to fill in the time until they could go home and draw their pay. This seems to me to be a plain case of what, in the old cases, was sometimes called 'going out on a frolic of their own'. It has most tragic consequences, but it does not seem to me that it is possible to hold (though I would like to do so if I could), looking at the realities of the situation, that on the course of that journey the second defendant was doing anything that he was employed to do'.

Hilton v. *Burton (Rhodes) Ltd* [1961] 1 All E.R. 74

Hilton v. *Burton (Rhodes) Ltd* (Case study 5.4) is only one of a number of cases littered around the Law Reports concerned with the scope of employment after a tort has been committed by an employee. Employers have been held vicariously liable even for actions which were expressly prohibited.

In *Rose* v. *Plenty* (1976), for example, a milkman in Bristol, contrary to an express prohibition from his employer, allowed a milkboy to travel on his float, and help with the round. The milkman drove carelessly, and the boy's leg was badly injured. The Court of Appeal held that the milkman was within the course of his employment, despite the prohibition. Lord Denning said:

> In considering whether a prohibited act was within the course of employment, it depends very much on the purpose for which it was done. If it is done for his employer's business, it is usually done in the course of his employment, even though it is a prohibited act.

It might be though that this was something of a 'policy' decision. The court was faced with a 13-year-old boy with a smashed leg on one side, and an employer with an insurance policy on the other. If the employer

Policy decision is the term given to a 'creative decision' by a court. Where a judge finds that the precise situation in dispute before him is not already covered by an authority, or where a previous denial of a duty of care is challenged for the first time at the appellate level, the court has to make a creative choice whether or not a duty of care is raised by the facts before it, for '. . . how wide the sphere of the duty of care in negligence is to be laid depends ultimately upon the courts' assessment of the demands of society for protection from the carelessness of others' (*Hedley Byrne and Co. Ltd* v. *Heller and Partners* (1964)).

Winfield and Jolowicz on tort: 'The use of the word "policy" indicates no more than that the court must decide not simply whether there is or is not a duty, but whether there should or should not be one, taking into account both the established framework of the law and also the implications that a decision one way or the other may have for the operation of the law in our society'.

Lord Denning M.R. in *Home Office* v. *Dorset Yacht Co. Ltd* [1969] 2 Q.B. at p. 246: 'It is, I think at bottom a matter of public policy which we, the judges, must resolve. This talk, of "duty" is simply a way of limiting the range of liability for negligence'.

KEY CONCEPT 5.6

POLICY DECISION

were to be held vicariously liable, the party best able to pay would shoulder the burden. Policy decision is defined in Key concept 5.6.

In the workplace, difficulties sometimes arise with employees who are 'practical jokers', and as a consequence of their horseplay they injure others – particularly fellow-employees. Are such tricks inside or outside the 'course of employment'? Recently, in *Harrison* v. *Michelin Tyre Company* (1985) p. 220, Comyn J. devised a test in the form of two mutually exclusive questions:

☐ Was the incident part and parcel of the employment in the sense of being incidental to it although and albeit unauthorized or prohibited?
☐ Was it so divergent from the employment as to be plainly alien to and wholly distinguishable from the employment?

If the answer to the first question is yes, the defendants are liable. If the answer to the second question is yes, they are not.

Here they were liable. The injury was caused when a trolley was pushed off its route along a passageway, as a joke, injuring a fellow-employee. The answer to the first question above was yes. Within our system based on precedent, the last word of the superior courts is always followed, so this is the current approach to this problem.

(c) Independent contractors

The basic rule, as we have seen is that there is no vicarious liability for independent contractors. They are hired for their special expertise, and they are expected to insure against tortious liability, and to pay for themselves.

However, as with many simple rules in law, there are exceptions to this

Independent contractor An Independent Contractor is a person employed under a contract of services to achieve a specific task. Such a person is not usually under the control of his or her paymaster/client and is usually in business on his or her own account.

one too. The employer must answer vicariously for even his or her independent contractor when:

☐ The tort committed is one of 'strict liability' (e.g. *Rylands* v. *Fletcher*) (Chapter 2).
☐ The work to be done directly affects the highway, or some other place ordinarily accessible to the public at large.
☐ The contractor allows fire to spread from the employer's land to another's.
☐ The tort involves a breach of some duty which is personal, and thus not susceptible to delegation to others so as to avoid the responsibility;
☐ The task undertaken is of an extraordinarily hazardous nature.

In order to protect himself against the possibility of vicarious liability (Key concept 5.5) the employer's line of defence is clearly careful selection, training and supervision as appropriate. The Employer's Liability (Compulsory Insurance) Act 1967 requires an employer to carry insurance against his potential vicarious liability to his employees for personal injuries. The fact that a business is regarded generally as being in a sounder financial position than an individual plus the requirement that it carry insurance cover means that inevitably it is the firm which will be sued when one of its employees has caused loss.

Constraints imposed by employment legislation

A further constraint on the production function may be caused by the general law relating to employment of individuals. As has previously been discussed in Chapter 2, all employees have to be engaged under a contract of employment, with written particulars of employment containing details such as job title, hours of work, etc., issued within 13 weeks of commencement (Chapter 7 gives a detailed review of written particulars of employment).

Rapidly changing technology, round the clock communications or improved manufacturing processes could result in the employer's requirement for a more flexible workforce, but the law relating to unfair dismissal inhibits him or her if the employee refuses to co-operate in changing job duties, or working hours, or is just not able to cope with new work requirements or re-training. Similarly, if a new process or product means that some jobs disappear, the employer may be constrained by the law relating to redundancy. In these cases, employees with more than two years' continuous service will be entitled to compensation, under certain circumstances, which can be prohibitive to a small employer. (Both unfair dismissal and redundancy will be discussed in more detail in Chapter 7.)

Occupiers' liability

In this section we shall examine the company's liability in civil law towards third parties injured on company property, whether they are there by invitation, expressly or impliedly, or trespassing. The result of the production process, whether goods or services, will necessitate third parties coming to the company's premises; whether it be as a delivery driver, a representative of a supplier or buyer, a customer, a HSE inspector, or even

> The Occupiers' Liability Act 1957 provides that: 'An occupier of premises owes the same duty, the "common duty of care" to all his visitors . . . a duty to take such care as in all the circumstances of the case is reasonable to see that the visitor will be reasonably safe in using the premises for the purposes for which he is invited or permitted by the occupier to be there'.

KEY CONCEPT 5.7

OCCUPIERS' LIABILITY

a group of business studies students viewing the company's production process as part of their programme of studies.

Under the Occupiers' Liability Act 1957 there is imposed on the business a form of statutory negligence liability. It is a statutory duty of care which the occupier of premises (i.e. the person in control of them and not necessarily the owner) owes to lawful visitors (not trespassers) (Key concept 5.7). These may have been expressly invited (potential customers or clients, consultants, trade union officials), or they might impliedly have been invited (milkman, health and safety inspector).

In most places of work, for example a factory, or a shop, there could be said to be a 'line of lawful presence'. It might be marked with a 'staff only' sign, or a barrier of some kind, but it is clear that beyond such a line the statutory duty of care will probably not apply. This is not to say that there can therefore be bear traps behind the door. The occupier owes something of a duty towards even the trespasser, as will be seen later.

Under the 1957 Act the mental and physical state of the visitor will always be relevant – so that children and the mentally or physically disabled will be owed a higher standard of care than, say, consultants called in to work in their specialist field on the employer's premises. In *Roles* v. *Nathan* (1963) two sweeps were killed, but the occupier was not liable. He had done enough to satisfy the requirements of the Act. On the other hand, in *Reffell* v. *Surrey C.C.* (1964), the County had not done enough to prevent a 12-year-old girl from running into a thin plate glass door. Likewise in *Ward* v. *Tesco Stores* (1976) the company policy, under which floors in the shop were cleaned several times a day, was not in itself sufficient to escape liability when a customer slipped in a puddle of yoghurt. They were liable under the 1957 Act because they could not show exactly when the floor had last been cleaned.

There will be no liability for injuries caused by independent contractors under the Act, provided that the business selected its contractors in a reasonable way. Simply putting up warning signs will not necessarily be enough to escape liability. They will be taken into account, of course, but if the presence of children or the blind is reasonably foreseeable, then they will be insufficient in themselves. Also, under the Unfair Contract Terms Act 1977 (Chapter 2) it is impossible to exclude liability for personal injury caused by negligence, and only possible to exclude liability for damage to property if the exclusion satisfies the statutory test of 'reasonableness'.

However, where visitors to business premises are present for recreational or educational purposes, and this is not the business of the occupier (e.g. a manufacturer allowing a group of business studies students to visit his

premises to view his production methods), then, under the Occupiers'
Liability Act 1984, it is possible for the occupier to exclude liability for
personal injury. He will still be responsible for their health and safety as far
as reasonably practicable under S.3 Health and Safety at Work etc. Act
1974, and failure to do so could lead to his prosecution (see section on
health and safety above).

Occupiers' liability towards trespassers is an uncertain thing. It is clear
that the occupier owes a trespasser a 'duty of common humanity', and that
this duty is far less onerous than the statutory duty under the 1957 Act, or
that owed under the 'neighbour principle' in negligence, but there have
been problems in recent years for occupiers of premises which are
trespassed upon by children. Trespassing adults are, it seems, owed no
more duty than the avoidance of setting traps. However, where children
are reasonably to be expected, near a railway line crossing public land
(*British Railways Board* v. *Herrington* (1972)), near a bonfire (*Pannett* v.
P. McGuiness & Co. Ltd (1972) p. 221), in a lime quarry with tall slag
heaps (*South Portland Cement* v. *Cooper* (1974)), and in a closed house
which had been re-opened by vandals (*Harris* v. *Birkenhead Corporation*
(1976)), occupiers have been held liable for injuries sustained by the trespassing children.

More recently, however, there has been a trend in the decisions away
from this and towards a reaffirmation of parental responsibility, particularly
with regard to young children. In *Ryan* v. *London Borough of Camden*
(1982) the defendants were not liable for the injuries sustained by a child
who crawled near hot pipes in a council-owned property, and in *Simkiss* v.
Rhondda B.C. (1983) they were not answerable for injuries sustained by a
child sliding down a steep slope on a blanket. In both cases it was held that
the occupier was not liable as he was entitled to assume that prudent
parents would have taken steps to warn their children of such obvious
perils.

These general common law principles have now been replaced by statute,
the Occupiers' Liability Act 1984:

> An occupier of premises will owe a duty to trespassers if he is aware (or
> ought to be) of danger, knows (or has grounds to believe) that the
> trespasser is or may be in the vicinity of the danger, and may reasonably
> be expected to offer some protection to the trespasser against the danger.
> The duty is said to be to take such care as in all the circumstances is
> reasonable to see that the trespasser does not suffer injury. The duty
> may in appropriate circumstances be fulfilled by appropriate warnings of
> the danger, and it does not apply to property damage.

This provision adds little or nothing to the common law, and it seems clear
that the courts will have recourse to the cases decided before the 1984 Act
when interpreting its provisions.

Nuisance

Another area of concern for businesses is the liability the law imposes on
them to care for their neighbours and the general public at large in the way
that they operate their business. The section earlier in this chapter on

health and safety at work has already examined the criminal law aspects of safety towards the general public; in this section we shall now look at an example of the civil law in this area, namely the tort of nuisance (Key concept 5.8) (Nuisance: Case study 5.6).

A business may be liable in private nuisance if the use to which it puts its premises unreasonably interferes with the use to which those who own or occupy the neighbouring land and properties wish to put their land. Nuisance can be public or private. A public nuisance affects the public generally and is a crime; it is also actionable in civil law by anyone who suffers more than the public does generally. A private nuisance affects only the neighbouring property.

KEY CONCEPT 5.8

NUISANCE

A road in Fulham, London, contained the line between that land which had been zoned for residential use, and that zoned for industrial use. The plaintiff lived opposite the defendant's oil depot. Acid smuts damaged his car parked in front of his house, and his washing on the line at the back of his house. There was a nasty smell coming from the factory, and a lot of noise at night from the boilerhouse, and huge tankers calling at the depot. The smell had not actually hurt the plaintiff, but the noise rattled his windows and doors, and kept him awake at night.

The defendants were held to be liable in private nuisance for damaging the clothing (i.e. injury to property resulting from the activity on neighbouring land), for the smell (it was not necessary to show damage to health, the uncomfortable atmosphere was enough), and for the noise in the depot and from the tankers whilst in the depot. They were also liable in public nuisance for the damage to the car; it was on a public road, but the plaintiff had suffered more than the general public.

As if this was not enough, the defendants were also liable in both public and private nuisance for the noise from the tankers whilst they were using the public highway, (public because at that hour it was an unreasonable use of the highway which had particularly affected the plaintiff, and private because it materially affected the plaintiff's enjoyment of his property). The defendants were also liable in the tort called 'Rylands v. Fletcher' (after the case in 1868 which established that, as Blackburn J. said: '. . . a person who, for his own purposes brings on his land and collects and keeps there anything likely to do mischief if it escapes, must keep it at his peril, and if he does not do so, is prima facie answerable for all the damage which is the natural consequence of its escape'). This is an adapted form of nuisance. The defendants were liable in Rylands v. Fletcher in respect of the damage to the clothing and the car, that is, for the damage caused by the escape of a harmful substance from their premises.

Halsey v. Esso Petroleum Co. Ltd (1961) 1 W.L.R. 683

CASE STUDY 5.6

NUISANCE

What makes the interferance 'unreasonable' is a question of degree. In nuisance, the character of the neighbourhood is a relevant consideration, as is the reasonableness of the defendant's conduct (*Christie* v. *Davey* (1893) and *Hollywood Silver Fox Farm Ltd* v. *Emmett* (1936)). We all live on a crowded island and we must put up with the consequences of living near other people (*Robinson* v. *Kilvert* (1889) and *Bridlington Relay Ltd* v. *Yorkshire Electricity Board* (1965) p. 220).

Nuisance is that branch of the law most closely concerned with 'protection of the environment'. Typical nuisance actions have concerned pollution by oil or noxious fumes, interference with leisure activities, offensive smells from certain work premises, noise from industrial installations. The common law of nuisance has now been supplemented, and to a large extent replaced, by many statutory powers designed to control environmental damage, including Public Health Acts, the Control of Pollution Act, Clean Air Acts, etc. The enforcement of these statutory measures rests in the hands of public bodies (often the local authority) and they do not generally give rise to civil liability. However, the usual remedy sought by most victims of nuisance is an injunction to prevent its continuance, and nowadays a complaint to the relevant enforcing body will bring the same result without the necessity of personally taking a long, complicated, slow, expensive civil law action in the courts. The common law of nuisance remains necessary where the plaintiff seeks damages or where the enforcing body are unwilling to take action. Hence public law is gradually replacing private law.

The end product

Introduction

It is clear, then, that there are a number of aspects of the production function of a business enterprise which are regulated by both the civil and criminal law in regard to the ways in which the business operates. Having overcome these constraints the production process will result in goods or services being produced. In this section we will briefly examine the area of law which is sometimes referred to as 'product liability', which is concerned with the obligations imposed by the law onto businesses for injuries sustained by those to whom the goods are distributed or used.

Where the end product is services the producer is bound by the Supply of Goods and Services Act 1982 and by the common law of negligence, particularly applicable where professional advice is given (Chapters 6 and 2 respectively). The business must, as part of its decision-making processes consider structuring the organization of the production processes in such a way as to minimize the dangers of incurring liabilities for product-related injuries, as well as, as we have already seen, structuring the pattern of employment procedures, controls, discipline, methods of working, etc. so as to minimize vicarious laibility, and liability at criminal law for infringement of the many statutory provisions on safety and health.

A manufacturing business will be subject to contractual liability. That is, it will have to answer if it fails to deliver the products which were ordered, and which were the subject matter of the contract. This contractual liability is strict, i.e. it is no answer to a claim for breach of contract for the business to argue that the fact that the goods did not match the agreed description, or were delivered late, or not delivered at all was not their fault. Contractual liability does not depend upon fault. The goods are either right or not. If they are not right then the business can be held liable, at least on the face of it, for breach of contract.

This form of responsibility only extends to the other party to the contract. There is no contractual liability towards anyone else. Up until very recently, the third party to a contract, say, for the sale of goods – perhaps the recipient of a birthday present – could look for redress only to the law of tort.

The most important of the torts these days, and especially for the business enterprise, is the tort of negligence.

An action based on negligence depends upon the breach of a duty of care, owed by the defendant to the plaintiff, which resulted in reasonably foreseeable damage.

We will pick the bones out of that definition in a moment; the important point here is that negligence liability is fault based. That is to say, the plaintiff must establish that it was the defendant's fault that the injury complained of was suffered and that the defendant was blameworthy, (i.e. breached a duty to take care). So the basis of product liability law in the UK is contractual between the buyer and seller and tortious towards anyone else. Contract law is a strict liability system. Tort law (at least as far as negligence is concerned), is fault based (Case study 5.7).

It is crucial to remember that the tort of negligence does not require you to get it right, just to be careful. So simply because you have suffered an injury, it does not follow that you will be able to obtain compensation in the tort of negligence (Chapter 2).

CASE STUDY 5.7

NEGLIGENCE v. CONTRACT

A man visited a pub (the 'Falcon Arms', in Battersea, London). He bought a jug of beer and a bottle of lemonade. He returned with this afternoon refreshment to his home, where his wife was waiting. He poured out two glasses nearly full with beer, and topped each up with the lemonade. They drank together. They spat the mixture out together. The lemonade contained carbolic acid. They suffered the same injury at the same time in the same way, together. However, the English law regarded their potential for redress very differently. The husband was able to recover compensation from the landlady of the pub, Mrs. Tabard. His wife was not, because, of course, she had not been a party to the contract under which the lemonade had been sold. She was not 'privy' to the contract. She was left to establish that the manufacturers had been negligent in their production process, and that she had suffered a reasonably foreseeable injury as a consequence. Almost unbelievably, she lost. The Judge was satisfied that the process used for washing and checking the bottles had been adequate (actually, it consisted of a girl sniffing the empty bottles!)

Daniels and *Daniels* v. *R. White and Sons* (1938) 4 All E.R. 258

The Consumer Protection Act 1987

The difficulty faced by a plaintiff in proving breach of duty and the consequent difficulty in recovering compensation in many cases led to a good deal of dissatisfaction and a powerful consumer lobby. The idea of imposing strict or no fault liability on the producer of defective goods was first adopted in the United States. After nine years of debate it has now been accepted by the European Community. The idea behind the change is to allow the victim of a defective product to recover compensation for the injury simply on proof of causation and defect without the need to prove the producer was at fault, i.e. that he or she knew or ought to have known of the defect. The Consumer Protection Act 1987 implementing the European Product Liability Directive came into force on 1 March 1988. It is still too early to say whether it will produce a flood of claims, as the CBI feared, or whether producers will improve their quality control in advance of possible suits. The effect of the Act is to introduce product liability (Key concept 5.9) into English law.

S.2(1) of the 1987 Act provides that:

> ... where any damage is caused wholly or partly by a defect in a product, every person to whom subsection (2) below applies shall be liable for the damage.
> (2)   This subsection applies to –
> (a) the producer of the product;
> (b) any person who, by putting his name on the product or using a trade mark or other distinguishing mark in relation to the product, has held himself out to be the producer of the product;
> (c) any person who has imported the product into a member state from a place outside the member states, in order, in the course of any business of his, to supply it to another.

This is a very important reform. It can be clearly seen that there is no requirement of fault. It says 'shall be liable'. There is no limitation to the purchaser, as in contract. It says 'where any damage is caused'; it does not specify who has to be the victim of the damage.

In short, if the product is defective and if the defect causes injury, then the producer must answer to the victim. All the plaintiff needs to show is the defect and causation.

This brings the English law into line with that found in many of the United States: of course, each of the 50 States has its own jurisdiction in such matters and each has its own legal system. However, this is not to say that we will have a product liability system like the Americans, of which producers are so nervous, with millions of pounds awarded on a regular basis, because our lawyers do not work on contingent fees nor do we have juries in negligence or breach of contract actions to set the level of dam-

Contingent fees A lawyer representing his or her client in a case will only be paid if he or she wins. Usually this payment will be based on a percentage of the total amount awarded, often as high as 30% or even 40%. If the lawyer loses he or she receives no fee.

KEY CONCEPT 5.9	Product liability means the liability of a producer for injury caused by a defect in his or her product to any person. This liability is strict, i.e. there is no need for the plaintiff to prove fault.
PRODUCT LIABILITY	

ages. Moreover we do not award 'punitive' damages, except in the most extraordinary of cases.

This statutory product liability is additional to the contractual and tortious liability discussed in Chapter 2. There are limitations on the liability:

☐ The damage must be worth more than £275.
☐ The defect must not have been traced to 'game or agricultural produce' which had not undergone an 'individual process' (whatever that is!). It seems, for example, from the debate in the House of Lords during the enactment of the 1987 Bill, that harvesting of the produce is not an industrial process for the purposes of this law.
☐ The producer will escape from liability if it can be established: 'that the state of scientific and technical knowledge at the relevant time was not such that a producer of products of the same description as the product in question might be expected to have discovered the defect if it had existed in his products while they were under his control (S.4(e)). This is known as the 'state of the art defence'.

'State of the art' defence

'The state of the art' defence (Key concept 5.10) was not bound to be incorporated in UK legislation as each member state was left the choice. Indeed, it is likely that the Directive would never have been agreed without such a choice being left up to member states. The opposition to its incorporation into our law is both practical and political. Across the Community the approach has varied. France is as bitterly opposed to incorporation as we were in favour. Belgium and Luxembourg too left it out; West Germany incorporated it, but not for pharmaceuticals. Hardly the 'harmonization' process envisaged when the Community was established!

Further, and on a more openly political basis, the incorporation of this defence has left the manufacturer with an escape route from liability which could have been closed to him or her, leaving the manufacturer to insure, and the rest of us to share the premium costs in the form of higher prices, consistent with market forces. There is no doubt that insurance would have been available. The incorporation of this defence has left the possibility that a severely injured consumer will be left to shoulder personally and alone the entire consequences of the injury caused by a defect in a product which happened to be there and a surprise to us all.

The EC Defective Product Directive specifically allowed member states to include, if they wished, a defence to a producer that at the time of the manufacture he or she did not know and had no reason to know of the defect causing the injury (S.4(e)). The effect of including this defence is in many ways to reintroduce the element of fault although the burden of proof has shifted from the plaintiff to the producer, i.e. if the plaintiff can prove the defect caused the damage the producer will be liable unless he can establish a defence. Although the plaintiff is relieved of the positive burden of proving fault the state of the art defence does provide a substantial loophole from the apparent social ideal of strict liability.

KEY CONCEPT 5.10

STATE OF THE ART DEFENCE (CONSUMER PROTECTION ACT 1987)

Nevertheless, this defence is now part of our law, and available to any manufacturer who can show that the defect which caused the injury sustained by his or her complaining consumer was of a kind which might not have been expected to have been discovered by a producer like him or her. That is, the producer was up with the state of testing within his or her field. The consequences predicated by us here, and by others elsewhere, are only theoretical – experience and the power of the Courts to interpret the statute law as they see fit will show us the truth. Nevertheless, this insertion of blameworthiness (was he or was he not up with the state of the art?) goes against the whole concept of the attempted change in the law: to introduce a regime of strict liability for injuries caused by defective products.

Product safety and the Consumer Protection Act 1987, Part II

The Consumer Protection Act 1987, Part II, brought into effect on 1 October 1987, gives more cause for concern to the business enterprise, for it provides further potential liability. It consolidates the earlier legislation in the field of consumer safety under which it is possible for Regulations to be made by the Secretary of State to ensure that consumer goods are safe, and that appropriate instructions are provided with them, and so on. Indeed, a number of Regulations exist, covering such goods as childrens' nightwear, electrical goods, toys, pedal cycles, prams, even toy watersnakes and expanding novelties!

KEY CONCEPT 5.11 **GENERAL SAFETY DUTY (CONSUMER PROTECTION ACT 1987)**	PART II of the Consumer Protection Act 1987 has introduced a 'general safety duty', under which it will be a criminal offence to supply, offer or agree to supply, or indeed possess for the purposes of supply, consumer goods which are not safe; that is, which do not comply with generally accepted or approved standards of safety.

The pre-1987 Regulations remain in force. New ones will be made from time to time. The emergency powers to act quickly (prohibition notices and orders) remain. But there is now a kind of 'backstop' provision – *a general duty to trade in safe goods* (Key concept 5.11). It is long overdue, and much welcomed by those who are required to enforce this legislation which is designed to protect consumers from goods which are perhaps complicated beyond their knowledge, and dangerous beyond their wellbeing. These are important innovations in our law – and compliance with them must be a feature of the production process of any business organization.

Summary

In this chapter we have examined the areas of law most relevant to the production function of a business. The initial definition, that production is a 'transformation process which takes a variety of inputs such as materials and labour and turns them into goods and services', illustrates that the production function exists in a far wider context than the pure manufacturing of goods. The law we have looked at in detail covered the producer's liability in both civil and criminal law. The Health and Safety at Work Act imposes duties on employers, manufactuers, designers, suppliers and importers to ensure the health and safety of employees and others (non-employees and the public at large) as far as is reasonably practicable, and we examined the main duties under this Act, as well as the method of enforcement by the Health and Safety Executive.

Under the heading of vicarious liability we then examined the liability of the producer for the actions of his employees towards third parties; and under occupier's liability, the company's liability in civil law towards third parties injured whilst on company premises. Nuisance concerned the liability towards neighbours and other persons not on company premises but affected by the production activity.

Having overcome these constraints the production process will result in goods and services being produced, so we concluded the chapter by looking at the law relating to product liability, both at common law and under the Consumer Protection Act 1987.

Further reading

Selwyn's, *Law of Health and Safety at Work* (Butterworths), a very easy to read style and very comprehensive book. C. Drake and F. Wright, *Law of Health and Safety at Work: The New Approach* (Sweet and Maxwell), more detailed than previous book but again very understandable. Winfield and Jolowicz, *Tort* (Sweet and Maxwell), the leading textbook on tort and should be used as a reference book for all areas of tort law in this book, including negligence, nuisance and occupiers' liability. C.J. Miller, *Product Liability and Safety Encylcopaedia* (Butterworths): this is a regularly updated loose-leaf work and is by far the best in the field.

Exercises

1. What are the main duties imposed on employers by the Health and Safety at Work Act 1974?

2. Fred is injured as a result of not wearing the protective clothing which is made available by his employer. Advise the employer of what he will have to prove to the Health and Safety Inspector if he is to escape prosecution under the Health and Safety at Work Act 1974.

3. What powers does a Health and Safety Inspector have to visit a premises and investigate an accident? Why would he normally issue on Improvement or a Prohibition Notice rather than bring a prosecution before the courts?

4. John was injured when Sam, a fellow employee, indulged in 'horseplay' and tipped the machine on which John was standing to talk about foot-

ball to another worker on the other side of a six foot high partition. John's employers are contesting his claim for compensation for his injury on the grounds that he was not in the course of employment when the accident happened.

Discuss.

5. Briefly outline the differences between the 'tests' used by the High Court and the Industrial Tribunal to decide whether or not an individual is an 'employee' in law.

6. In the weeks leading up to their marriage, Margaret and Denis were buying various household goods for their home together.

At Norman's 'Cut Price Bicycle and Hardware' store, they chose a boxed 'brass style' coal bucket. Denis paid the full price of £15 in cash. At Geoffrey's 'Electrical Emporium' they selected a 'Family Washtime' brand washing machine. Margaret paid the price of £250 using her 'Instantcredit' credit card. They declined the offer of an extended guarantee insurance policy for £30.

At Michael's 'Hi-Fi Superstore' the couple chose a 'Multimemory' video cassette recorder. Denis entered into a hire purchase contract with Fleecem Finance Ltd in order to finance the transaction; the hire purchase price was £420. At Nigel's 'Real World Domestic Goods' store they selected a '4 slice' toaster for £28, which Denis paid for with his 'Instantcredit' credit card.

When they unpacked their coal bucket they found that it was not made of brass, or of metal at all, but of a dingy yellow coloured plastic. They did, however, find that it was strong enough to hold a full load of household coal.

After nearly a year the couple were blessed with a son, Mark. During the six months following his birth, the washing machine was in daily use. Twenty months after they bought the machine it broke down. They have had the necessary repair estimated at £100.

The video cassette recorder did not give satisfactory service for very long either. Within a few weeks it began 'chewing' tapes, one of which was a recording of the wedding ceremony, which had been made by their close friend, Arthur. Another destroyed tape belonged to the local video rental shop.

One early morning, Margaret was preparing breakfast for herself and Denis, whilst at the same time, watching 'Breakfast Television' and changing Mark. For reasons which are not entirely clear, she sustained a serious burn while trying to remove two pieces of toast from the toaster whilst changing channels on the television. Margaret says that she 'just touched the thing and it was red hot'.

Advise Denis and Margaret.

Marketing, selling and advertising 6 |||||

Introduction

In this chapter we will examine the various ways in which the law exerts control over the marketing activity of a business enterprise. First we will focus upon the controls which exist outside the business – the environmental controls. Then we will deal with certain structural considerations, e.g. the way in which a number of businesses have seen fit to join together in trade associations, and the rise of the Code of Practice as a regulator of business, and finally consider the legal rules related to the provision of credit in consumer transactions.

Attracting business/advertising

The law relating to advertising is both civil and criminal. The display of goods in a shop window, on a shelf inside a retail outlet or in a newspaper or magazine advertisement is an invitation to treat rather than an offer to sell. This is basic contract law. The criminal law has a role here too; legislation controls the manner in which goods, services, accommodation and facilities are described.

Legislative controls

The Trade Descriptions Act 1968 and the Consumer Protection Act 1987 lay down criminal offences which may be committed by anybody advertising or providing goods or services in the course of business. For breach of these provisions a fine may be imposed of up to £2000 if the case is heard by the magistrates or an unlimited fine and/or two years imprisonment if a more serious case is brought in the Crown Court.

(a) The Trade Descriptions Act 1968

The Act has two sections which create criminal offences: SS.1 and 14. Section 1 provides:

> Any person who, in the course of a trade or business –
> (a) applies a false trade description to any goods; or

(b) supplies or offers to supply goods to which a false trade description is applied;

shall, subject to the provisions of this Act, be guilty of an offence.

In general terms, the offence in (a) can be said to apply to manufacturers and packers, whereas that in (b) applies to retailers. Of course, a business could be charged under both offences if it was found to have 'applied' and 'supplied'. A classic instance is the dealer in secondhand cars who winds back the mileometer, or 'clocks' the car, and then proceeds to sell it. He or she has 'applied' a false trade description, in that he or she has misdescribed the vehicle's previous use, and then has 'supplied' in that he or she has sold the car. Indeed, the Act does not actually require a sale at all. The display of the clocked car on his or her forecourt would be enough. He or she has 'offered to *supply*' under S.6.

S.6:

A person exposing goods for supply or having goods in his possession for supply shall be deemed to offer to supply them.

Section 14 of the 1968 Act provides that it is a crime knowingly or recklessly to make a statement which is false about services, accommodation or facilities. This section has been most often used against holiday tour companies who have advertised hotels as having balconies, sea views, entertainment, air conditioning, and so on, which they did not – and even advertised hotels which did not exist at all!

An instance is in *R.* v. *Clarksons Holidays* (1972) where a holiday bro-

---

CASE STUDY 6.1

MISLEADING TRADE DESCRIPTIONS: THE TESCO CASE

In September 1969 Tesco Supermarkets Ltd was selling Giant Size packets of Radiant washing powder at a price of 2s. 11d. This represented a discount of 1s. from the manufacturers recommended price of 3s. 11d. They had advertised this in national and local newspapers, and at their branch at Northwich in Cheshire there was a large poster in the window: 'Radiant 1s. off Giant Size 2s. 11d'. There were flash packs in stock to start with. By 25 September they had run out, but the poster was not removed. The shelves had been filled with packs at the normal price. Thus the shop was advertising goods at a price at which they were not prepared to sell them. This was an offence under the old S.11 of the 1968 Act. Tesco Supermarkets were prosecuted. They defended themselves with the 'act or default of another' defence within S.24, citing the store manager, Mr. Clement, as the other person. They were able to establish that the chain of authority between the central management of Tesco and the local branch manager was long enough to enable him to be regarded as 'another' person, and that the in-house checks and control systems were adequate to amount to 'reasonable precautions and due diligence'. So Tesco escaped conviction.

This is a case that would reward study of the full report. It is a rare example of the House of Lords in action in a consumer law area.

(*Tesco* v. *Nattrass* (1972))

chure described hotels as having been selected for their cleanliness, efficiency of service and good food. There was a picture of a large, modern hotel with a pool. This was actually an artist's impression. The hotel had not been built. It was not built when the holidaymakers arrived. Furthermore, construction was not running late: the hotel was never planned to have been ready by that date!

There is a technical problem with S.14 which does not arise with S.1: that the prosecution must establish a mental ingredient in the crime ('knowingly' or 'recklessly'). This has created a number of uncertainties in the law (e.g. *Wings* v. *Ellis* [1984] p. 221).

Defences

There are defences available for those charged under this Act. S.24 provides that

... it shall be a defence for the person charged to prove –

(a) that the commission of the offence was due to a mistake or to reliance on information supplied to him or to the act or default of another person, an accident or some other cause beyond his control; and

(b) that he took all reasonable precautions and exercised all due diligence to avoid the commission of such an offence by himself or any person under his control (Misleading Trade Descriptions: Case study 6.1).

It is important to note that the two elements of the statutory defence are cumulative. That is, it will not be enough just to establish one of the five answers to the charge unless the accused can also show that reasonable precautions and due diligence were present. For example, it will probably not be enough for a businessman or woman to show that he or she chose reputable suppliers, if he or she did not also test the products supplied in some way so as to ensure compliance with the law (*Garrett* v. *Boots* (1980)).

KEY CONCEPT 6.1

THE STATUTORY DEFENCE (TRADE DESCRIPTIONS ACT 1968)

(b) Consumer Protection Act 1987

Under S.20 of this Act it is an offence to give a false or misleading price indication with regard to goods, services, accommodation or facilities. If the indication was neither false nor misleading when made, but it later becomes so, it is an offence not to take reasonable steps to say so

These generalized offences represent a philosophical change in criminal consumer law – away from listed offences to generalizations. In this instance the change is even more marked because behind S.20 there is a code of practice which sets out good 'trading practice'. That is, it sets out pricing practices which do not amount to offences under S.20. However, as a result of long and detailed argument during the implementation stages of this new law, the Code is only of evidential value. That is, to breach the code is not necessarily to breach S.20, neither is compliance a defence. In reality it seems unlikely that an over-stretched Trading Standards service will institute proceedings against traders who comply with the Code.

As an example of the content of this Code, when comparing with previous prices it is suggested that the previous price quoted should be the last one at which the goods, etc., were available in the previous six months; that last price should have applied for at least 28 consecutive days in the previous six months; it should have applied at the same shop; otherwise comparisons should be fair and meaningful and give clear and positive explanation for the period and circumstances regarding the higher price.

Self-regulation

There is a great deal more criminal law which affects advertising. Indeed, there are some 80 separate statutes, orders and regulations. Their main function, taken as a whole, is a negative one in that they restrain the publication of misleading and/or indecent material. However, advertising is a fast developing business, often escaping precise definition and classification. There is a need for wider and voluntary control. As a working party within the Department of Trade reported in 1980:

> Codes of practice provide a positive approach to advertising control. They can reflect the spirit rather than the letter and can be readily reviewed and updated to take account of changing social conditions and public attitudes. They command a high degree of commitment from the business community and encourage high standards of advertising to the benefit of consumer and advertiser.

Examples of successful self-regulation include curbs on cigarette advertising and limits on advertising to children (Advertising: The Magic Mirror: Case study 6.2).

The principal self-regulatory control in the United Kingdom is that administered by the Advertising Standards Authority in the print, cinema and poster media. There are two Codes operated by the ASA: the British Code of Advertising Practice and the British Code of Sales Promotion Practice. They are not law. Enforcement is achieved by the media themselves by, for example, denial of advertising space to offending advertisers. Probably the most effective sanction, however, is the deterrent effect of the adverse publicity which always accompanies an ASA finding of transgression.

This pattern of control has now been enhanced by the implementation of a Directive from the European Community on Misleading and Unfair

CASE STUDY 6.2	In November 1989 the IBA banned a £1 million series of children's cartoons called The Magic Mirror because it contained too much advertising for the film's sponsor, Kellogg. The IBA held that the use of Kellogg's famous K logo on the frame of the Mirror amounted to over exposure, despite the fact that this had been done by the series producer as an act of courtesy to the sponsor rather than with any intention of increasing the advertising content.
ADVERTISING: THE MAGIC MIRROR AND KELLOGG'S	

Advertising. The Department of Trade and Industry issued a statement after the adoption of this Directive:

> The Directive ... is intended to protect consumers, traders and the public in general against misleading advertising. Member states must ensure that adequate and effective means exist for the control of such advertising; including arrangements permitting persons or organisations to take legal action against misleading advertisements, and/or to bring such advertisements before administrative authority empowered to take appropriate action.

In the UK the Director General has the power to obtain court orders to restrain the activities of miscreant advertisers. But this power is held in reserve behind the existing legal and self-regulating controls which have already been discussed. It has been used only twice since the directive was implemented into English law.

The sale

All sales (Key concept 6.2) are governed by the law of contract. The particular terms depend upon the type of sale. In principle the parties to the contract are left to decide the nature, quality and contents of the transaction themselves. However, overlaying this broad principle is the rising tide of consumer protection and the terms implied by statute (Key concept 6.3).

The original Sale of Goods Act was passed in 1893 – having been little more than a codification of the existing common law at that time by Sir Mackenzie Chalmers. Over the years there have been a number of other statutes which have amended the so-called 'parent' Act of 1893. In 1979 Parliament passed the Act in its present form, making the 1979 Act a con-solidated code. Sections 12–15 of the 1979 Act are concerned with implying terms into those contracts to which the Act applies. These are, of course, contracts for the Sale of Goods, as defined by S.2.

The contracts covered by the Act are those where the buyer acquires the title to goods, and the seller gets money. Certain other important contracts – such as hire purchase, hire, contracts for services only and contracts for goods and services together (commonly called contracts for work and

'A contract for the sale of goods is a contract by which the seller transfers or agrees to transfer the property in goods to the buyer for a money consideration called the price' (S.2 Sale of Goods Act 1979).	KEY CONCEPT 6.2 **THE SALE (SALE OF GOODS ACT 1979)**
Into each kind of contract there will be terms implied by law, by custom or by necessity. In relation to contracts of sale, statutory terms are implied by the Sale of Goods Act 1979.	KEY CONCEPT 6.3 **IMPLIED TERMS (SALE OF GOODS ACT 1979)**

materials) are covered by statutes, but not the 1979 Act. We will examine these other transactions later.

The implied terms of Sale of Goods Act

Section 12 of the 1979 Act implies into contracts of sale a condition that the seller will have the right to sell the goods to the buyer. It may be recalled that a condition is a contractual term which is important enough, if breached to give the innocent party the right to treat the contract as discharged, and himself or herself freed from all obligations under it (Chapter 2).

In a consumer context, this will usually amount to a right for the consumer to obtain a refund of the price he or she paid for the goods if it appears the seller had no right to sell them. It seems hardly surprising that such a term should be implied into contracts for the sale of goods, since the property in the goods, the ownership of them, is a fundamental part of the deal. It is, after all, from the buyer's point of view, the point of making the contract in the first place. For example, in *Rowland* v. *Divall* (1923), the plaintiff bought a car from the defendant. He used it for about three months, then discovered that the car had been stolen. It had to be returned to the original owner, but the buyer was entitled to the return of all his money from the person who had sold the car to him because he had not received the ownership – the basis of the contract. Although he had, however, received three months' free motoring!

S.13 implies a similarly important term:

> Where there is a contract for the sale of goods by description, there is an implied condition that the goods will correspond with the description.

This is a very strict requirement. Any deviation from the contractual description gives the buyer the right to reject the goods (*Arcos* v. *Ronaasen* (1933) p. 222, *Re Moore and Landauer* (1921) and *Beale* v. *Taylor* (1967).

It follows that a careful businessman or woman will allow for a margin or error. As Lord Atkin said (in *Arcos* v. *Ronaasen*) p. 222:

> If the written contract specifies conditions of weight, measurements or the like, those conditions must be complied with. A ton does not mean

KEY CONCEPT 6.4	The phrase 'merchantable quality' is itself defined. S.14(6) provides: 'Goods of any kind are of merchantable quality within the meaning of subsection (2) above if they are as fit for the purpose or purposes for which goods of that kind are commonly bought as it is reasonable to expect having regard to any description applied to them, the price (if relevant) and all the other relevant circumstances.' The concept of merchantable quality lies at the very heart of consumer protection in civil law. N.B. it seems likely that this definition will be modified as a result of the Private Member Bill introduced in the 1989–90 session by Martyn Jones, M.P. The new definition will probably include such elements as 'durability', 'freedom from minor defects' and 'compliance with safety standards'.
MERCHANTABLE QUALITY	

about a ton, or a yard about a yard. Still less, when you descend to minute measurements, does half an inch mean about half an inch. If the seller wants a margin he must, and in my experience does, stipulate for it.

Such tolerance clauses are now widely used by business, a premium being charged the tighter the buyer's specification. It is no excuse that the goods are suitable for the purpose for which they were bought, if they do not match their description.

The requirements about quality and fitness for purpose (Key concept 6.4) are given in S.14(2):

> Where the seller sells goods in the course of a business, there is an implied condition that the goods supplied under the contract are of merchantable quality.

It is important to note that there is no such implied condition where the seller sells as a private individual. In a private sale a buyer must rely on S.13, and the general law on misrepresentation (Chapter 2). He or she has no protection under S.14.

Where this protection does exist it is subject to limitations: except that there is no such condition –

(a) as regards defects specifically drawn to the buyer's attention before the contract is made; or
(b) if the buyer examines the goods before the contract is made, as regards defects which that examination ought to reveal.

Broadly, then, the buyer is entitled to expect that the goods will be reasonably fit for their usual purposes, and that he or she will get reasonable value for money. It is interesting to note that, whereas quality is not important when assessing correspondence with description within S.13, description *is* relevant when considering merchantable quality within S.14.

Like all statutory definitions, 'merchantable quality' (Key concept 6.4) is constantly subject to refinements of meaning developed by the courts when deciding cases. There have been several cases recently concerning the right to reject unsatisfactory cars which have shown that the definition probably contains a requirement of durability which does not appear in the Act itself.

For example, in *Bernstein* v. *Pamsons Motors* (1987) the plaintiff bought a brand new Nissan car. After having driven it for a little under three weeks (part of which he was ill in bed) and for a little over 140 miles, the car broke down on the M3 motorway. The seller was happy to repair the car, but would not accept the buyer's rejection. The matter was heard in the High Court by Mr. Justice Rougier. He declared that the car was not of merchantable quality, but that the passage of time and the 140 miles of use deprived the buyer of the right to reject. The buyer was deemed to have accepted the car, was awarded damages for car hire and general aggravation. He decided to appeal. The Court of Appeal listed the case, but it was settled out of court. We are left with the decision on the loss of the right to reject. This is unsatisfactory law, and should be revised as soon as possible.

Also relevant are *Rogers* v. *Parish*, p. 221 and *Shine* v. *General Guarantee*,

All (1987). This aspect of durability has been troublesome in the past. Strictly, it appeared that the obligation to deliver goods of merchantable quality arose at the time of delivery and did not continue beyond that time. So that if the goods broke down later this was nothing more than evidentiary value that the goods were not merchantable when delivered ('they cannot have been of merchantable quality or they would not have broken down so soon'). However, this analysis leaves open the door to answers involving buyer misuse and wear and tear, and so on.

This problem, and others, led the Law Commission to a reconsideration of the definition of 'merchantable quality' within the Act. After long consideration they have reported (1987 Cmnd 137). A new definition has been proposed, but the Commission notes that

> . . . it is doubtful how far a process of 'patching' the Sale of Goods Act can continue . . . the law does not stand still and no-one should suppose that even such reforms as we now propose can be the last word for more than a few years.

They recommend, amongst other things, that the new definition of merchantable quality should consist of a basic principle that the quality of goods should be such as would be 'acceptable' (Key concept 6.5) to a reasonable person.

They had considered a detailed list of buyers' remedies, but abandoned the task. They do, however, recommend a distinction between consumer and non-consumer (e.g. business to business contracts) remedies, such that business buyers should be restricted in their right to reject the goods where the breach of the contract is so slight that repudiation of the whole contract would be unreasonable. There would remain, of course, the right to compensation. These recommendations would require legislation. Indeed the Report contains a draft Bill, a version of which was included in a Private Members Bill on the 1989–90 Parliamentary session.

S.14(3) of the 1979 Act implies another term, holding the seller to his professed expertise:

> Where the seller sells goods in the course of a business and the buyer, expressly or by implication, makes known to the seller any particular purpose for which the goods are being bought, there is an implied condition that the goods supplied under the contract are reasonably fit for that purpose, whether or not that is a purpose for which such goods are commonly supplied, . . .

KEY CONCEPT 6.5	The Law Commission suggest a number of aspects of quality which should be embraced within a new definition of 'acceptable' quality: the fitness of goods for all their common purposes; their appearance and finish; their freedom from minor defects; their safety; and their durability. These suggestions may well pass into law in 1990.
THE LAW COMMISSION'S PROPOSED 'ACCEPTABLE' QUALITY	

KEY CONCEPT 6.6

S.14: FITNESS FOR THE BUYER'S PURPOSE

S.14, taken as a whole, is a cornerstone of consumer protection in civil law, and it is essential for the successful business enterprise to ensure that the goods supplied to customers meet the statutory requirements – set out in the Act and interpreted over the years by the courts.

So if the buyer relies on the skill of the seller, then it does not matter that the goods are fit for a normal purpose (against which merchantable quality within S.14(2) would be assessed), the goods must be fit for the 'purpose made known' by the buyer. Again, this protection is subject to limitations:

... except where the circumstances show that the buyer does not rely, or that it is unreasonable for him to rely, on the skill or judgement of the seller ...

There have been a number of important examples of such judicial interpretation (*Wilson* v. *Ricketts* [1954], *Jackson* v. *Rotax Motor & Cycle Co.* [1910], *Sumner Permain* v. *Webb* [1922] p. 222, *Brown* v. *Craiks* [1970] p. 222, *Cehave NV* v. *Bremer Handelsgessellschaft mbh (The Hansa Nord)* [1976], *Bartlett* v. *Sydney Marcus* [1965] p. 222, *Baldry* v. *Marshall* [1925], *Bristol Tramways* v. *Fiat* [1910], *Priest* v. *Last* [1903], *Frost* v. *Aylesbury Dairy* [1905], *Chaproniere* v. *Mason* [1905], *Vacwell Engineering* v. *BDH Chemicals* [1969] p. 223, *McAlpine* v. *Minimax* [1970], *Godley* v. *Perry* [1960], *Grant* v. *Australian Knitting Mills* [1936] and *Griffith* v. *Peter Conway* [1939]) (Key concept 6.6).

Businessmen, and indeed consumers, often contract on the basis of samples the buyer has examined. For example, a retailer might order a bulk consignment of goods from a sales representative, or a consumer might order a carpet from a piece of carpeting from a book of such samples. The basic principle here is that the sample should 'speak for the bulk'. The 1979 Act implies into contracts such as these much the kind of terms that might be expected:

S.15(2):

In the case of a contract for sale by sample there is an implied condition –
(a) that the bulk will correspond with the sample in quality;
(b) that the buyer will have a reasonable opportunity of comparing the bulk with the sample;
(c) that the goods will be free from any defect, rendering them unmerchantable, which would not be apparent on reasonable examination of the sample.

A classic illustration of the operation of SS.14 and 15 is *Godley* v. *Perry* (1960) where a six-year-old boy bought a sixpenny catapult from a local shop. While he was playing with it the toy broke, and part of the fork damaged his eye. He sued the shop under S.14 (lack of merchantability), and the shop brought in the wholesalers on a S.15 argument (lack of correspondence with sample) and they similarly brought in the importer. All the actions succeeded. So in effect the importer paid the boy – and rightly so – but this 'chain of contracts' route is no answer to the need for consumer protection from injuries caused by defective products. Any of these links in the chain of contractual liability could have been weak, any of the parties could have been weak or impecunious or out of business. This is why the new law on product liability (discussed in Chapter 5) is of such great importance.

Exclusion of terms

It remains to consider the extent to which these implied terms can be excluded by the parties. After all, it is their contract, and for all the supposed improvement in consumer protection legislation over the past twenty years or so, the basic principle of English contract law remains *caveat emptor* – let the buyer beware.

The relevant statute here (Key concept 6.7) is the Unfair Contract Terms Act 1977:

KEY CONCEPT 6.7

BUSINESS CONTRACTS: EXCLUSION OF IMPLIED TERMS UNDER SALE OF GOODS ACT 1979

The consumer is always protected by the implied terms, but the businessman or woman may find this protection excluded by a contract term – provided that a court is prepared to declare that exclusion in those circumstances is reasonable. S.11 of this 1977 Act (Unfair Contract Terms Act) sets out a so-called 'test of reasonableness', and in Schedule 2 to the same Act there are a number of 'Guidelines' for the application of the reasonableness test. Nothing here extends the meaning much further than to say that reasonableness is a question of fact in the circumstances of each case (*George Mitchell* v. *Finney Lock Seeds* (1983) p. 223).

S.6:

(1) Liability for breach of the obligations arising from –
   (a) section 12 of the Sale of Goods Act 1979 (seller's implied undertakings as to title, etc.); . . . cannot be excluded or restricted by reference to any contract term.
(2) As against a person dealing as consumer, liability for breach of the obligations arising from –
   (a) sections 13, 14 or 15 of the 1979 Act (seller's implied undertakings as to conformity of goods with description or sample, or as to their quality or fitness for a particular purpose); . . . cannot be excluded or restricted by reference to any contract term.
(3) As against a person dealing otherwise than as a consumer, the liability specified in subsection (2) above can be excluded or restricted by reference to a contract term, but only in so far as the term satisfies the requirement of reasonableness.

Service and supply contracts

Having considered the way in which the 1979 Act implies terms into contracts of sale we can now say that other contracts are affected in very

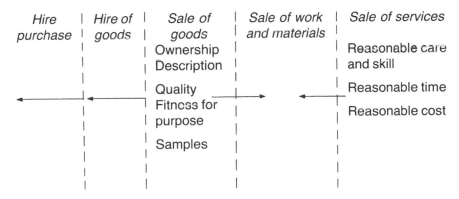

Hire purchase	Hire of goods	Sale of goods	Sale of work and materials	Sale of services
		Ownership Description		Reasonable care and skill
		Quality Fitness for purpose		Reasonable time
		Samples		Reasonable cost

Figure 6.1 Comparison of Terms Implied into Contracts under Supply of Goods Implied Terms) Act 1973, Sale of Goods Act 1979 and Supply of Goods and Services Act 1982.

similar ways by other statutes: contracts of hire purchase by the Supply of Goods (Implied Terms) Act 1973, and contracts of hire, contracts for work and materials, and contracts where the exchange is not ownership of goods for money (e.g. barters) by the Supply of Goods and Services Act 1982. Contracts for trading stamps are covered by the Trading Stamps Act 1964. The 1982 Act implies terms into contracts for services alone (e.g. bankers, lawyers, insurers, etc.) so as to provide that such service must be provided with reasonable care and skill, within a reasonable time, at a reasonable cost. In the case of contracts for work and materials (e.g. plumbing, car repairing, home double glazing supply etc.) the materials must be of merchantable quality, and the service must be provided with reasonable care and skill, etc. The overall effect of all this can be seen in Figure 6.1.

Five kinds of contracts are shown here, by means of which the buyer seeks to obtain goods and/or services. The implied terms we have discussed from the Sale of Goods Act are listed, and arrows indicate that terms of a substantially similar nature are to be found elsewhere. In the case of contracts for just services, three special implied terms are to be found. In the case of contracts for work and materials a combination of implied terms can be seen, some of which relate to the service element of the deal and others to the goods, or materials, supplied under it.

The role of public bodies

There are a number of organizations which play a part in the overview of business activity. They vary from those which are formally constituted and directed towards consumer protection – such as the Consumers' Association and the National Consumer Council, to Trade Associations whose primary aim is to enhance the prospects of those businesses which are members, and the Office of Fair Trading, which is a kind of Government Department with clearly defined and very extensive supervisory functions.

The Consumers' Association

CA was set up as long ago as 1957. In its somewhat self-congratulatory 30th Anniversary publicity it cites the Moloney Report on Consumer Protection (which, incidentally, was produced in 1962):

The business of making and selling . . . is highly organized often in large units, and calls to its aid at every step complex and highly expert skills. The business of buying is conducted by the smallest unit, the individual unit, relying on the guidance afforded by experience, if he possesses it, and if not, on instinctive but not always rational thought processes.

The Consumers' Association came into being to help redress this imbalance between the power of the seller and the power of the buyer. CA's work has been to provide independent and technically based guidance on the ever-increasing variety of goods and services available to the consumer.

CA's method is to test products and investigate services, and then to publish frank comparative reports on the performance, quality and value of the brands tested. This information is published complete with the brand or supplier's name in *Which?*, *Holiday Which?*, and *Gardening from Which?* – these magazines are available only on subscription.

The size and importance of this organization is not to be underestimated. It now has over a million members. In 1957 it was housed in a converted garage, with no paid staff and £18 in the bank. In 1988 it has an operation split between London, Hertford and Harpenden with a staff of over 400, and an income approaching £30 million each year.

In terms of its campaigning success – the debt all consumers owe to its activities, whether or not they are members of the organization is enormous. CA can be credited with having done crucial work leading to the addition of such measures as the Unfair Contract Terms Act 1977, the Consumer Safety Act 1978 and the Supply of Goods and Services Act 1982, to the statute book, and also with advice, assistance and representation which has led to certain important judicial interpretation of legislative provisions (*Woodman* v. *Photo Trade Processing* [1981]).

CA is said to be founded upon 'seven basic principles':

☐ CA is and takes care to be seen to be, independent of all interests other than those of the consumer.
☐ CA accepts no money from government, trade or industry (other than for specific services rendered which could not compromise CA's independence).
☐ CA takes no advertising in any of its publications.
☐ CA accepts no free samples, free holidays, free meals or any other hand-outs from those whose products and services are under review, from suppliers, or from anyone else who might threaten CA's integrity.
☐ CA refuses to allow any of its findings or recommendations to be exploited by interested parties – producers, sellers, advertisers; tour operators, hoteliers, restaurateurs, etc.
☐ CA campaigns under no party label; in politics it is strictly cross-bench, representing no-one but consumers.
☐ CA does not allow principals from trade or industry to sit on its Governing Council.

The National Consumer Council

NCC lacks the high profile of CA. However, it does not share in the aspersion sometimes cast (rarely with justification) upon CA that it is a rather 'bourgeois members' club', seen to 'do good works'. In its own publicity, NCC explains:

> The NCC is a body set up and financed by government. It started in 1975. Its job is to persuade government to change its policies or introduce new ones to better the lot of consumers, to influence business to meet the needs of its consumers more efficiently, and economically, and to induce the public services to give better value for money and to be more responsive to the needs of users.

NCC has a central Council and a Chairman, most of whose members come from consumer organizations and voluntary services of various kinds. They are appointed by the Secretary of State for Trade. There is a staff of about 30, but NCC often use outside help and expertise when compiling their various reports – on such matters as poorly made shoes, 'gobble-degook', the Police, the repair industry, and many more. Sometimes their proposals are taken directly into new legislation, as was the case with the NCC Report on Services ('Service Please', 1981), containing a draft Bill, most of which became Part II of the Supply of Goods and Services Act 1982.

NCC has no powers, it says that:

> it relies on the quality of its research and of its campaigning to persuade policy-makers, both in and out of government, to meet consumer demands.

An obvious criticism is that, being government-funded, it might well feel unable to be entirely free of government control. It replies:

> Although our money comes from government, the NCC has never hesitated to criticize the policies of successive governments where these conflict with the interests of consumers. Governments say they want an independent consumer voice, and that is what they get. The NCC's job is to represent the interests of consumers frankly to whatever government is in power.

Trade associations

Having considered the CA and NCC, it is important to realize that the traders are interested in mutual support and representative campaigning as well (Key concept 6.8). Any sensible businessman would consider joining a

---

KEY CONCEPT 6.8

TRADE ASSOCIATIONS

There are Trade Associations in a wide and increasing number of sectors of industry, both in the goods and service sectors. None of them is a consumer protection agency, but many of them operate conciliation and/or arbitration schemes with a view of obtaining redress for the properly aggrieved consumer, and a hearing at least for the rest. These are designed to protect the good trader from the rogue within the same industry more than to protect the consumer from the trade as a whole (e.g. ABTA).

trade association – perhaps to share experience of unreliable buyers and suppliers, and to exchange other useful scraps of information. Many associations also organize training schemes, programmes and materials, and publish codes of practice to which all their members adhere, e.g. Motor Vehicle Manufacturers and Traders Association.

The Office of Fair Trading

Without doubt, the most important of the government-funded organizations which exerts significant controls over business enterprises is the OFT. It was created using powers given to the Director General of Fair Trading in the Fair Trading Act 1973 (which, incidentally, created the post of DGFT). The DGFT, and his staff, the OFT, have been set a wide variety of supervisory and regulatory tasks and responsibilities over the years since 1973: in relation to monopolies, mergers, restrictive trade practices and uncompetitive practices; and power to seek assurances of future good conduct from traders who persistently flout the law, civil and/or criminal, adversely affecting the interests of consumers. For example, refusing refunds or 'clocking' cars. That is, apart from facing civil action for the refund, or criminal prosecution for the misdescription of the car, the trader may be faced with the DGFT asking for a 'Part III Assurance' – a promise to avoid such action in future. This is a personal matter. It would not matter if the trader closed that business and opened another. Should he or she continue in unlawful ways, the DGFT can have the trader taken before a court to repeat his or her promise, subsequent breach of which would amount to contempt of court for which the trader could be imprisoned. Thus, interestingly, a trader can be jailed for a breach of the civil law!

The DGFT is required to keep under review commercial activities in the UK, to collect and collate information about trade practices which may adversely affect consumers and where necessary to recommend changes in the law.

The DGFT supervises the operation of the Estate Agents Act 1979 and is responsible for the operation of the complex licensing scheme imposed upon the consumer credit industry by the Consumer Credit Act 1974. Under this scheme everyone involved in the trade: canvassers and brokers, debt adjusters, counsellors and collectors, credit reference agencies and others must be licensed. To lend without a licence is a crime. The DGFT can refuse and/or revoke such licences. In theory, therefore, the OFT controls the consumer credit industry and all those who trade within it. Some of the rules covering the giving of credit to consumers are as follows.

Credit

Most businesses consider some sort of credit as part of their marketing provision. The principle being that the less a customer has to pay at the moment of agreement the greater the chances of making the deal. This is as true of a company issuing shares to the public, e.g. the new water companies, as it is of a High Street retailer. There are various ways in which a business can protect itself when offering credit, the most common of which we shall look at here.

The principal concern any lender has is how to ensure that he or she can recover the outstanding credit. With well-known customers this may not be a problem, but with a smaller client or an unknown company this may be a genuine difficulty.

Leaving aside those businesses whose whole purpose is to lend money at interest, e.g. banks and building societies, there are really two options available in terms of providing credit; provide it yourself or arrange it through a professional.

Where a business chooses to provide credit itself it will usually be of a short-term variety, e.g. a monthly account, or a 28-day invoice, and to established or known customers. Most businesses are happy to make such arrangements and do not have great difficulty. Where longer term credit or less well known customers are concerned it often makes good business sense to use the services of a professional lender. Many of the large retail stores have their own finance houses whose job it is to provide the credit for the stores' customers. In this way the store is paid promptly at an agreed discount, leaving the finance company to chase the debtor if need be. A recent newspaper article found how easily a totally unknown teenager could obtain thousands of pounds in unsecured credit from a number of London stores. Accepting a customer's credit card from a credit company such as Visa or Access gives the supplier the same right to discount payment.

Where a company wishes to supply its own credit, and therefore carry the risk of non-payment, there are various forms of legal transaction which it can use. Where goods are being sold the agreement can be a credit sale, where the goods are transferred without full payment but the purchaser nevertheless becomes the owner; a conditional sale, where the goods are transferred to the purchaser but the ownership of the goods remains with the seller until the price is paid; this means that in the event of non-payment the owner, the seller, may recover the goods from the purchaser and is not limited to an action for money against someone who may have become insolvent; or thirdly instead of an outright sale, the goods may be supplied on hire-purchase, in this case the supplier retains the ownership of the goods and the hirer acquires the right to buy on payment of the final agreed instalment, thus using the goods as security again. At a practical level most businesses who wish to supply goods on hire purchase first sell the goods outright to a finance house and do not themselves supply the credit.

The Consumer Credit Act 1974 was passed to provide protection for borrowers who could easily be over reached by more powerful lenders (Key concept 6.9). Any business wishing to offer credit itself to those within the terms of the Act should take care to comply with its provisions. These are detailed and complex but in outline they require the following: the business wishing to provide credit must obtain a licence from the Director General of Fair Trading, any unlicensed loan is irrecoverable without a court order; the charge for credit, the APR, must be notified in writing; the agreement itself must be in writing signed by the debtor personally and by or on behalf of the creditor, and the debtor must always be given a copy

KEY CONCEPT 6.9

THE CONSUMER CREDIT ACT 1974: CONDITIONAL SALES AND HIRE PURCHASE AGREEMENTS TO CONSUMERS

Conditional sales and hire purchase agreements are governed by the Consumer Credit Act 1974. The Act applies only to personal credit agreements, therefore not to loans made to corporate bodies or companies (NB partners are regarded as individuals) and subject to a maximum outstanding loan of £15 000.

of any agreement he or she signs. Where the agreement is signed other than on the trade premises of the lender, or any dealer with whom the debtor negotiated, there is a statutory cooling off period, i.e. the debtor has a right to cancel the agreement within five days, and must be so notified.

One of the main reasons for using the goods as security against the loan of credit is the increased protection this gives to the creditor, i.e. he or she has the right to recover the goods themselves in the event of non-repayment of the loan; however, in a case to which it relates, the Consumer Credit Act has placed restrictions on the lender's rights to repossess the goods. Under the Act a creditor must now give seven days notice of default before taking any steps to recover the goods: no dawn raids! He or she may not enter property to recover goods without a court order and after one-third of the purchase price, including initial deposit or down payment, has been made, again the creditor will need a court order to recover his or her goods.

Thus whether or not to offer credit and if so on what terms is very much a marketing decision. Where a good deal of business is to be funded on credit it may well be worth a business dealing with individual as opposed to trade customers to set up its own finance company to take care of the credit side, or to allow customers to use the credit facilities offered by the major charge cards. A business that wishes to give credit on its own account in cases covered by the Consumer Credit Act 1974 must be very careful to observe the legal formalities, which are quite complicated.

Summary

In this chapter we have reviewed the impact of the law on the marketing function covering the initial advertisement of goods and services, the statutory terms implied into contracts of sale or supply of goods and services, the limits to which such clauses may be excluded, the role of various public bodies in monitoring and reviewing the operations of business in the market; and some of the rules covering the giving of credit to consumers.

Further reading

The law relevant to the marketing function has very little in the way of specific written provision made for it. Newspapers, journals and other periodicals are usually the best places to look in order to keep pace with this fast-changing area of law. Examples would include *Consumer Law Today*, *Which*, *New Law Journal* and the marketing journals such as *Marketing* and *Marketing Week*. The 'better' newspapers all carry specialist articles from time to time.

Amongst the books that do exist, by far the best (and cheapest!) general introduction is Borrie and Diamond, *Consumer, Society and the Law* (Pelican). Other useful works include Harvey, *The Law of Consumer Protection and Fair Trading*; Atiyah, *Sale of Goods*; Dobson, *Sale of Goods and Consumer Credit*; Lowe and Woiodroffe, *Consumer Law and Practice*; Miller and Harvey, *Consumer and Trading Law – Cases and Materials*.

Exercises

1. Susan is a Legal Executive. In her lunch hour she visited the local 'interstellar Megastore'. She wanted to buy a dress for a party. She usually took a size 12. She chose a dress which was labelled 'size 12'. She did not try it on. The dressing rooms at the store were communal, and Susan was shy. Wandering around the store, she picked out a pair of bright yellow jeans. She did not try those on either. She also bought a blouse which was labelled 'shopsoiled', and a set of hair rollers marked 'price was £25, special clearance offer only £10'. The last item she bought was from the 'Megahealth Wholefood Counter'. It was a 'crunchybake crispbread pineapple and cottage cheese lunchpack'. She paid at the check-out till and went into the park.

   She soon observed that the crispbread was soggy. Further inspection revealed teethmarks – perhaps made by mice. When she arrived home that evening she tried on the dress. It did not fit. The blouse had a hole in the cuff, and dirty marks around the neck. When her boyfriend Sebastian came around later she showed him the jeans. He said they were revolting. The next evening she said she could not go out with Sebastian because she had to wash her hair. The hair rollers remained cold.

   Disappointed, Susan returned the next day to the store. She laid the dress, the jeans, the hair rollers and the blouse on the counter. She asked to speak to the Manager. She showed him the remainder of the crispbread which she had kept in her handbag. She asked for all her money back. The Manager simply pointed to a sign near the till which read 'it is not the policy of this store to give refunds, but we will gladly exchange any goods which prove faulty'. Susan said that she did not wish to exchange any of the goods. The Manager shrugged and walked away.

   Discuss the legal position

2. Sharp sells secondhand cars. Charlie was looking for one. He noticed a classified advertisement in his local evening paper: 'For Sale Vauxhall Astra 1984 15 000 miles VGC £4000 call 214534'. Charlie called. Having been told the address, he found himself at Sharp's saleroom. The car

was there, and Charlie took a test drive. Sharp extolled the virtues of the vehicle. He pointed out the low mileage as registered on the mileometer. He explained that the car had only one previous owner, and that she was a little old lady who had treated it like a baby. Charlie was impressed. He agreed that the car would be a bargain, but he was not able to afford the asking price. Sharp explained that finance was the least of Charlie's worries, and he helped him complete the hire purchase proposal form from Fleecem Finance Ltd which he happened to have about his person. Charlie, in due course, entered into this hire purchase contract.

A few days after delivery the car broke down in the fast lane of the M3 motorway. The engine had ground to a halt. It appeared to have lost lubrication. The subsequent garage inspections revealed that the car was not a 1984 model at all, but a 1983, and that the true mileage was something like 80 000 miles. The engine, clutch and gearbox were badly worn. The tyres were worn below the legal minimum. It would cost some £900 to put the car back on the road.

Discuss the legal position.

The personnel function 7 |||||

Introduction

The state, operating through government policies and the legal system, has brought considerable change to the work of the personnel officer in the past few years via legislation, manpower policies and income policies. These issues are addressed in more detail in Chapter 8 of the core text in this series, 'Business in Context'. The purpose of this chapter is to examine the current legislation relating to employment which has a direct impact upon the day to day work of the business. Personnel management has developed quite clearly as a result of managers reacting to external constraints and pressures, especially to the increasing role played by legislation in the employment situation.

The employer has no say in whether to operate within this law; it is the law, and it must be followed. Legislation has decreed that employers who do not comply with the law will have to pay compensation to the aggrieved individual, whether he or she be a potential employee, an employee or an ex-employee. The personnel manager has to perform his or her day-to-day work within the existing legal environment.

In this section we will consider recruitment and selection, the actual contract and terms of employment, wages administration, discipline and termination of employment, including redundancy, personnel records and finally the law relating to trade unions and industrial relations.

Recruitment and selection

Discrimination

Recruitment is not a totally free market exercise – certain criteria are no longer regarded by law as acceptable in choosing between candidates. Parliament has provided quite complex rules which must be carefully followed.

Two major Acts of Parliament attempt to deal with the problem of discrimination in relation to recruitment and selection – the Race Relations Act 1976 and the Sex Discrimination Act 1975 (as amended by the Sex Discrimination Act 1986). Both Acts are very similar in relation to employment, and both contain similar definitions of discrimination which may be actionable.

There are three main types of discrimination defined in the legislation.

(a) Direct discrimination

Direct discrimination is prohibited by (S.1(1)(a) Sex Discrimination Act 1975 and S.1(1)(a) Race Relations Act 1976). The questions to be asked in relation to sex discrimination are:

☐ Was the woman less favourably treated than a man would have been in that situation? and
☐ Was she less favourably treated because she was a woman?

Direct racial discrimination arises where a person treats another person less favourably because of their colour, race, nationality (including citizenship) or ethnic or national origins.

A good example of direct discrimination is the case of: *Grieg* v. *Community Industry* (1979) I.R.L.R. 158 where Miss Grieg accepted employment as a painter and decorator together with another female. On what was supposed to be her first day at work the personnel officer refused to permit her to commence her new job because the other female had failed to turn up, and Miss Grieg would therefore have been the only female working in the gang. He offered her alternative work which she refused. It was held that she had been treated differently solely because she was a woman, and that that amounted to unlawful, direct discrimination.

In another case, *Coleman* v. *Skyrail Oceanic Ltd* (1981), it was said:

> ... An assumption that men are more likely than women to be the primary supporters of their spouses and children is an assumption based on sex. Therefore the dismissal of a woman based upon on assumption that husbands are breadwinners and wives are not can amount to direct discrimination.

'Ethnic origins' is defined in Selwyn's *Dictionary of Employment Law* (Butterworths, 1985) – an ethnic group must regard itself, and be regarded by others, as a distinct community by virtue of certain essential characteristics. These include

☐ A long shared history, of which the group is conscious as distinguising it from other groups, and the memory of which keeps it alive and
☐ Cultural traditions of its own, including family and social custom, often (but not necessarily) associated with religious observance. In addition the following characteristics are relevant; namely
☐ A common geographical origin or descent from a small number of common ancestors:
☐ A common language, not necessarily peculiar to the group;
☐ A common literature peculiar to the group.
☐ A common religion different from that of neighbouring groups; and
☐ Being a minority or an oppressed or dominant group within a larger

KEY CONCEPT 7.1 ──────── **DIRECT DISCRIMINATION**	Direct discrimination occurs where someone is treated differently because of their sex, race, colour, nationality, ethnic or national origins.

community. This definition would include converts (e.g. persons who marry into the group), but excludes apostates. Provided a person who joins the group feels he is a member, and is accepted as such, then, for the purposes of the Race Relations Act, he is a member (*Mandla* v. *Lee* [1983] I.R.L.R. 209).

Other cases on direct discrimination to which reference might usefully be made are: *Gubala* v. *Crompton Parkinson Ltd* [1977] I.R.L.R. 10, *Horsey* v. *Dyfed C.C.* [1982] I.R.L.R. 395, *Ministry of Defence* v. *Jeremiah* [1979] I.R.L.R. 436, *Owen* v. *Briggs and Jones* [1981] I.R.L.R. 133, *Porcelli* v. *Strathclyde Regional Council* [1985] I.C.R. 177, *Marshall* v. *Southampton and S.W. Hants Area Health Authority* [1986] I.R.L.R. 140.

(b) Indirect discrimination

Indirect discrimination is covered by S.1(1)(b) Sex Discrimination Act 1975 and S.1(1)(b) Race Relations Act 1976. Indirect discrimination is a more difficult concept (Key concept 7.2).

Indirect discrimination occurs when a condition is applied equally to both sexes (race, colour, nationality, ethnic or national origins) but it is such a condition that a smaller proportion of one sex (etc.) than the other can comply with the condition.	KEY CONCEPT 7.2 **INDIRECT DISCRIMINATION**

A good example of indirect discrimination occurred in *Hussein* v. *Saintes Complete House Furnishers Ltd* (1979) I.R.L.R. 337 when the employers advertised for a sales assistant: ' . . . must reside more than 5 miles from the city centre' (of Liverpool). The condition was applied equally to both white and coloured applicants, but it was such a condition that a greater proportion of white people than coloured could apply. Five miles from the city centre is the 'stockbroker belt' and obviously predominantly white, whereas the centre of Liverpool has a very high coloured population. The requirement was therefore unlawful indirect discrimination.

In *Price* v. *Civil Service Commission* [1977] I.R.L.R. 291, it was held that the requirement that applicants had to be aged between 17 and 28 years was unlawful indirect discrimination, as there were more men than women between these ages who are available for work, due mainly to the fact that many women are at home bringing up a young family!

Other controversial decisions have followed this case: *Home Office* v. *Holmes* (1984) where a requirement for 'full time' working was held to be unlawful indirect discrimination; *Wright* v. *Rugby Borough Council* (1985) where set hours (i.e. 9 a.m. to 5 p.m.) was held to be indirect discrimination; *Huppert* v. *University of Cambridge* (1986) where a maximum age requirement was held to be indirect discrimination; *Griffiths and Robertson* v. *Strathclyde Regional Council* (1986) where a refusal to allow job-sharing was held to be indirect discrimination; *Ojutiku and Oburani* v. *Manpower Services Commission* (1981) where a requirement for MSC sponsorship that applicants must have managerial experience was indirect discrimination, as it was more difficult for overseas applicants to gain this experience.

Bayoomi v. *British Railways Board* [1981] I.R.L.R. 431, where requiring applicants for the post of telex operator to become competent in the use of a particular British machine within six months and without any formal training, was held to be indirect discrimination as it was much more difficult for immigrants to get this experience.

Indirect discrimination is unlawful unless it can be justified. The requirement that a VR4 radial drill operator had to be 5 ft 8 in. tall and 14 stones in weight was accepted by the industrial tribunal, after medical evidence that it was necessary to be of these proportions to operate this heavy machinery without damage to the operator's health (*Thorn* v. *Meggitt Engineering Ltd* (1976) I.R.L.R. 241).

A requirement for an accountant to work 9.30 a.m. to 5.30 p.m., Monday to Friday, was challenged as being indirect discrimination against orthodox Jews. The tribunal took into account the employer's organizational needs, the requirements of the company's clients, and the training requirements and procedures of the Institute of Chartered Accountants, and concluded that the stated conditions of service were justifiable, and therefore not unlawful indirect discrimination. This case, *Fluss* v. *Grant Thornton Chartered Accountants* (1987), is unfortunately unreported.

Out of the thousands of cases heard in courts each year only a very small minority actually end up being reported in the official law reports or in the commercial law reports (e.g. Industrial Relations Law Reports). 'Unreported cases' have just as much authority in law as those reported, but are more difficult to research. A copy of the transcript of an unreported employment law case can be obtained from the Central Office of Industrial Tribunals, or from the relevant regional office (if known), or via computerized legal information retrieval systems, such as LEXIS.

Another interesting unreported case, *Leavers* v. *Civil Service Commission* (1987), accepted a maximum age qualification of 32 years as 'justifiable', bearing in mind that it is dealing with 'high flyer' competition for entry into a service (the Diplomatic Service) for which the retirement age is 60 years. The tribunal said Ms Leavers could have entered the service at a lower grade, for which the maximum entry age was 45 years. The case illustrates the 'lottery' involved in industrial tribunal cases, and is in direct conflict with *Huppert* v. *University of Cambridge* (1986) (see above).

(c) Marital Status Discrimination

By S.3(1) Sex Discrimination Act 1975 it is unlawful to discriminate (either directly or indirectly) on the grounds of marital status, but not unlawful to discriminate against someone because they are single, e.g. *Watkins* v. *Jubilee Club and Institute* (1982) (unreported). Mrs Watkins' husband was employed as club steward and she worked under a separate contract as a barmaid. There was no express requirement that they had to work under a joint contract. A large stock deficiency was discovered and both Mr. and Mrs. Watkins were dismissed. Mrs. Watkins argued that, as a barmaid she had no responsibility for stock or stock control and there was no evidence that she had misappropriated any of it.

The tribunal held she had been dismissed because she was the wife of the steward, i.e. because of her marital status. They said an unmarried barmaid with no responsibility for stock would not have been dismissed in these circumstances; therefore she had been unlawfully discriminated against on the grounds of her marital status.

For other case examples see: *Hurley* v. *Mustoe* [1981] I.C.R. 490, *Thorndyke* v. *Bell Fruit Co. Ltd* [1979] I.R.L.R. 1, *Bick* v. *Royal West of England School for the Deaf* [1976] I.R.L.R. 326.

Having explained the complicated definitions of 'discrimination' we can now examine the various component parts of the recruitment and selection process to illustrate the way in which the law constrains the working of the personnel manager, and imposes limits on the freedom of the employer to choose whom he or she would like to be his or her employee, i.e. job advertisements, short-listing and interviews.

Job advertisements

Both the Sex Discrimination Act and the Race Relations Act make it unlawful to discriminate in job advertisements, short-listing of candidates for interview and the interview itself. The Acts state that it is unlawful to publish or cause to be published an advertisement which indicates, or might reasonably be understood as indicating, an intention to discriminate. The Equal Opportunities Commission's Guidance Notes on Employment Advertising (available free of charge from the Commission) make the following important points:

☐ Consider the impact of the advertisement as a whole.
☐ Words with a sexual connotation should not be used (S.38 SDA). Advertisers must be very careful therefore when using words like 'manager' to make sure the job is clearly offered to both sexes; (*E.O.C.* v. *Robertson* [1980] I.R.L.R. 44).
☐ Only use the abbreviation 'm/f' in lineage advertising.
☐ Make sure that advertisements for jobs which have in the past been done mainly by one sex (e.g. typist, HGV driver) are not understood to indicate a preference for one sex.
☐ If pictures are used ensure that men and women are shown fairly in both numbers and prominence.
☐ Avoid indirect discrimination by specifying only the essential qualifications or job requirements, for example, 'Business Studies degree essential' may be interpreted as indirect discrimination as more men than women can comply with the requirement.

Short-listing of candidates

During the short-listing stage all applicants must be treated equally, irrespective of sex, race, colour, nationality, ethnic or national origins. Relevant cases for reference include: *Wilkie* v. *Strathclyde Regional Council* (unreported) where the employer was unable to justify his failure to shortlist and interview a very well-qualified female applicant. In *Bentham* v. *North-East Regional Airport Committee* (unreported) the applications from men and women were sorted separately, and only men were selected as security staff. Refusal to interview the female applicants was unlawful.

Equal Opportunities Commission (EOC) and the Commission for Racial Equality (CRE)   The EOC has the duty of working towards the elimination of discrimination on grounds relating to sex and marital status and promoting the equality of opportunity between men and women generally. The CRE was created by the Race Relations Act 1976 with the same composition, rights, duties, responsibilities and powers as the EOC, but with the aim of working towards the elimination of racial discrimination.

A tribunal has the power to extend the normal three months time limit for bringing a discrimination action if ' . . . in all the circumstances of the case, it considers it just and equitable to do so' (S.68(6) Race Relations Act, S.76(5) Sex Discrimination Act). In *MacMillen Bloedel Containers Ltd* v. *Morris* (1984) (unreported) the tribunal permitted an action to be brought 10 months after the event. Unless the employer has been very formal when short-listing candidates, will he or she be able to remember, and therefore justify the non-selection of a certain candidate for short-listing almost a year after the event? Very careful record-keeping is called for.

Instructions to persons involved in the short-listing of candiates (or indeed the interviewing as well) that they should discriminate will also be a criminal offence under both Acts (S.30 Race Relations Act, S.39 Sex Discrimination Act).

Interviews

At the interview stage all interviewees must again be treated equally, and reference should be made to the EOC booklet, 'Fair and Efficient – Guidance on Equal Opportunities Policies in Recruitment and Selection Procedures'. This booklet also covers job descriptions, application forms, short-listing and assessment tests, as well as interviews. It makes clear that today questions relating to an applicant's marital status, marriage or family intentions, children and parental responsibilities, etc. are ' . . . regarded as impertinent, are resented and should never be asked'. Relevant cases on interviews include: *Saunders* v. *Richmond B.C.* [1977] I.R.L.R. 362, *Thorndyke* v. *Bell Fruit Co. Ltd* [1979] I.R.L.R. 1, *Brennan* v. *J.H. Dewhurst Ltd* [1983] I.R.L.R. 357.

The EOC booklet mentioned in the above paragraph contains details of further unreported cases relating to discriminatory practices during interviews. In relation to assessment tests there has recently been concern in the US that certain psychometric tests may indirectly discriminate against ethnic minorities and thus render them illegal. They are banned in some states. It must be remembered, however, that there are some exceptions to the legislation, including where a person's sex, or colour, etc. is a 'genuine occupational qualification' for that particular job, for example, a photographic model, a counsellor for welfare services to females, or males, or a particular racial group, etc. For full details of 'genuine occupational qualification' exceptions see Sex Discrimination Act S.7 and Race Relations Act S.5.

Employee references

Having decided which person would be offered the vacant position it is normal practice for the employer to take up references. There is no law which requires an employer to give a reference for his or her ex-employee, but if the employer does decide to give one it will be deemed to be an honest reference. Indeed, knowingly to give a false reference will be a criminal offence under the Servants' Characters Act 1792.

It has long been established that a referee could be liable under civil law of negligence to pay damages to the person to whom a negligent reference was given (*Hedley Byrne and Co. Ltd* v. *Heller and Partners* [1963] 2 All E.R. 575 and *Anderson and Sons Ltd* v. *Rhodes (Liverpool) Ltd* (1967) 2 All E.R. 850). It is only recently, however, that courts have considered the liability of the referee to the person who was the subject of the reference. In *Lawton* v. *BOC Transhield Ltd* [1986] I.R.L.R. 405 the ex-employer's reference to the new employer stated that Lawton's general conduct, ability, reliability, timekeeping, and attendance were 'poor', and his health 'fair', and that he would not be re-employed. The new employer thought this intriguing as the man had been with his ex-employer for 10 years so he telephoned the company, only to receive verbal confirmation of the bad reference. The consequent dismissal from the new job resulted in Lawton's unemployment for two years, and consequent loss of pay of over £7500.

The Court carefully considered each statement made in the reference and concluded that the referee had not been negligent. They stressed, however, that a negligent reference causing loss to the subject would result in the referee being held liable for the subject's loss.

In the same way, the subject of the reference could take a defamation action if any statement made tended to lower the ex-employee 'in the eyes of right-thinking people'. Generally an ex-employer would claim that the reference he or she gave was subject to qualified privilege; i.e. being made in good faith by a person who has a legal, social or moral duty to make it, to a person who has a similar interest or duty to receive it, i.e. the prospective employer. The sucess of the defence depends on the statement having been made carefully, honestly and without malice.

The Unfair Contract Terms Act 1977 has made it difficult to avoid liability by putting in a disclaimer clause. These are only effective if the referee can show that the clause is reasonable. If a reference has been given without making proper inquiries, it is hard to see how such a clause could be reasonable. It seems essential now that personnel files are not only accurate as far as they go, but also up to date and complete.

Rehabilitation of Offenders Act 1974

Some mention must be made in this chapter of this important legislation, though it has far wider implications than just for employee references. The Act seeks to rehabilitate ex offenders by restricting or forbidding the disclosure of 'spent convictions', which means convictions for offences in respect of which the offender has received a sentence of less than 30 months imprisonment, and the specified 'rehabilitation period' has elapsed since the last conviction. The more serious the offence, the greater the length of the 'rehabilitation period', and full details can be obtained by reading S.5 of the Act.

A rehabilitated person is then to ' . . . be treated for all purposes in law as a person who has not committed or been charged with or prosecuted for or convicted of or sentenced for the offence . . . the subject of that conviction' (S.4(1)). This is severely limited, however, in respect of proceedings for defamation. S.8(3) provides that nothing shall prevent a defendant in such an action from 'relying on any defence of justification or fair comment or of absolute or qualified privilege which is available to him or restrict the matters he may establish in support of any such defence'. The Act then goes on, however, that the defendant shall not be entitled to rely upon the defence of justification if the publication is proved to have been made with malice (S.8(5)).

'Malice' is not defined, but its normal meaning is that the statement is either made without belief in its truth or for an improper purpose.

Prospective employees are under no obligation to disclose such spent convictions when seeking a new job, and if dismissed for failure to disclose, or because of the past criminal record, the dismissal will be automatically unfair.

Certain classes of employee are excluded from the legislation, e.g. members of the legal profession, chartered accountants, dentists, veterinary surgeons, nurses, pharmaceutical chemists, traffic wardens, social workers, etc.

Contracts of employment

Having decided to recruit new staff, interviewed, taken up references and appointed the successful candidate, the company is still subject to the general law of employment. All employees are employed under a contract of employment. There are no formal requirements for the contract of employment; as with most other contracts it can be oral, by conduct, partly written or entirely written: it must, however, comply with the general rules governing all contracts.

This section will now examine the main sources of contractual terms for employment contracts. It will be clear that modern employment legislation places many constraints on the freedom of the employer by imposing minimum rights for all employees in many areas. Space will not permit a detailed discussion of all these rights; such detail is better left to a specialist textbook on employment law (Further reading). However, we will examine, albeit very briefly, the law regarding written statements of terms and conditions of employment, time off work rights and maternity rights, as examples of the 'new' statutory rights granted to all employees. The section also contains an actual example of the written particulars of employment, disciplinary rules and procedures which should be given to all full-time employees (naturally the name of the company has been changed).

Express terms

The express terms (Key concept 7.3) will usually include the wages to be paid, hours to be worked, broad nature of the duties, holiday entitlements, etc. Special terms can be inserted for particular employees, e.g. not to disclose confidential information, possession of a clean current driving licence, etc.

Since the express terms are the basis of the contract, they cannot generally be changed without mutual agreement. However, the employer may always lawfully terminate the contract and offer a new contract based on the new terms. Whether or not this would amount to an unfair dismissal will, of course, depend upon all the circumstances (p. 185).

Express terms are those to which the parties have expressly agreed.   KEY CONCEPT 7.3

EXPRESS TERMS OF AN EMPLOYMENT CONTRACT

One example of a particular express term commonly found in contracts of employment is a 'restraint clause' (i.e. one which seeks to restrict the future activities of an employee after the termination of his or her current contract of employment). These clauses are dealt with in detail in Chapter 4.

Implied terms

As Lord Wright stated in *Luxor* v. *Cooper* (1941): . . . It is well recognized that there may be cases where obviously some term must be implied if the intention of the parties is not to be defeated, some term of which it can be predicated that 'It goes without saying'; some term not expressed but necessary to give the transaction such business efficacy as the parties must have intended . . .

And as per Scrutton L.J. in *Reigate* v. *Union Manufacturing Ltd* (1918):

. . . A term can only be implied if it is necessary in the business sense to give efficacy to the contract; that is, if it is such a term that it can be confidently said that if at the time the contract was being negotiated someone had said to the parties – 'What will happen in such a case?', they would both have replied: 'Of course so and so will happen; we did not trouble to say that; it is too clear'. Unless the court comes to some such conclusion as that, it ought not to imply a term which the parties themselves have not expressed.

Today there is a tendency to imply terms (Key concept 7.4) when it is reasonable to do so (*Shell UK Ltd* v. *Lostock Garage Ltd* [1977]). However, in every contract of employment, there are certain implied terms which have been recognized for many years, including:

☐ The employer will treat the employee with respect, *Wood* v. *Freeloader* (1977).
☐ The employer will pay the agreed wages promptly, *Hanlon* v. *Allied Breweries (UK) Ltd* (1975).

Implied terms are those not actually discussed and agreed upon by the parties, but which may be presumed to have been the intention of the parties when they entered into the contract.   KEY CONCEPT 7.4

IMPLIED TERMS OF AN EMPLOYMENT CONTRACT

☐ The employer will not treat employees ' . . . arbitrarily, capriciously or inequitably in matters of remuneration', *F.C. Gardner Ltd* v. *Beresford* (1978).

☐ There must be trust and confidence between the parties, *IOW Tourist Board* v. *Coombes* (1976), *Robinson* v. *Crompton Parkinson Ltd* (1978).

☐ The employee will exercise reasonable care and skill when doing his job, *Lister* v. *Romford Ice and Cold Storage Co Ltd* (1957).

☐ The employee will obey all reasonable and lawful orders, *Dennis and Co.* v. *Campbell* (1977).

☐ The employee will give faithful service, *Wessex Dairies* v. *Smith* (1935), *Hivac Ltd* v. *Park Royal Scientific Instruments Ltd* (1946) p. 224, *Bent's Brewery Co. Ltd* v. *Hogan* (1945), *Seager* v. *Copydex Ltd* (1967).

The real significance of the implied term is that is frequently used as a basis for a constructive dismissal claim (p. 185). A breach of a term, whether express or implied, by an employer amounts to a breach of contract by him or her. An employee may 'accept' the breach and claim that he or she has been constructively dismissed. If the breach is of an express term there is usually little dispute, but since the implied terms are not 'known' by the parties until a court or tribunal has pronounced them, there are many problems which may arise if the breach is of an implied term (p. 186).

Collective agreements

Relevant here are *Robertson* v. *British Gas Corporation* [1983] and *Marley* v. *Forward Trust Group Ltd* [1986]. Collective agreements are presumed to be not legally enforceable as between the parties unless containing a written statement to the contrary, unless made between between 1st December 1971 and 16th September 1974, when they were presumed to be legally enforceable.

KEY CONCEPT 7.5	A collective agreement is an agreement made between an employer (or employers' association) and a trade union or unions. A collective agreement will usually deal with many matters, including recognition of the union, disputes procedures, wages and hours of work of trade union members, etc. Some of the terms of this agreement can become incorporated into an individual's contract of employment, for example in *Galley* v. *National Coal Board* (1958) a mining deputy's contract expressly stated that his wages were to be regulated by '. . . the national agreement for the time being in force'.
COLLECTIVE AGREEMENTS	

Works rules

ACAS Advisory, Conciliation and Arbitration Service.

Today works rules are necessary for the employer to comply with the ACAS Code of Practice on Disciplinary Rules and Procedures, the law relating to unfair dismissal, and the Health and Safety at Work Act. The practical effect of such rules is that they become incorporated into the individual contract of employment.

Statutory rights

Modern employment legislation has conferred a number of rights on employees, and any attempt by an employer to take away these minimum rights by agreement with the employee will be void. The main statutory rights are listed in Figure 7.1.

These rights are enforceable by an application by the employee to an industrial tribunal (Key concept 7.6).

(a) Written statement of main terms of employment

As it is impossible in a work of this nature to consider all of these in detail, a number are picked by way of illustration. Full details on all these rights

1. Written statement of terms and conditions of employment.
2. Itemized pay statements.
3. Guaranteed payments.
4. Medical suspension payments.
5. Trade union membership and non-menbership.
6. Time off work (some with pay) for trade union activities and duties, public duties, to look for work when under notice of redundancy, ante-natal care, and to act as a safety representative.
7. Maternity pay.
8. Maternity leave and the right to return to work afterwards.
9. Written reasons for dismissal.
10. Not to be unfairly dismissed.
11. Redundancy pay.
12. Certain rights if the employer becomes insolvent.
13. Not to be unreasonably expelled or excluded from a trade union.
14. Equal pay.
15. Not to be discriminated against on grounds of sex, race, colour, nationality, cthnic or national origins.

Figure 7.1 Statutory rights of employees.

Industrial tribunals were set up by the Industrial Training Act 1964, and their procedure is now governed by the Industrial Tribunal Regulations 1985. From a modest beginning they now have jurisdiction for almost all employment law matters; although the majority of cases are concerned with unfair dismissal. Each tribunal consists of a legally qualified chairman (either full time or part time) and two lay persons, representing both sides of industry. Each has an equal vote (even on points of law) and the tribunal has to reach at least a majority decision (96% of all decisions are unanimous!). The Regulations relating to procedure are designed to ensure simplicity, absence of legal formalities, speed, cheapness and flexibility.

KEY CONCEPT 7.6

INDUSTRIAL TRIBUNAL

can be obtained from job centres on Department of Employment free leaflets.

Within 13 weeks of the commencement of employment, the employer must issue to every employee (subject to the exceptions detailed below) a written statement of main terms of employment (S.1 Employment Protection (Consolidation) Act 1978) (Figure 7.2). Any changes to these terms must also be notified to the employee in writing within one month of the change taking place (S.4).

Figure 7.2 Written statement of main terms.

The written statement must include:

1. The identity of the parties.
2. The date when employment began, with a statement about whether employment with a previous employer counts towards the employee's period of continuous employment.
3. The scale or rate of remuneration and the intervals at which payment is to be made.
4. The hours of work and any terms relating to overtime requirements.
5. Terms and conditions relating to holidays, holiday pay, public holiday rights, etc.
6. Details of sickness scheme in operation (if any). Additionally the Statutory Sick Pay scheme requires employers to notify employees in writing of the agreed 'Qualifying Days' for calculation purposes, and of the rules of notification of absence.
7. Pension rights (if any).
8. The length of notice the employee is obliged to give and to receive on termination of the contract.
9. The job title.
10. Any disciplinary rules and procedures applicable to the employee (need not be given if fewer than 20 people are employed under the Employment Act 1989).
11. The name of the person (or position in the company) to whom the employee can apply if he or she has any grievance relating to their employment; and the manner in which such an application should be made.

Excluded classes of employment

These written particulars do not have to be issued to part-time employees (i.e. those working less than 16 hours per week, unless they have been working between 8 and 16 hours per week for five years or more) or casual workers employed for a period of three months or less. Both these classes will be included in new legislation if and when the EEC Directives on Part-Time Workers and on Temporary Workers are finally adopted (Chapter 1 on the effect of EEC Directives on UK law]. Crown employees, and merchant seamen are also excluded.

It must be noted that the written particulars are not the contract of employment, they are only evidence that a contract exists. This is a very important point and was confirmed recently in *System Floors (UK) Ltd* v. *Daniel* (1981) where the E.A.T. stated:

> ... It provides very strong prima facie evidence of what were the terms of the contract between the parties, but does not constitute a written contract between the parties. Nor are the statement of the terms finally conclusive; at most they place a heavy burden on the employer to show that the actual terms of contract are different from those which he has set out in the statutory statement.

Prima facie Prima facie = at first sight.

There is no sanction against an employer who fails to provide the written statement, other than the employee's right to apply to an industrial tribunal for a declaration of what should be contained in such a statement: this could cause many problems for the employer. Also his or her failure to issue the statement means that no disciplinary rules and procedure will have been issued, so any dismissal, other than for the most serious kind of gross misconduct, is likely to be held to be unfair solely because of the failure to issue rules and procedures. This can be very costly as compensation up to a maximum of £23 049 can be awarded under certain circumstances for unfair dismissal (as at 1 April 1990).

Figure 7.3 gives an example of a Written Statement of Terms and Conditions of Employment.

XYZ GARDEN CENTRE, SOMEWHERE, DEVON.

Figure 7.3 Example of Written Statement of Terms and Conditions of Employment.

This statement sets out particulars of the terms and conditions of your employment, in accordance with S.I of the Employment Protection (Consolidation) Act 1978.

Employee's name: Fred Bloggs

Date of commencement of employment: 1 May 1983.

Any period of employment with the former owners of XYZ Garden Centre immediately prior to the takeover of the business has been included as part of your continuous period of employment.

Any alterations in the terms of the following conditions and/or legislation will be duly recorded and dated in the master copy which is held in the Office, where it can be seen if necessary. Notification that there has been an amendment to this Contract will be published to you as and when required.

1. *Job Title.* General Assistant (Shop and Garden Centre).

2. *Wages.* Your rate of pay is as stated on your employment sheet, which is available for inspection in the Office. Your wages are paid weekly in arrears.

3. *Hours of work.* Your normal hours of work will be from 8.45 a.m. to 4.30 p.m. on weekdays, and from 8.45 a.m. to 5.00 p.m. on Saturday, and from 9.00 a.m. to 4.00 p.m. on Sunday.

Your normal week consists of 40 hours, and all employees are required to work alternate weekends, as per the shift rota agreed with the employer.

4. *Overtime.* Any hours worked above 40 hours per week, or after 5.00 p.m. will be considered as overtime, and you will be expected to work a reasonable amount of overtime when called upon to do so. Hours worked above the standard week will be paid by time off in lieu or at the agreed rate, at the discretion of the employer.

5. *Sick pay.* The company does not operate a formal sickness scheme over and above the normal Statutory Sick Pay scheme. However after one year's continuous service the company will normally make up wages to the basic wage level for employees certified as unable to work due to sickness, or injury arising out of or in the course of employment, as follows:

> After 1 year's continuous employment – for 2 weeks;
> After 2 years' continuous employment – for 4 weeks;

Any periods of absence due to sickness or injury (however caused) must be self certified by the employee, using the employer's certificate, for absences up to 7 days, after which a doctor's certificate must be submitted.

For the purposes of the Statutory Sick Pay scheme your Qualifying Days will be those days in any week when you are expected to work, and all absences must be notified on the first day of absence. Failure to comply with this rule of notification of absence may lead to non-payment of the statutory sick pay due.

6. *Holidays.* During the first year of employment you will be entitled to 1 day's paid holiday per completed calendar month worked. After one year's service you will be entitled to 20 days' holiday per year, plus the normal Statutory and Bank holidays.

All employees must agree to work on 50% of the Statutory and Bank Holidays, with time off in lieu as agreed with the employer.

All holidays are to be agreed in advance with the employer, and normally no holiday periods will be permitted between 1 March and 14 June each year.

All holidays are paid on an accrued basis, and the company holiday year runs from 1 November to 31 October. There can be no carry forward of holidays from one year to another: such days as have not been taken will be treated as having been forfeited.

7. *Pension.* The company does not operate a formal pension scheme.

8. *Grievance procedure.* If you have any grievance relating to your employment you should apply to Mr Cole who will arrange a private interview at the earliest possible convenience.

9. *Disciplinary procedure.* Details of the Company's disciplinary rules and procedure are shown below.

10. *Notice of termination.* After 4 weeks' continuous employment, the employer is required to give the following notice should it wish to terminate your employment:

☐ Less than 2 years' continuous service = 1 week.
☐ 2 years, but less than 12 years = 1 week for each year of continuous service.
☐ 12 years or more continuous service = 12 weeks.

You are required to give the employer one week's notice, irrespective of length of service; such notice to be given in writing by noon on a Friday.

The foregoing particulars in this statement are correct as at 1 August 1987. [This statement does not of itself constitute a contract.] Employee's signature to acknowledge receipt of this statement:
.... Date.......................

Disciplinary rules and procedure

The key to the ability of the employers to continue to provide work for all employees is the continuing provision to customers of produce and service of the highest standards and at a competitive price. This requires high standards of work from every member of the company. It is far better that this is achieved by a sense of commitment and common purpose to strive for success, rather than by a long list of rules and regulations. However, it is necessary to have standards of performance, achievement and behaviour that must be met to ensure that the business does not suffer. It is to protect all members of the company against the possibility that someone may not pull his or her weight that the following rules will apply.

These rules and the disciplinary procedure are also issued in order to comply with current employment legislation and codes of practice.

1. *Gross misconduct.* The following is a list, but not an exhaustive list, of acts which will be considered gross misconduct which will lead to summary dismissal without notice:
   (a) Theft of the employer's property or property belonging to another.
   (b) Obscene language or insolence or offensive behaviour towards a customer or visitor.
   (c) Fighting with, or striking fellow employees, customers or visitors.
   (d) Serious infringement of any of the company's safety rules.
   (e) Serious misconduct outside working hours which has a detrimental effect on the employee's performance, or his or her ability to do the work he is employed to do, or which results in a breach of trust between the employer and the employee.

(f) Any other reason sufficiently substantial to warrant summary dismissal without notice.

2. *Other misconduct.* The following is a list, but not an exhaustive list, of the types of misconduct which will lead to a formal warning, as per the Disciplinary Procedure below.

(a) Unnecessary absenteeism without previous permission.

(b) Misconduct in the course of employment, e.g. bad language, insubordination, refusal to obey a lawful order, failure to comply with the company safety rules or other procedures, smoking in restricted areas, working under the influence of alcohol or drugs, etc. This is not an exhaustive list.

(c) Lateness for work.

(d) Misconduct outside working hours which has a detrimental effect on the employee's performance, or his ability to do the job he is employed to do, or which results in a breach of trust between the employer and the employee.

(e) Carelessly or negligently damaging the property of the employer or of another person.

(f) Any other reason sufficiently substantial to justify dismissal.

3. Disciplinary procedure

It is of the utmost importance that, where a written warning may be considered necessary, all the relevant facts are recorded within 24 hours. An employee will not, except in the case of gross misconduct, be dismissed for a first offence.

1st Stage. If it is considered that a written warning may be warranted, the employee concerned will be asked to attend the main office. The employee will always be given the opportunity to state his or her case and have the right to be assisted by any other employee of the company if he or she so wishes. Only after the employer has assured himself that he has heard all the facts, and is completely satisfied that a written warning is justified, will such a warning be issued.

2nd Stage. The written warning will be recorded on the official warning form. It will be read to the employee, dated and signed, and it will set out the circumstances and the disciplinary action to which the employee will be liable if he commits a further offence.

If a second warning is not given within the following 6 months, the 1st warning will be rescinded.

If the employee commits another offence justifying a 2nd written warning within the following 6 months from the date of the 1st warning, a 2nd written warning will be issued. The procedure will be the same as for the 1st warning.

If there is no further offence within 6 months from the date of the 2nd warning, both 1st and 2nd warnings will be rescinded.

A third offence justifying a written warning within 6 months of the 2nd warning will lead to a dismissal, but only after a full inquiry has been carried out by the employer.

3rd Stage. A written statement of reason for the dismissal will be given to the dismissed employee.

NB. The employer expressly reserves the right to give a final written warning to any employee whose conduct warrants such serious action, even though this may conflict with the foregoing procedure. This final written warning will not be on the official warning form but will be in the form of an individual letter.

Suspension from work. The employer expressly reserves the right to suspend an employee from work, with pay, at any stage of the above disciplinary procedure.

Right of appeal. All employees have the right to appeal against any disciplinary action providing such appeal is lodged in writing within 5 days of the action.

(b) Time off work rights

Employers can no longer refuse time off work to employees who wish to participate in certain public functions or duties. For example, in the recent past an employee who was invited to sit on the local magistrates' bench would have to agree to sit for between 20 and 26 sessions per year (depending on the area of the country). His or her employer could, and usually did, refuse to give the employee any time off work and consequently most magistrates' benches consisted of owners of businesses, self-employed persons and retired professional people. Today all employees have the right to 'reasonable' time off work to participate in public duties, which includes serving on the magistrates' bench; and consequently most benches now contain a growing proportion of 'working-class' members.

Ss.27–32 E.P.(C) Act 1978 confers the following rights to time off work for employees:

☐ 'Reasonable' time off, with pay, for employees who are officials of recognized trade unions for industrial relations activities and approved training.
☐ 'Reasonable' time off, without pay, for employees who are trade union members for 'trade union activities'.
☐ 'Reasonable' time off work, without pay, to all employees for 'public duties', which include magistrates, councillors, members of statutory tribunals, members of Regional or Area Health Boards, governor of state educational establishments and lay members of water authorities (*Emmerson* v. *Commissioners for Inland Revenue* [1977] I.R.L.R. 458, *Corner* v. *Buckinghamshire County Council* [1978] I.R.L.R. 320).
☐ 'Reasonable' time off, with pay, for employees who are under notice of redundancy to seek alternative employment and/or re-training.

CASE STUDY 7.1

TIME OFF WORK

Mr. Ratcliffe was a lecturer at the Bournemouth and Poole CFE, and was elected to Bournemouth Borough Council. He asked his employers for time off to carry out his public duties and the college re-organized his timetable in order to free him during afternoons so that he might attend council and committee meetings. They still expected him to perform his full functions as a lecturer, however, which meant he had to do some work at home, in the evenings and at weekends. He also had to cover for other lecturers who took his classes whilst he was absent on council business.

The tribunal concluded that such an arrangement did not comply with the Act. 'Swapping time around is not giving time off. . . . The applicant was still required to be on the premises for 30 hours and that is not giving him time off. He still has to do the work at some time or the other, often in his own time.'

Thus 'time off work' means doing less work than that which the individual concerned is contracted to do.

(*Ratcliff* v. *Dorset C.C.* [1978] I.R.L.R. 191)

☐ 'Reasonable' time off, with pay, for pregnant employees for ante-natal care (added by S.13) Employment Act 1980).

What does 'time off' mean? (Case study 7.1)

It is also relevant to add that employees who have been appointed as safety representatives by their independent recognized trade unions, have the right to 'all the time off work necessary' to carry out the rights and functions listed by the Safety Representatives and Safety Committee Regulations 1977 and the Health and Safety at Work etc. Act 1974.

The draft EEC Directive on Parental Rights, if and when adopted, will include more rights to time off work for working parents, e.g. for the illness of their children.

(c) Maternity rights

It is not possible to review in detail the law relating to maternity rights in a business law book; such a review is better placed in a specialist textbook on Employment Law (Further reading). This area is very complicated and has changed considerably since first introduced, in stages, between 1976 and 1978.

> . . . These statutory provisions (on maternity rights) are of inordinate complexity exceeding the worst excesses of a taxing statute; we find that especially regrettable bearing in mind that they are regulating the everyday rights of ordinary employers and employees. [*Lavery* v. *Plessey Telecommunications Ltd* (1983) I.C.R. 534, E.A.T.]

Current legislation confers four rights on a pregnant employee: first a right not to be dismissed because she is pregnant, or for reasons related to her pregnancy; secondly a right to reasonable time off work, with pay, for ante-natal care; thirdly a right to maternity leave and to return to her job after her maternity leave; and fourthly a right to receive maternity pay, from her employer, and statutory maternity pay from the State. Each of these rights is subject to qualification; for example, she may only claim unfair dismissal if she has been dismissed because she is pregnant if she has two years continuous service with her employer as at the eleventh week before the expected date of confinement. Also to be qualified to return to work after maternity leave she must have given notice in writing of her intention to return at least three weeks before she started her maternity leave (or as near to three weeks as is reasonably practicable).

It could be argued that the maternity rights in the UK are generous compared with some countries (but not many!). However, a quick review of maternity rights in Eastern Europe (for example in Bulgaria) would suggest the contrary. In Bulgaria working mothers cannot be dismissed because they are pregnant (irrespective of length of service). Leave entitlement is up to two years on full pay for the first three children, and six months for any subsequent children. A further period of one year, without pay, can also be taken. After maternity leave the original job is guaranteed for the mother. It is also possible for both the mother and the father to share the maternity leave periods if both are employed.

The UK law permits up to 40 weeks maternity leave (subject to two years service qualification) but only 6 weeks will be paid by the employer (at 90% of normal wages) and a further 12 weeks of statutory maternity pay by the state (both subject to qualifying periods of service and levels of pay). It must be remembered that the political and economic systems of Eastern Europe are different from those of the UK and these rights must be seen as against these different systems.

The law relating to the payment of wages

The law relating to the payment of wages is one area where there has been an easing in the restrictions imposed on employers. The Wages Act 1986 repealed the restrictive Truck Acts 1831–1940 and the Payment of Wages Act 1960, which had controlled the method of payments and amounts of deductions from wages for all manual workers. Since 1 January 1987 the employer can now pay all workers by whatever method he or she considers best for the business (subject to the right of existing manual workers on that date to payments in cash if their existing contract gave them that right). For example, an employer can pay by cash, cheque or direct credit.

The control on deductions from wages has also been eased. An employer can now deduct any amounts from the wages packet of his or her employees provided such deductions are:

☐ Sanctioned by another statute, e.g. income tax and national insurance contributions; or
☐ Covered by an express term in the individual contract, e.g. a check-off arrangement for trade union subscription; or
☐ Agreed in writing by the employee concerned prior to the deduction being made. This is the most controversial provision in the 1986 Act, as

it leaves the door open for unscrupulous employers to deduct any amount for any reason, the employee 'forced' to agree in writing under 'threat' of losing his or her job. Such an action by the employer is clearly unlawful but with the current levels of unemployment some workers might prefer less wages than no wages at all, and if the worker has less than two years continuous employment he or she is not able to challenge his or her dismissal for refusing to accept the unlawful deduction (p. 185).

The only real constraint imposed on employers by this Act is that in retail employment deductions from wages cannot amount to more than 10% of gross wages in any one week, except from the last wage packet of a worker leaving his or her employment, when there is no limit to the deduction that can be made.

Itemized pay statement

Section 8 E.P.(C) Act 1978 also gives the employee the right to an itemized pay statement, at or before the time at which wages/salary are paid, which must show the gross amount of wages or salary, the amount of any deductions and what they are for, and the net wages or salary. Fixed deductions need not be itemized separately if the total amount is specified in the statement and the employer provides an annual statement of the amount, interval and purpose of these fixed deductions.

Equal pay

An employer's ability to fix wage levels is affected not only by commercial considerations but also by the law. The Equal Pay Act 1970, as amended by regulations in 1983, provides for the principle of equal pay, irrespective of sex, for like work, work rated as equivalent, or work of equal value. This is achieved by implying into contracts of employment a statutory equality clause. An employer may use different rates of pay but he or she must be able to justify these by reference to external factors unrelated to sex. There have been a number of important decisions on the application of the Act; for further discussion reference should be made to the sources listed at the end of this chapter and to the free publications of the Equal Opportunities Commission which are designed to be as simple and helpful as possible.

Termination of employment

Perhaps the most important changes made by modern employment law on the employer/employee relationship have been in the area of termination of employment contracts. This section will briefly examine the different ways in which employment contracts can be brought to an end, before concentrating on the more important areas of unfair dismissal and redundancy.

The individual contract of employment can come to an end in a variety of different ways:

Resignation by the employee

If an employee voluntarily resigns he or she has not been dismissed and normally there will be no legal consequences attached to the resignation. If the words of resignation used are ambiguous, the question is whether a reasonable employer would have understood the words as amounting to a resignation (*Barclay* v. *City of Glasgow D.C.* (1983)). Also if an employee is given the alternative, 'resign or be dismissed', a consequent resignation will usually be regarded as a dismissal (*Croft* v. *Formica Ltd* (1975)).

Frustration of contract

Where the performance of the contract of employment becomes impossible because of some intervening event the contract is said to be terminated by frustration (Chapter 2) (and not dismissal). In *Murphy* v. *Hare Bros Ltd* (1973) it was held that an employee who was imprisoned could not after serving his sentence seek his old job back again because his contract of employment had been frustrated by his non-availability for work during his imprisonment.

Consensual termination

A contract of employment is terminated if the parties have expressly agreed that the happening or non-occurrence of an event will terminate the contract. For an interesting line of cases on the industrial tribunal attitude to this area students should read: *British Leyland Ltd* v. *Ashraf* [1978] I.R.L.R. 330, *Midland Electric Manufacturing Co. Ltd* v. *Kanji* [1980] I.R.L.R. 185, *Igbo* v. *Johnson Matthey Chemicals Ltd* [1985] I.R.L.R. 189 and [1986] I.R.L.R. 215 C.A.

Completion of task

This normally concerns casual workers who are taken on for a specific task, e.g. the harvest, the construction of a house, etc. When the task is completed the contract is automatically at an end.

Fixed-term contract coming to an end

Various occupations, including seasonal workers, teachers, football club managers, etc. are taken on for a specified period of time. It is quite common, for example, for a tourist hotel worker to be taken on from 'Easter until 30 September' (i.e. the holiday season). The hotel will close down from 1 October until the following Easter, and the contract automatically comes to an end on the specified date. Directors are usually employed on such fixed-term contracts expecting them to be renewed with appropriate financial reward.

Termination by notice

In the past it was always assumed that employment was on the basis of a yearly hiring; the modern view however is that an employee is employed for an indefinite period (unless there is express indication to the contrary) subject to termination of the contract by the giving of a reasonable period of notice. The common law implied that such a period must be 'reasonable in all the circumstances' but normally today contracts of employment are governed by the statutory minimum notice periods now found in the E.P.(C) Act 1978. S.49 states that employees are entitled to the following minimum notice:

☐ after four weeks continuous service – one week's notice;
☐ after two years continuous service – one week per completed year of service;
☐ after 12 years continuous service – 12 weeks, which is the maximum entitlement.

After four weeks continuous employment employees are required to give seven days notice to terminate their contract, irrespective of the length of service. These periods may be increased by agreement in writing in the written particulars of employment.

These statutory minimum periods do not prevent either party from waiving their right to notice, affect their right to terminate without notice for good cause, or prevent payment of money in lieu of notice.

Wrongful dismissal

Prior to the modern law of unfair dismissal, first introduced by the Industrial Relations Act 1971, an employee dismissed without due notice, or otherwise in breach of contract had, and still has today, the right to bring an action at common law for wrongful dismissal (Key concept 7.7). However, either party has the right at common law to terminate the contract on the giving of reasonable notice, so this common law remedy is little used today. It might still be appropriate where an employee is not within the protection of the unfair dismissal law, or is a very highly paid employee (because the damages for wrongful dismissal are not subject to the statutory maximum compensation applicable to unfair dismissal), or where a contract for a fixed term, for example a football club manager on a five-year contract, is terminated unlawfully.

KEY CONCEPT 7.7	Wrongful dismissal means dismissal in breach of contract.
WRONGFUL DISMISSAL	

KEY CONCEPT 7.8	Unfair dismissal means dismissal without a statutorily fair reason or a fair manner of dismissal.
UNFAIR DISMISSAL	

Unfair dismissal

The right not to be unfairly dismissed was first introduced into English law by the Industrial Relations Act 1971, and is now contained in the E.P.(C) Act 1978, as amended by the Employment Acts 1980 and 1982, and the Sex Discrimination Act 1986. The concept of unfair dismissal (Key concept 7.8) is not based upon breach of contract, but on the idea that an employer must always act reasonably when dismissing employees.

For example, if the employer had less than the full facts, if the situation did not warrant dismissal, if there were mitigating circumstances, if the disciplinary rules and procedures had not been made clear to the employee, etc., the dismissal will probably be held to be unfair.

The right not to be unfairly dismissed applies to all full-time employees (i.e. normally employed for 16 hours or more per week, or for 8 hours per week or more for five years or more), who have been employed continuously for two years or more, and are under retirement age. A dismissal for 'inadmissable reasons', i.e. for a reason related to the membership of an independent trade union, or participation in the activities of the union at an appropriate time, is not subject to the service or age exceptions.

The applicant must register his or her claim with the Central Office of Industrial Tribunals (COIT) within 3 months of the 'effective date of termination' of his or her contract.

The Act places the burden of proof on the applicant to show that he or she had been dismissed, and there are three ways in which dismissal may take place:

☐ Where the contract is terminated by the employer, with or without notice (Case study 7.2). Also relevant are *Morton Sundour Fabrics Ltd* v. *Shaw* (1967) and *Martin* v. *Yeoman Aggregates Ltd* (1983).

☐ Where a fixed-term contract has come to an end without being renewed on the same terms (*Wiltshire C.C.* v. *Guy* (1978)).

☐ Constructive dismissal, i.e. where the employee himself or herself

Effective date of termination Defined in S.55(4) Employment Protection (Consolidation) Act as the last day of the notice period if the contract has been terminated by notice, given by either the employer or the employee; or if terminated without notice, the date when the termination takes effect; or the last day of a fixed term contract which expires without being renewed.

CASE STUDY 7.2

TERMINATION OF EMPLOYMENT

F was a fish filleter with 4 years' service, and was renowned for his argumentative nature. One day, whilst arguing again, his foreman told him, *'If you do not like the job, fuck off'*. F left the job and claimed he had been dismissed; he claimed the words used meant 'you are dismissed'. The Tribunal held that where an employer uses what is known as 'ambiguous language' the words used had to be taken not in isolation – but against the background of the job on Hull fishdocks, where obscene language was very common.

The case confirms that the burden is on the applicant to an action to prove that he had been dismissed, and in the case of ambiguous language the 'test' is really how would the reasonable employee in that situation have interpreted those words.

(*Futty* v. *D and D Brekkes Ltd* [1974] I.R.L.R. 130)

terminates the contract, with or without notice, in such circumstances that he or she is entitled to resign without notice by reason of the employer's conduct. In *Western Excavations (ECC) Ltd* v. *Sharp* (1978) it was held that the conduct of the employer must be such as to amount to a breach of contract.

As mentioned earlier in this chapter, constructive dismissal is today closely linked with the implied terms of the contract (as a result of the *Western Excavations (ECC) Ltd* v. *Sharp* decision), as the following example cases illustrate:

In *B.A.C. Ltd* v. *Austin* [1978] I.R.L.R. 332, the employers failure to respond to their employee's complaint about the unsuitability of safety wear was held to be a breach of the implied term to 'act in accordance with good industrial relations practice'.

In, *Gardner Ltd* v. *Beresford* [1978] I.R.L.R. 63 the E.A.T. found an implied term that the employer would not treat employees ' . . . arbitrarily, capriciously or inequitably', with regard to increases in pay.

In *Wigan B.C.* v. *Davies* [1979] I.C.R. 411 the E.A.T. found an implied term that the employer would take reasonable steps to ensure that the employee could do her job without harassment from fellow workers.

These cases resulted from the industrial tribunal 'discovering' an implied term (Key concept 7.4) in the contract with which the employer had failed to comply. He was therefore technically in breach of contract, and the employee's consequent resignation was held to be a constructive dismissal. There are many other examples of these kinds of decision in the law reports, and they clearly illustrate the freedom with which industrial tribunals are permitted to operate. There are many lawyers who would like to see a strict system of precedent operated in regard to the decisions of industrial tribunals, but this would surely only serve to work against the interests of the weaker party in employment disputes.

S.57 of the 1978 Act then requires that an employer has to justify a dismissal in two stages; firstly by showing that the principal reason for dismissal was a 'valid' reason specified by the Act (Key concept 7.9) and secondly, that he acted reasonably in all the circumstances surrounding the dismissal (S.57(3) as amended by S.6 Employment Act 1980).

Space does not permit a full review of the current attitudes of industrial tribunals to employer reasonableness in any particular situation. However,

KEY CONCEPT 7.9	These are:
SPECIFIED VALID REASONS FOR DISMISSAL	☐ related to the capability or qualifications of the employee for performing work of the kind he or she was employed to do; or ☐ related to the conduct of the employee; or ☐ that the employee was redundant; or ☐ that continued employment of that employee would be contrary to a duty imposed by statute; or ☐ was 'some other substantial reason' of a kind such as to justify the dismissal.

the following guide may provide material for seminar discussion or essay, and students ought, by careful reading of relevant textbooks and law reports, to be able to prepare a similar list of questions to be asked by a tribunal for each of the other valid reasons for dismissal listed above.

(a) Capability

S.57(4) (a) – definition of 'capability'. Example relating to unsatisfactory work performance:

- [ ] Is there evidence of incompetence?: *Lewis Shops Group Ltd* v. *Wiggins* [1973] I.C.R. 335, *Taylor* v. *Alidair Ltd* [1978] I.R.L.R. 82
- [ ] Did the employee receive adequate training?: *Fox* v. *Findus Foods Ltd* [1973] I.R.L.R. 8, *Jones* v. *London Co-operative Society* [1975] I.R.L.R. 110, *Connor* v. *Halfords* [1972] I.R.L.R. 109.
- [ ] Was the employee adequately supervised?: *Davidson* v. *Kent Meters Ltd* [1975] I.R.L.R. 145, *Okereke* v. *The Post Office* [1974] I.R.L.R. 170.
- [ ] Was a proper warning given?: *James* v. *Waltham Holy Cross* U.D.C. [1973] I.R.L.R. 202, *Lumb* v. *Charcon Pipes* [1972] I.R.L.R. 73
- [ ] Was the employee given a chance to state his case?: *Sutton and Gates Ltd* v. *Boxall* [1979] I.C.R. 67
- [ ] Was the employee's previous record taken into account?: *Sibun* v. *Modern Telephones Ltd* [1976] I.R.L.R. 81.
- [ ] other relevant cases: *Lancaster* v. *Anchor Hotels Ltd* [1973] I.R.L.R. 13, *Hathaway* v. *F.W.D. Merchants Ltd* [1975] I.R.L.R. 108

You should also consult *Discipline at work* published by ACAS (1987). Remedies for unfair dismissal are dealt with in Key concept 7.10.

KEY CONCEPT 7.10

REMEDIES FOR UNFAIR DISMISSAL

Where the industrial tribunal is satisfied that the dismissal was unfair it has the power to order re-instatement, re-engagement or compensation, subject to maxima in regard to age, length of service and wages at the date of termination. An employer can refuse to implement an order to reinstate but in this case he or she will have to pay extra compensation to the unfairly dismissed worker.

Redundancy

Reinstatement The employee is taken back to the same job.

Re-engagement The employee is taken back to another job.

The Redundancy Payments provisions of the 1978 Act are contained in Ss.81–120. The legislation acts as a constraint upon employers who decide that they need to cut their workforce, or to change their production process or products, as every full-time employee, with two years or more continuous employment, who is dismissed in these circumstances will be entitled to a redundancy payment.

In a redundancy situation (Key concept 7.11) an employee who unreasonably refuses an offer of 'suitable alternative employment' will disqualify himself or herself from receiving a redundancy payment. However, the offer made by the employer must have complied with the provisions of the

KEY CONCEPT 7.11	'Redundancy' arises if: the employer has ceased, or intends to cease carrying on the business at a particular place; or the need for the particular work done by the employee has ceased or diminished, or is about to do so.
REDUNDANCY	

Act, and whether or not a refusal is 'unreasonable' is a question of fact in every case, with the burden on the employer to show that his offer was unreasonably refused.

In these circumstances the legislation has given employees a right to a four week trial period in the new job, during which time they are free to terminate the new contract if they consider it unsuitable, without affecting their right to claim a redundancy payment if the job is in fact unsuitable. There are no statutory definitions of 'suitability' for these alternative jobs, but employers must have regard to such things as the skills of the employee, the nature of his or her previous job, the new earnings compared with the previous job, where the new job is in a different location the difficulties this might cause to the employee, and the accepted custom and practice in such situations in that particular job or industry.

The redundancy payment is calculated according to the employee's age, length of service and wages at the date of redundancy, subject to a specified maximum level of earnings and a maximum of 20 years service. All employers now have to bear the full cost of their redundancies since the Wages Act 1986 repealed the provisions relating to rebates.

In selecting for redundancy an employer must act fairly, according to predetermined objective criteria. Unfair redundancy selection amounts to unfair dismissal.

(b) Other relevant areas of law

Whilst it is clear that employers do have some choice in the above areas when making decisions, they nevertheless have to act within the legal environment existing at the time. An example of choice would be that they can choose which payment system to use, e.g. payment by cash, or direct credit, etc. but having made that decision they are then bound by the law relating to the payment of wages. They can also choose whether or not to dismiss an employee, but again, having decided to dismiss, they must comply with the unfair dismissal law.

The latter part of this chapter is devoted to a discussion of some areas of law which may influence a business when making certain organizational or strategic decisions: for example, should they take over another business as a going concern? Should they computerize all their personnel records? Should they recognize and negotiate with a trade union? If the company decides against one of these strategies they will be untouched by that area of law: should they decide to go ahead, they will be obliged to comply with the relevant law, e.g. the law on transfer of undertakings.

Transfer of undertakings The new owner of a business will by law take over the rights, powers, duties and liabilities of the former owner towards those transferred employees.

> Most businesses today will be using a computer for many purposes, e.g. accounts, personnel records, wages systems, mailing lists of suppliers and customers, etc. Most of these records are now subject to the Data Protection Act 1984, which is based upon the Council of Europe's Convention for the Protection of Individuals with regard to Automatic Processing of Personal Data (1981).
>
> KEY CONCEPT 7.12
>
> **THE DATA PROTECTION ACT 1984: PERSONAL DATA ON COMPUTERS**

The Data Protection Act and personnel records

The Data Protection Act 1984 is full of complicated definitions and principles which will no doubt lead to many expensive, complicated legal actions. The main thrust of the legislation, however, is quite simple:

☐ Data users must register the fact that they have information about living individuals, or from which individuals can be identified, with the Registrar of Data Protection.
☐ Data must be collected, stored, processed and disclosed only in accordance with the specified data protection principles.
☐ Data subjects (i.e. living individuals) have the right to view the Register, and make application to any data user who may have personal data about them held on computer, to view the data. Such information must be revealed within 40 days of the request by the data subject, in a form easily understandable to a layman.
☐ Under certain circumstances the data subject will have the right to correct inaccurate information, request erasure, and receive compensation for any loss suffered due to incorrect data.
☐ The Act has created the Registrar of Data Protection, and a new Data Protection Tribunal (similar to the industrial tribunal) for the resolution of disputes.

The Registrar

The Registrar has many rights, including, on authority of a warrant, the right to enter, search, inspect, operate and if necessary seize any documents or equipment. He or she can issue enforcement notices, which can require rectification or erasure of data, demand insertions that the sources of the data are considered inaccurate, or misleading, insert supplementary statements, and order compliance with the Data Protection Principles. He or she can also issue a de-registration notice which has the effect of immediately prohibiting further processing of the data by the data user. Finally he or she has the right to bring prosecutions in the Magistrates' Court (maximum penalty a fine of £2000) or the Crown Court (maximum penalty an unlimited fine).

Registration

All data users and computer bureaux must register on the relevant forms, available free of charge from all main post offices. The forms are very comprehensive and contain lists of standard purposes, sources, etc., which in practice means a data user has only to tick boxes to complete a registration. If data users fail to register in accordance with the Act, there is an absolute prohibition on their holding and processing personal data via their computers. This is an example of 'strict liability' in criminal law, the proof of possession of a personal data being sufficient to establish guilt. The first prosecution of a company which failed to register by the deadline date resulted in a fine of £500 in February 1988 (registration for a three-year period would have cost £40!)

Each entry on the register must contain the name and address of the data user, a description of the data to be held and of the purposes for which it is to be held; the sources of the information; the persons to whom the information may be disclosed; the countries or territories outside the UK to which the information may be sent; and the address to which data subjects should send their requests for access to the data.

The Act makes it unlawful to hold any data other than that described in the register, or use or collect information from any source other than those ways described, or to disclose to persons other than those detailed in the entry.

Exceptions

There are some exceptions to the Act, and exemptions are granted for one of two reasons:

☐ The data does not pose a threat to the privacy of the individual data subject, so its inclusion would place an unnecessary burden on the data user; or

☐ The interests of the state require that the data is exempt on grounds of national security, proper administration of justice and detection of crime, or the collection of taxes.

Principal exemptions (Ss 26–34, Data Protection Act 1984).

☐ Payroll, pensions and certain accounting data
☐ Names and address files used only for distribution purposes
☐ Data held for statistical and research purposes
☐ Crime and tax data
☐ Text processed data
☐ Certain corporate data
☐ Manual data
☐ National security
☐ Data relating to legal proceedings.

Administrative implications of the Act

The main administrative implications for businesses who wish to comply with this legislation are, firstly to appoint a person within the company to co-ordinate all data protection matters, which includes conducting a census of the personal data used within the company, informing all staff of the implications of the Act, and setting up and maintaining appropriate training programmes. Secondly it is necessary to complete the registration with the Data Protection Registrar, and set up a system for keeping the register entry up to date. Finally a system must be designed for processing requests by data subjects (employees and/or customers), and also to ensure that computerized records relating to individuals are relevant and kept up to date.

Trade unions and industrial relations

The present law relating to trade unions cannot properly be appreciated without studying the long history of the movement, a subject which is outside the scope of this book. A discussion on the wider issues involved in industrial relations legislation and the direction it has taken in the 1980s is offered in the Business in Context text. Here it is intended briefly to summarize the legal aspects relating to collective bargaining, trade union recognition and the rights of an employee to trade union membership as against his or her employer. Continuing the theme of organizational choice and the law, the concluding part of this chapter relates to the legal consequences of an organization choosing to recognize an independent trade union for collective bargaining purposes.

Union

The Employment Protection Act 1975 set out a statutory procedure for trade unions to achieve recognition (Key concept 7.13) by reluctant employers if voluntary recognition was not possible. The Conservative government, however, repealed this statutory procedure by the Employment Act 1980, and once again recognition disputes can now only be resolved voluntarily by the parties. The current Labour Party policy is to restore the statutory method of recognition if and when they are returned to power. This area of law clearly illustrates the 'see-saw' effect of party politics.

Recognition of a union by an employer is an important step for both parties in terms of both legal rights and the development of the bargaining relationship. The legal consequences of recognition (Key concept 7.13) include:

(a) The right of the union to negotiate collective agreements

S.29–30 TULRA 1974 defines a collective agreement as any agreement between union(s) and employer(s) relating to one or more of the following matters:

The business organization must have a strategy with regard to trade unions, as recognition of an independent trade union has legal consequences for the business.	KEY CONCEPT 7.13 **UNION RECOGNITION**

☐ Terms and conditions of employment or the physical conditions in which any workers are required to work
☐ Engagement, non-engagement, termination or suspension of employment of workers
☐ Allocation of work between workers or groups of workers
☐ Disciplinary matters
☐ Workers' union membership or non-membership
☐ Facilities for trade unions
☐ Negotiating, consultative or procedure machinery relating to any of these items, and including trade union recognition.

The legal status of a collective agreement is governed by S.18(1) of TULRA 1974, which provides that a collective agreement:

shall be conclusively presumed not to have been intended by the parties to be a legally enforceable contract unless the agreement:
(a) is in writing, and
(b) contains a provision which (however expressed) states that the parties intend that the agreement shall be a legally enforceable contract.

Thus unless there is a provision to the contrary, a collective agreement is not legally enforceable by the parties to it.

However, as far as the individual employee/trade union member is concerned, the terms of a collective agreement may be incoporated into his or her individual contract of employment, either expressly or by implication.

(b) The right to disclosure of information

Sections 17–21 of the Employment Protection Act 1975 detail that at all stages of collective bargaining it is the duty of an employer to disclose to the representatives of any independent trade union recognized by him, all such information relating to his undertaking without which the representatives would be, to a material extent, impeded in carrying on such collective bargaining, and which it would be in accordance with good industrial relations practice to disclose. If requested by the representatives the information disclosed must be in writing.

The ACAS Code of Practice, 'Disclosure of Information to Trade Unions for Collective Bargaining Purposes', gives examples of what might be disclosed:

☐ Information relating to pay and benefits: pay structure; job evaluation schemes; grading criteria; total pay bill; fringe benefits; non-wage labour costs.
☐ Information on conditions of service: recruitment policies; training; equal opportunity; promotion; health and safety matters.
☐ Information on manpower: age and sex of labour force; labour turnover; absenteeism; manning levels; overtime working; investment plans; changes in working methods.
☐ Information on performance: productivity data; sales; level of order book; rate of return on capital, output figures.
☐ Financial information: gross and net profits; cost structures; assets; liabilities; allocation of profits.

Disclosure of information is not required where it would be contrary to some legislation, would involve a breach of confidence by the employer, or affect a particular individual (unless he or she consents to disclosure) or would cause 'substantial injury' to the employer's undertaking for reasons other than its effect on collective bargaining.

If an employer fails to disclose information, the recognized trade union may apply to the Central Arbitration Committee (CAC). The CAC can ask ACAS to conciliate. If the CAC decides to hear a complaint and finds it proved, it can order the employer to disclose information requested. The CAC may also make a 'one-off' award based on what a settlement would have been had the information been available.

(c) The right to disclosure and consultation on the transfer of a business

Under the Transfer of Undertakings (Protection of Employment) Regulations 1981 there is a duty to inform representatives of recognized trade unions of certain matters about the transfer. These matters include details of when and why the transfer is to take place, the legal, social and economic implications of the transfer for employees, and any measures which may be taken by the transferor or transferee in relation to employees. The employer has a duty to consult with the trade union and consider any representations the union may make. If the employer rejects any such representations he or she must give his reasons for doing so.

(d) The right of consultation in case of redundancies

The Employment Protection Act 1975 introduced a new procedure for handling redundancies by an employer who recognized a trade union for collective bargaining purposes. He or she must consult relevant unions about all proposed redundancies before any employee is actually made redundant. This consultation must take place whether or not the intended redundant workers are union members, and even though the individuals concerned may not be qualified to receive a redundancy payment. The Act says that the consultations shall take place at the 'earliest opportunity', and specifies certain minimum periods for consultations depending on the numbers to be made redundant. It also gives the trade union(s) the right to receive certain information which must be disclosed by the employer.

Failure to consult by the employer may result in a 'protective award' being made by the industrial tribunal which will in effect extend the individual's contract of employment by up to a maximum of 90 days (depending on numbers involved).

Central Arbitration Committee (CAC) The CAC replaced the Industrial Arbitration Board in 1975, being set up by the Employment Protection Act 1975. It consists of a chairman and representatives of both sides of industry, and its work consists mainly of making awards under the provisions relating to disclosure of information for collective bargaining purposes, hearing references relating to collective agreements and Wages Councils awards which may contravene the Equal Pay Act 1970 (as amended) and voluntary arbitration of disputes.

Union membership agreements (closed shops)

Current legislation requires that all closed shop agreements are 'approved'. Approval requires that the union(s) holds a secret ballot every five years and secures the support of at least 80% of those affected by the agreement, or 85% of those voting. A ballot on a closed shop has, so far as is reasonably practicable, to be conducted in such a way that all those entitled to vote can do so, and are able to vote in secret. Guidance on the organization and conduct of ballots is contained in the Code of Practice, 'Closed Shop Agreements and Arrangements' (1983), issued by the Secretary of State for Employment under the powers conferred on him or her by S.3 Employment Act 1980. Since the 1988 Employment Act a closed shop is no longer enforceable, i.e. any industrial action to support a closed shop is unlawful, as is any dismissal for refusing to join a trade union. There are proposals now to outlaw the closed shop altogether, as has already been done in some other countries.

Trade union membership and individual rights

The E.P.(C) Act 1978 as amended (unless otherwise stated) confers the following rights on all employees.

☐ A right not to be dismissed for 'trade unions reasons', i.e. for being a member of, or wishing to join, an independent trade union, or having joined for participation in reasonable trade union activity at an appropriate time (S.58(1)).

☐ A right not to be dismissed, or have action short of dismissal taken against him or her for refusing to join a 'non-independent' trade union (S.58(1)). Actions short of dismissal which might be held to infringe employee's rights include such matters as disciplinary measures, docking of pay or benefits, unjustified refusal of promotion, training or job transfer, and threats of dismissal or redundancy (S.23(1) and (6)).

☐ A right to 'reasonable' time off work to take part in trade union activity, or if an official of an independent recognized trade union, to carry out 'industrial relations activities' and approved training (S.27(1)).

☐ A right to all the time off work necessary, with pay, to fulfill his or her functions if he or she is a duly appointed safety representative (Safety Representative and Safety Committees Regulations 1977).

☐ A right not to be unreasonably excluded or expelled from membership of a trade union which is a party to a closed shop agreement with his or her employer or prospective employer (S.4 Employment Act 1980).

Recent legislation (e.g. Employment Acts 1980, 1982 and 1988, and the Trade Union Act 1984) has dramatically affected the legal relationship between employers and trade unions, between trade unions and their members, and as a consequence between trade union and trade unions.

A very brief summary of the new rights given to individuals and to employers under this new legislation illustrates how power has been taken from the unions and put into the hands of the members, and at the same time increased the rights of the employers.

(a) Employment Act 1980

Individuals given:

☐ Protection against dismissal or discrimination for non-union membership in a closed shop in the case of strongly held personal convictions.

Employers given:

- ☐ Freedom to decide for themselves whether or not to recognize trade unions.
- ☐ Right to restrain unlawful picketing.
- ☐ Right to restrain indiscriminate secondary action.
- ☐ Freedom from inappropriate restrictions in determining pay levels.

(b) Employment Act 1982

Individuals given:

- ☐ Increased protection and compensation if dismissed because of a closed shop.

Employers given:

- ☐ Freedom to take legal action for injunctions and damages against trade unions.
- ☐ Right to restrain industrial action which is not about employment-related disputes between workers and their employer.
- ☐ Right to restrain secondary action intended to establish or maintain labour-only contracts.

(c) Trade Union Act 1984

Individuals given:

- ☐ Right to regular ballots to decide whether their union should undertake political activities.
- ☐ Right to elect by secret ballot all voting members of their union's executive.

Employers given:

- ☐ Right to restrain industrial action unless there has been a properly conducted secret ballot.

(d) Employment Act 1988

Individuals given:

- ☐ Right to restrain their union from calling any industrial action not supported by a properly conducted secret ballot.
- ☐ Protection against dismissal for non-union membership in all circumstances.
- ☐ Right to inspect their union's accounting records.
- ☐ Protection against unjustifiable discipline by their union, including working during a strike action.
- ☐ Right to elect all principal union leaders by secret postal ballot under independent scrutiny.
- ☐ Right to take legal action against trustees if they permit union funds to be used unlawfully.
- ☐ Right to apply to the Commissioner for the Rights of Trade Union Members for assistance in taking certain court proceedings against their trade union.

Employers given

☐ Right to restrain industrial action intended to establish or maintain any closed shop practice.

This complex area of trade union law cannot, unfortunately, be explored in depth in this book; the further reading section, however, contains references to specialist books in this area of law.

Summary

This has been a long and complex chapter covering many aspects of law which relate most closely to the operation of the personnel function within an organization, and affecting the way in which a personnel manager has to operate. The review of the law relating to recruitment and selection illustrated the constraints now placed upon employers when advertising jobs, seeking applications from potential employees, short-listing and interviewing candidates, and taking up of employment and character references.

Once employees have been engaged the law demands certain written particulars be given to all full-time workers outlining the main terms and conditions of their employment, and recent legislation has imposed a 'basic floor of rights' for all employees. These include minimum rights relating to time off work, maternity leave, etc. The chapter also suggested that UK law could be altered considerably by proposed EEC Directives which, whilst acceptable to most European states, are objected to most strongly by the current UK government. A quick review of maternity law in Bulgaria illustrated that even the EEC has a long way to go to catch up with Eastern European standards.

The chapter then examined the law relating to the termination of employment, especially in relation to unfair dismissal and redundancy, and concluded with an examination of the effect of trade union recognition on company policies regarding, amongst other things, collective bargaining, disclosure of information and closed shop arrangements.

Further reading

J. Bowers, *A Practical Approach to Employment Law* (Financial Training Ltd) – a good practical employment law book, perhaps too detailed for business students in some areas. Another excellent textbook is R. Lewis, *Labour Law in Britain* (Blackwell). S. Anderman, *The Law of Unfair Dismissal* (Butterworths) – the leading book on unfair dismissal, but sometimes too academic. An easier book (and more up to date) is M. Mead, *Unfair Dismissals Handbook* (Oyez Longman). There are several cases and materials books but perhaps the best is P. Benedictus and B. Bercusson, *Labour Law: Cases and Materials* (Sweet and Maxwell). Other books covering parts of this chapter include N. Savage and C. Edwards, *A Guide to The Data Protection Act 1984* (Financial Training Ltd), D. Pannick, *Sex Discrimination Law* (Clarendon Press) and F.P. Davidson, *A Guide to The Wages Act 1986* (Financial Training Ltd) and B. Perrins, *Trade Union Law* (Butterworths). A good revision book for this chapter is Holmes and Painter, *Employment Law* (Blackstone Press Ltd) which is one of the SWOT series of law books. R.

Kidner, *Statutes on Employment Law* (Blackstone Press Ltd) and Bowers and Auerbach, *The Employment Act 1988* (Blackstone Press Ltd) are up-to-date books regarding the new employment and trade union legislation.

Exercises

1. Consider these examples of actual advertisements from national and local newspapers in 1987; are they lawful advertisements, and, if not, how would you propose to re-draft them in order to comply with relevant legislation?

   Van Driver/Person – Clean driving licence and automotive battery or motor experience essential, age 20–23 years old. Apply by telephone . . .

   DESIGN DRAUGHTSMAN. We are looking for an experienced Design Draughtsman for our Plymouth factory. The ideal candidate will be aged 22–35 and be qualified in pattern cutting, draughtsmanship, or the field of graphics and design.

   ***** HOTEL, London. Two Chambermaids required urgently, with experience, wages negotiable, please telephone for interview.

2. Read the following cases, materials and article, and then discuss the legal status and business relevance of the written particulars of employment: *Robertson and Jackson* v. *British Gas Corporation* (1983) I.R.L.R. 302, *System Floors (UK) Ltd* v. *Daniel* (1981) I.R.L.R. 475, *Mears* v. *Safecar Security Ltd* (1982) I.R.L.R. 183; Article: 'Written Particulars of Employment' I.R.L.I.B. 269, 20/11/84 pp. 2–10.

3. Jim was employed as a shop assistant in a town centre branch of a local store. Pedestrianization of the centre resulted in a loss of business and several members of staff were made redundant. Shortly afterwards the manager left to work for another company. Jim was then promoted to store manager but after only four months was dismissed because he had made several silly and a few very expensive mistakes.

   With reference to decided cases discuss the industrial tribunal's likely attitude to Jim's dismissal.

4. By reference to the relevant sections of the Data Protection Act 1984 define the following: (a) data; (b) data subject; (c) data user; (d) computer bureau; (e) processing; (f) data protection principles.

5. Professor Kahn-Freund has said, 'The content of the contract of service remains in a state of uncertainty. It is still not unusual to find the parties to such a contract have failed to settle expressly many important points'.

   In the event of a dispute what sources of contractual terms may be available to determine the rights of the parties?

6. The UK has the lowest rates of return to work for women following childbirth in the EEC. Discuss the ways in which our current law is designed to assist a female to return to work after childbirth. Do you consider that improvements should be made in our law along the lines of the other EEC states, or even Eastern European countries?

8 The finance function

Introduction

When a business organization is created it will require finance. This will come from one of three main sources; the owner's private capital, bank loans, or share issue. Once established the same mechanisms are used, plus internally generated funds.

In this chapter we will be considering, in outline, the ways and means by which this finance is attracted and administered. We will not be attempting to provide a description of business accounting, that is the purpose of another book in this series. We shall first consider different forms of capital and the use of credit including factoring. The new provisions on wrongful trading will be outlined and we will then conclude with an outline of the law relating to business insurance, because whilst there are significant problems and risks which entrepreneurs will have no choice but to shoulder themselves, there are others which they may well be able to transfer to their insurers.

Share capital or contributed capital

When a registered company is created a Memorandum of Association is necessary. We considered this in Chapter 3 of this book. Each of the subscribers to this document is required, under the Companies Act 1985, to take at least one share in the new business enterprise. One of the sources of business finance, therefore, is known as 'contributed' capital. As a proportion of the whole, however, it is not a massive amount – about 12% of capital for new companies is obtained in this way. Incidentally, figures such as this can be checked each year by consulting the Financial Statistics, an information source which is available in most reference libraries.

Every company limited by shares must state in its memorandum the number of shares with which it proposes to be registered, and the nominal value of those shares. The total value is called the share capital and it sets the maximum number of shares (Key concept 8.1) which that company may issue. In practice, however, the company will only issue the number of shares necessary to provide the initial working capital required.

The nominal value of a plc's issued capital must be at least £50 000 (Chapter 3); there is no minimum for a private company. The nominal value of shares is usually fixed at £1, but this is not a reflection of its true value; it simply means the liability of the shareholder is limited to that £1 if

The most common division between shares is into ordinary shares and preference shares:

KEY CONCEPT 8.1

ORDINARY AND PREFERENCE SHARES

Ordinary shares
Full voting rights
Equal rights to profits

Share of surplus assets on winding up of company

Preference shares
Limited voting rights
Right to a fixed dividend expressed as percentage of nominal value
Preference to payment of dividend and repayment of capital on winding up of company.

the company folds for any reason. The nominal value is also used as a base for calculating dividends.

Value of shares

The real value of shares =

$$\frac{\text{net assets of company} - \text{repayment of outstanding debts}}{\text{total number of shares}}$$

This real value is, however, subject to several variable factors, including:

☐ *Capital cover*, i.e. the extent to which a company's net assets are sufficient to repay the share capital to the shareholders.
☐ *Dividend yields*, i.e. the proportion of dividend paid to the price of shares (e.g. if a company retains a high proportion of its profits and therefore distributes only a small dividend, the value of the shares may fall).
☐ *Actual earnings or profits*. Usually the higher the profits the greater the value of the shares.
☐ *Marketability*, which includes such things as personality of directors, corporate image, chances of reselling the shares, etc.

Since the decision in *Trevor* v. *Whitworth* (1889) it has been accepted that a company cannot buy its own shares. This has since been confirmed in S.143 Companies Act 1985. Gower has explained the rationale of the rule as follows:

Such acquisitions are dangerous, not only because they might result in the reduction of capital yardstick to the detriment of the creditors, but also because, if the company paid more than the true worth of the shares, it would dilute the value of the remainder while, if it paid too little, it would increase the value of the remainder and might be used by the directors to enhance the value of their own holdings. Moreover, such purchases might be used by the directors to maintain themselves in control.

Companies are only allowed to purchase their own shares under strictly controlled circumstances (Companies Act 1985, SS. 158–178) and these shares then become cancelled. The Green Paper, 'The Purchase by a

Company of its Own Shares' [1980] Cmnd. 7944, lists the advantages of allowing this facility as follows:

(a) It may enable the company to buy out a dissident shareholder;
(b) It facilitates the retention of family control;
(c) It provides a means whereby a shareholder, or the estate of a deceased shareholder, in a company whose shares are not listed can find a buyer;
(d) It is particularly useful in relation to employee share schemes in enabling the shares of employees to be re-purchased on their ceasing to be employed by the company;
(e) It may help with the marketing of shares by enabling the company to give a subscriber an option to re-sell to the company;
(f) It enables companies to purchase their shares for use later in stock option plans or acquisition programmes;
(g) if redeemable shares are quoted at below the redemption price it enables a company to save money by buying up in advance of the redemption date (a practice which our companies can, and do, adopt in the case of debentures but cannot in the case of redeemable preference shares);
(h) It permits the evolution of the open-ended investment company or mutual fund instead of having to operate through the mechanism of a unit trust;
(i) It provides a company with surplus cash with a further means of using it advantageously;
(j) It can be used to support the market for the shares if this is thought to be unduly depressed, thus preserving for the shareholders the value of their shares as marketable securities;
(k) If the company not only buys its shares but trades in the treasury shares thus acquired it may make money thereby.

Loan (or debt) capital

A similar proportion of finance is obtained from banks, as is raised from share, or contributed capital. Long-term loans are important as a source of financial support for new businesses, and these comprise what is known as loan, or 'debt' capital. In contrast to share capital there are fewer formal restrictions on the amount which a company can raise by way of loans. However, the problem with bank borrowing is that banks generally require a fixed and/or floating charge, and even personal guarantees from directors.

There may be a limitation on the ability of a company to raise funds by the issue of debentures (Chapter 3), and a loan represents a debt against the company, giving contractual rights to the lender, but not membership of the company as is given to the shareholder. In the event of a winding up of the company the holder of a debenture ranks alongside other creditors and is entitled to be repaid in full before capital is returned to the shareholders (*Salomon* v. *Salomon and Co. Ltd* and Chapter 3).

It is usual for the lender to require some form of security for the loan; he thus becomes a 'secured creditor' and thereby is entitled to the benefit of

Debenture A debenture is a document which creates or acknowledges a debt. The issue of debentures is the most usual form of borrowing by a company. Debenture holders are not members of the company, they are creditors.

Fixed charge This is a form of mortgage of distinct assets, e.g. land or heavy machinery, against which a loan is made.

Floating charge This involves a form of mortgage secured against the assets of the organization in general. It crystallizes or attaches to specific property only when the company needs to repay its debts.

Mortgage A form of real security where the borrower (mortgagor) normally retains possession of the property mortgaged but grants a right over the property to the lender (mortgagee).

the security in the event of a winding up of the company (Chapter 3). Secured creditors will take preference over unsecured creditors, such as normal trade creditors. An increasing proportion of corporate working capital is provided by borrowing from banks by way of overdraft facilities or fixed-term bank loans. Banks are, naturally, prudent and will therefore always insist on some form of security over corporate assets, or a personal guarantee from the directors.

The basic right of a creditor to demand security, and thus obtain priority over the creditors in the event of a winding up, is a matter of contract. As Lord MacNaughton said in *Salomon* v. *A. Salomon and Co. Ltd*:

> Every creditor is entitled to get and hold the best security the law allows him to take.

Company objects and borrowing

In *General Auction Estate and Monetary Co.* v. *Smith* [1891] 3 Ch. 432; S., a director, had lent money to the company and during the compulsory winding up of the company the liquidator argued that, as the objects of the company did not mention borrowing, the transaction with S. was *ultra vires* and therefore void. It was held that a 'trading company' (which this company was) must have an implied power to borrow money as reasonably incidental to the attainment of its objects.

In practice today objects clauses of all companies contain an express power to borrow money. A power to borrow, whether express or implied, carries with it by a further implication of law a power to give security for the loan, and to pay interest upon it. Again most companies would have express power for so doing, though this express power cannot override the Companies Act 1985 (e.g. S.120 makes it unlawful to charge the company's reserve capital).

Companies must have the capacity to enter into a particular transaction, which must be to pursue an object of the company as stated in its memorandum (Companies Act 1985, S.2(1)(c)).	KEY CONCEPT 8.2 ***ULTRA VIRES –*** **'BEYOND THE POWERS OF'**

Borrowing which is in excess of the company's powers renders the loan *ultra vires* and therefore void (Key concept 8.2) (*Fountaine* v. *Carmarthen Rail Co.* (1868) and *Re Introductions Ltd* (1969)). Any security given on such a loan is also void and cannot thereafter be ratified by resolution in general meeting, as per *Ashbury Railway Co.* v. *Riche* (1875). This does not mean, however, that there is no possibility of relief for the lender in such a situation. There could be remedy in the following cases:

☐ A guarantor of the company's obligation might be liable depending on the wording of his or her guarantee: *Garrard* v. *James* (1925).

☐ Directors who negotiated the transaction might be liable to the third party for breach of warranty of authority, i.e. appearing to have authority he did not in fact have deceit or negligent misstatement, provided the representation was in respect of fact and not law: *Collen* v. *Wright* (1857).

☐ Any payment could be recovered if it is possible to trace it in equity: *Sinclair* v. *Brougham* (1914).

☐ By subrogation. If the money is used to pay off an 'intra vires' loan the ultra vires lender has the right to 'stand in the shoes' of the intra vires creditor: Wrexham, Mold & Conah's Quay Railway Co (1899).

Tracing A process in equity which enables a person claiming property in one form to claim other property into which the original has been transformed, e.g. money, resulting from a sale.

Who can plead ultra vires?
1. The company;
2. the other party to the transaction;
3. a shareholder;
4. a debenture holder (other creditors generally cannot).

In November 1989, major City banks were caught unprepared by a High Court order declaring interest deals made by Hammersmith and Fulham Council with ratepayers' money *ultra vires* their powers as local authorities and therefore illegal and void, leaving the banks to bear the losses.

Retained profits and trade credit

Once the business has started trading it will (hopefully) generate profits, and these will be used, in whole or in part, as a source of internal finance as well as being distributed in the form of dividends to company members.

Trade credit of various kinds is important too. For example, delaying payment for goods and services which are bought in, and demanding payment in advance for products to be supplied. However, this can be unreliable because it will be affected by the pressures on other traders from their creditors in turn.

Hire purchase is also used by companies, but the cost is high. Expensive equipment is often hired rather than purchased. The plant hire trade is increasingly important, as are organizations which deal in the leasing of motor vehicles.

Many smaller companies are sometimes undercapitalized and, as a result, have to fight a daily battle against strained cash flow. This problem is made worse by the traditionally late payment of accounts by customers, whilst suppliers are demanding earlier payment of monies owing to them. The usual result of all this is ever-increasing overdrafts.

In recent times a new industry has emerged to help in this situation, that of credit-factoring (Key concept 8.3) Factors will make available to clients up to 80% of good trade debts outstanding, at a discount charge calculated on a day-to-day basis at normal overdraft rates. The unique quality of factoring is that funds increase automatically as sales grow; cash is therefore

KEY CONCEPT 8.3	Many companies factor their trade debts. That is, they deal with a credit factor who will 'buy' their debts, so that the company receives payment in advance, but at a discount. The factor will then collect the debts in full.
CREDIT FACTORING	

available to the client company to increase stocks, gain supplier discounts for prompt payment, and chase after new orders with the knowledge that they can be financed.

The factor is a company whose systems are entirely geared to the collection of monies owing; they are specialists, and usually shorten the collection period for debts. The average 'debt-turn' among the ten member companies of the Association of British Factors in 1989 was just 63 days. This shortening of the period when monies are outstanding obviously saves a great deal in borrowing costs alone for client companies.

The factor is not a high-pressure debt collection agency; its role is to act as the client's accounts department, operating strictly within the credit policy agreed by the client when they entered into the contract with the factor.

Export factoring is becoming more important today as '1992' rapidly approaches, and offers the exporter an alternative to the more traditional instruments of international trade. UK factors are developing relationships with similar factoring companies abroad who are experts in their own domestic market, thereby easing the problem of foreign debt collection. The features of export factoring are:

☐ The factor will relieve the exporter of the need to maintain a full sales ledger often in varying currencies, but the exporter will still have the benefit of up-to-date reports on the state of his or her clients' accounts.
☐ Credit control and collection of payments will be done locally in the language of the buyers.
☐ Resultant improvement in amount of credit taken should improve cash flow and reduce the amount and cost of finance required.
☐ Exporter will have 100% protection against bad debts on credit-approved accounts.

A factor will normally charge his clients in two ways:

☐ An administrative charge which relates to the service elements of factoring – sales ledger administration, credit control and protection against customer insolvency – and is usually calculated as a percentage of the total turnover managed by the factor;
☐ A discounting charge comparable to bank overdraft interest charges, which is applied to the advanced payments made to the client against invoices issued.

Most of the large clearing banks operate a factoring service.

Wrongful trading

Reference was made in Chapter 3 to Directors, but space does not permit a full discussion of directors' responsibilities and liabilities. One area of law which is very relevant to the running of a company, especially in regard to the raising of finance and proper running of the operations to prevent increasing debt, is that of 'wrongful trading' (Key concept 8.4).

The term 'shadow director' means 'a person in accordance with whose directions or instructions the directors are accustomed to act (S.741(2) Companies Act 1985). However, a person is not deemed to be a shadow

---

KEY CONCEPT 8.4

WRONGFUL TRADING

Although the company is normally considered a separate legal identity (*Salomon* v. *Salomon and Co. Ltd*), the Insolvency Act 1986 now allows the court to lift the veil of incorporation and to make a director, or shadow director, personally liable to contribute to the assets of the company if the director knew or ought to have known that the financial position of the company was precarious and insolvency was possible but nevertheless continued to trade without taking every step he or she ought to minimize potential losses to the company's creditors.

---

director merely because the directors act on advice given by him or her in a professional capacity.

A shadow director is therefore a person or body who exerts sufficient control over a company to be regarded as a director. This may include a bank requiring a company to improve its financial ratios, a management consultant implementing a policy of rationalization, an institutional investor instructing a board to develop the company in a particular manner, etc. All could be required to contribute to the company's assets on its insolvency.

Directors need not have an intention of cheating or defrauding creditors to be made subject to a court order for wrongful trading. Directors do not have automatically to cease trading immediately. Insolvent liquidation becomes probable, because if a company can continue to trade profitably in the short term, it should do so in order to reduce the loss to creditors at the time of winding up.

If directors believe that their co-directors are not acting responsibly, they should make their views known, otherwise they will not be taking

---

CASE STUDY 8.1

WRONGFUL TRADING: RE PRODUCE MARKET CONSORTIUM LTD

Two directors of Produce Marketing Consortium were ordered to contribute £75 000 (plus interest and costs) towards the company's debts. Their error was continuing to trade for some twelve months after they should have known that the company's insolvency was inevitable. They would have known this had the company's accounts been drawn up within the statutory time limits. They also continued to trade after being warned by the auditors of the risks of wrongful trading.

During this period the company's bank maintained its support, relying on unrealistic projections produced by the directors, and its request to reduce the overdraft was effectively financed by increased credit from the company's main supplier. The business collapsed when the bank and the supplier finally lost patience.

The law requires that directors take every step to minimize the loss to creditors, and clearly the directors of Produce Marketing failed to do this, as they continued trading and incurring credit for some twelve months after they should have closed down the company.

Halls v. *David* (*Re Produce Marketing Consortium Ltd* [1989])

'every step' to minimize loss. Although it will be difficult to convince a liquidator or the court that every step was taken to minimize creditors' losses, there are a number of measures which a prudent director should take to reduce wrongful trading risks, including:

☐ Ensuring that accurate financial information is produced and monitored.
☐ Ensuring that board meetings are regularly held and records of board decisions are kept with minutes of the discussions.
☐ Obtaining outside professional advice immediately from the company's auditors, management consultants and solicitors, if there are any doubts as to the company's viability.
☐ Setting out the responsibility of each director in writing, so that there is no doubt as to what specific matters each is responsible for.
☐ Taking particular care when companies owe considerable monies to the Crown, e.g. in PAYE, national insurance or VAT.

In the Produce Marketing case (Case study 8.1) the court accepted that directors in a small business having a number of different functions and operating simple accounting procedures could not be expected to have the same knowledge, skill and experience as a director in a multi-national plc with sophisticated resources. Nevertheless, the law does require a company director to show reasonable diligence in fulfilling the tasks allocated to him or her by the company, and directors having special skills are to be judged by the skills they actually have.

If a liquidator is of the opinion that the director has failed to meet the required standard he or she can make an application to the court to have him or her contribute to the company's assets available for distribution to its creditors. The court has a discretion as to whether to make such an order, and if it does, as to what amount shall be contributed.

If such a court order is made against a director this in turn could lead to the director being disqualified under the Company Directors Disqualification Act 1986, from being:

☐ a director of a company; or
☐ a liquidator or administrator of a company; or
☐ a receiver or manager of a company's property; or
☐ in any way, directly or indirectly, concerned in the promotion, formation or management of a company.

Insurance and the business enterprise

There is a wide variety of risks which are inevitable within the operation of a business enterprise. The careful businessman or woman will try to transfer as much of this burden as he or she can. Sometimes this can be done by contract (excluding certain liabilities) or by paying someone else to cover his losses: this means insurance.

Insurance began with the transfer of marine risks. Today, however, the businessman or woman will wish to lay off as many kinds of potential losses as he or she can. They can insure against fire, burglary, product liability, public liability, for motor vehicles, accident or industrial tribunal claims, legal costs, even the losses which might be sustained through the activities of dishonest employees (called 'fidelity' cover). Most businesses which trade in professional services of one kind or another, such as lawyers, accountants, surveyors, consultants, etc., acquire insurance against professional negligence and some are required to have cover by law (Professional Indemnity Insurance: Case study 8.2). These policies often carry 'excess' clauses, under which the insured would have to pay the first, say, £1000 of any claim and, perhaps, an exclusion of cover for such claims as defamation.

There are also certain risks which the business has no choice but to insure against, such as those arising from injuries to employees, a duty imposed by the Employers' Liability (Compulsory Insurance) Act 1969, and third party death or personal injuries in connection with road traffic accidents, under the Road Traffic Act 1972 (as amended).

There are a number of technical terms peculiar to insurance which we shall explain in context.

| CASE STUDY 8.2 PROFESSIONAL INDEMNITY INSURANCE (FIMBRA CASE) | A controversial scheme, due to start today, to make all financial advisers registered with the Financial Intermediaries, Brokers and Managers Regulatory Association (Fimbra) take out standard professional indemnity insurance has collapsed in disarray. |

Fimbra called an emergency council meeting yesterday to abort the whole excerise when it became clear the underwriters were not offering cover as wide-ranging as Fimbra and the broker, Pointon York Vos, had first believed.

Alec Sharp, the Lloyd's underwriter, wrote a week ago: 'We do not consider ourselves bound by the slip originally scratched on 31 August 1989'.

Fimbra had asked several brokers to tender for the contract to provide professional indemnity (PI) insurance, which would be mandatory for all Fimbra members. This was to provide cover for a minimum of £100 000, as well as meeting claims arising from the rulings of the Investment Referee. The referee has the power to make awards of £50 000 per claimant.

The misunderstanding arose over so-called class actions, where many people are in the same position and one ruling might cover numerous cases.

Fimbra believed that each investor should be covered to the limit of the award made on their behalf, while the underwriters shrank from this and limited cover to £50 000 per case.

Mr. Richard Youard, the referee, has complete discretion over which cases he hears and which he decides would be better handled by the courts.

He could hear a Barlow Clowes-type case involving hundreds of investors, but in practice he would be more likely to allow the law to take over the case. Mr. Geoffrey Pointon, of Pointon York Vos, said he was 'astonished' that Fimbra should halt the scheme at the last minute.

In hurried negotiations he offered a cap of £1 million for each event, but Fimbra was determined to get insurance without limit to cover the referee's awards.

The whole idea of forcing brokers to join a compulsory scheme is unpopular among many Fimbra members.

The 3500-member British Insurance and Investment Brokers' Association, whose members already have PI, opposed it and the Insurance Brokers Registration Council had gathered 1750 signatures calling for an end to the scheme.

Mr. Pointon believed Fimbra found it convenient to dump the scheme and blame the underwriter and broker rather than back down in face of opposition.

(*Source:* Vivien Goldsmith, 'Fimbra insurance scheme collapses: watchdog acts after underwriters place limit on indemnity claims',

The Times, 1 November 1989)

Indemnity and contingency insurance cover

There is a basic distinction within the legal framework of insurance. It divides 'indemnity' insurance cover from 'contingency' cover.

Indemnity insurance is designed to protect the business against loss from such calamities as fires, storms and burglaries. With insurance of this kind, the measure of the loss that has been sustained becomes the measure of the payment which will be made provided adequate cover was taken. That is, the insurers will see to it that the business does not actually lose at all.

Contingency insurance, on the other hand, is not intended to provide quite the same kind of protection. With this type of cover a set amount is paid upon the happening of a stipulated event; so much for a death, so much for the loss of a leg, so much if an event is 'rained-off', etc. The measure of the payment is pre-set in the policy; it does not necessarily reflect the loss sustained.

The contract of insurance

Insurance contracts (Key concept 8.5) are part of the normal law of contract, discussed in detail in Chapter 2. There are three essential elements to a contract of insurance:

KEY CONCEPT 8.5

INSURANCE AND ASSURANCE

There is a distinction which is sometimes drawn between the terms 'insurance' and 'assurance'. Insurance implies cover against something that might happen, such as damage by fire, or liability for defective products and having to compensate an injured consumer, for example. Whereas assurance arises where the insurer will pay the 'assured' or his or her representatives an amount when an inevitable event occurs, such as the death of the assured. There is, however, a trend towards these terms being used synonymously.

(a) Consideration

The insurer undertakes to pay out upon the occurrence of an event stipulated in the contract, in exchange for the policy holder's consideration, which normally takes the form of a single or periodical payment, called the 'premium'. Premiums are usually re-assessed each year to take into account inflation, any claims for the previous year and the current market forces.

(b) Uncertainty

An insurance contract must involve some degree of uncertainty. This might be as to whether or not the stipulated event will happen (e.g. damage by fire), or if it is bound to happen (e.g. death) about the date upon which it will happen. This may seem to suggest the insurance contract resembles a wager: 'I bet you that your factory will not burn down this year, and the stake in this bet is the agreed premium'.

The law normally frowns upon wagers (Key concept 8.6), although they are not illegal in themselves. Generally a wager is void (Gaming Act 1845, S.18) so that neither party can sue the other should the loser not pay up (Chapter 2).

KEY CONCEPT 8.6	'A wagering contract is one by which two persons professing to hold opposite views touching the issue of a future uncertain event, mutually agree that, dependent upon the determination of that event, one shall win from the other, and that other shall pay or hand over to him, a sum of money or other stake; neither of the contracting parties having any other interest in that contract than the sum or stake he will so win or lose, there being no other real consideration for the making of such contract by either of the parties.' (*Carlill* v. *Carbolic Smoke Ball Co.* [1892] 2 Q.B. 484 at 490, per Hawkins J.)
WAGERING CONTRACTS	

A wager may be on a present or past event when there is uncertainty in the parties' knowledge. Each party must stand to win or lose.

(c) Insurable interest

The uncertain event which is necessary to make the contract one of insurance, rather than a wager, must be an event which is prima facie adverse to the interests of the insured, that is, it would cause him or her loss or impose a liability upon him or her. If there is nothing to lose then the contract is probably not a contract of insurance.

In *Department of Trade* v. *St Christopher Motorists' Association Ltd* [1976] 1 W.I.R. 99 each member of the association paid an annual sum so that if an event occurred which prevented the member from driving, e.g. disqualification or injury, the member had the right to be provided with a chauffeur (and if necessary a car as well) for up to 40 hours per week for a maximum of 12 months. The Department of Trade contended that the association was carrying on an insurance business and was thereby subject to the Insurance Companies Act 1958 (then in force).

There was no difference in substance between the association paying for a chauffeur for a member and its agreeing to pay the member the cost of him providing his own chauffeur. It was therefore held that the contracts between the association and its members were contracts of insurance and insurance business was being carried on.

The contract of insurance is based upon the information given by the parties. From the insured's point of view this will be the responses written on the standard form (called the proposal form) which is normally provided. The answers on the proposal form will provide the prospective insurer with the information necessary to decide whether to accept the risk at all, and if the risk is to be carried, at what level to set the premium. It is, therefore, a crucially important document (*March Cabaret Club and Casino* v. *London Assurance* (1975)). As a matter of contract law, the form is an invitation to treat (Chapter 2). It is not an offer to insure, even if the rates the prospective insurer normally charges are included on the form.

When completing the proposal form the proposer (i.e. the person seeking insurance) is under a duty to disclose all material facts (Key concept 8.7). Such contracts as these are called *uberrimae fidei*, that is, they are contracts 'of the utmost good faith'. The failure to disclose any material fact will render the contract voidable at the option of the insurer (Chapter 2). This means, of course, that the insurer can simply refuse to honour his or her obligations under the deal and refuse to pay out if and when the specified event occurs.

In *Roselodge Ltd* v. *Castle* [1962] 2 Lloyd's Rep. 113 diamond merchants insured their diamonds against all risks. They failed to disclose that their sales manager had been convicted eight years before in America for smuggling diamonds into the USA, since they considered the fact to be immaterial. Later the director of the diamond merchants was robbed of diamonds with violence, and the merchants made a claim under their insurance policy. The insurers refused to pay out. The court held that the manager's offence and conviction were material facts and should have been disclosed; the claim was therefore dismissed.

It is common practice for a warning about non-disclosure of material facts to be included on the proposal form, together with a statement to the effect that if there is any doubt as to whether or not any particular fact is material, then it should be disclosed anyway. The standard forms generally used request information on matters which have been found to have been material to that particular type of policy in the past.

There is probably no duty to disclose matters which would reduce the risk, for example, failure to disclose the existence of a guard dog patrol when seeking burglary insurance, or a sprinkler system when seeking fire

---

A material fact is one which would have affected the deliberations of the insurer in determining whether or not to take the risk. The test of materiality is an objective test, and, if need be a court will decide whether or not any particular fact was a material fact.

KEY CONCEPT 8.7

A MATERIAL FACT IN AN INSURANCE CONTRACT

insurance. It is unlikely, however, that a careful businessman or woman would have forgotten to mention matters which may reduce the premium payable.

Obviously, if an accurate statement is made which later becomes incorrect through changed circumstances, particularly if the contract has yet to be finalized, then there is a duty to disclose the changes, otherwise again the contract will be voidable.

Averaging

There is a real danger for business people who are casual about the value they assign to risks they seek to insure. This danger lies in the notion of 'averaging'. If a risk is under-insured, then the insurer will be limited in his liability to the extent of the declared risk.

Thus in the case of buildings insurance, if the policy discloses a total maximum loss of, say, £100 000, whereas the total loss should have been £200 000, then if a loss occurs the insurer will be limited to £100 000 maximum. However, if there is an averaging clause in the policy (and there usually is), the insurer will be entitled to regard the insured as carrying the risk associated with 50% of the value of the premises. Thus, if a loss worth £50 000 were sustained, the insurer would only have to pay out 50% of the loss, i.e. £25 000. The careful businessman or woman obtains professional advice about the nature and extent of insurable losses, and he or she does so from a professional with professional negligence insurance.

Subrogation

Another important principle of insurance law for the business enterprise is 'subrogation'. This is where the insurer 'steps into the shoes' of the insured when he or she has indemnified the insured against all his or her loss. If the business loses a vehicle in a crash as the result of the fault of the other driver, and then claims against their insurer, they will generally be paid: the insurer will then proceed against the other driver in the same way as the insured could have done had he or she chosen not to claim under his or her policy. The insurer is placed in (subrogated to) the insured's position with regard to rights against third parties.

Subrogation does not apply to life assurance nor to personal accident policies. It applies only to what were described above as indemnity policies. Indeed, subrogation goes hand in hand with indemnity. If the insurer carries the losses sustained by the business so that the business does not actually lose at all, then it follows that if subrogation did not apply, the business could still sue the third party involved and make a profit out of the disaster!

Summary

In this chapter we have considered the financial aspects of setting up, running and liquidating a business, including a brief summary of the new area of law, wrongful trading, and the liability of directors of a company in regard to the raising of finance and proper running of its operations to prevent increasing debt. The chapter concluded with a summary of the law relating to business insurance, whereby a careful businessman or woman will try to transfer as much risk as they can in the running of their business to another person or company.

Further reading

Students will find the general texts in the company law field of use with this chapter; they vary from the inexpensive such as: Charlesworth and Cain, *Company Law* (Sweet and Maxwell) and Farrar, *Company Law* (Butterworths), to the very expensive but very detailed, Gower, *Modern Company Law* (Sweet and Maxwell) and Pennington, *Company Law* (Butterworths). Easier books to read include M.C.Oliver, *Company Law* (M and E Handbooks), and Keenan and Riches, *Business Law* (Pitman). A good revision aid is C. Ryan, *Company Law: A Revision Aid* (ICSA).

It may also be of use to consider the more specialist texts, such as: Bates and Holly, *The Financing of a Small Business* (Sweet and Maxwell), Burgess, *Corporate Finance Law,* (Sweet and Maxwell), Wine, *Buying and Selling Private Companies* (Butterworths), Airmic, *Company Insurance Handbook* (Gower), Birds, *Modern Insurance Law* (Sweet and Maxwell).

Exercises

1. Rob is a car mechanic, and he is a sole trader. Until the summer of 1988 the business had been expanding steadily, but then he decided to expand into car sales, and to incorporate the business. He assigned all the company assets to a company called Philpott Enterprises Ltd. In payment for this assignment he took 6000 fully paid shares in the new Company. However, for reasons which were not clear, the insurance relating to the business remained in his own name. Early in 1989 the business premises were destroyed by fire, and Rob has claimed upon the insurance policy. The insurers have refused to pay. Advise Rob.

2. Consider how far it is true to say that preference shareholders suffer the same disadvantages as do debenture and ordinary shareholders, and at the same time they enjoy very few of the advantages that the others possess. Why would an investor choose to be a preference shareholder in a new business?

3. Are there any circumstances in which it is legally permissible for a private company to give financial assistance to others, to facilitate the purchase of its own shares?

4. How far is it true to say that the information that a company director receives in his or her capacity as a company director is part of the

property which belongs to that company, and that he or she is not entitled to use that information without accounting to the company?

5. Distinguish between: (a) authorized capital; (b) issued capital; (c) unpaid capital; (d) reserve capital.

Appendix
Case summaries

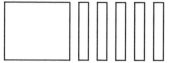

Chapter 2

Harris v. *Nickerson* [1873] L.R.8 Q.B. 286
The defendant, an auctioneer, advertised in the London newspapers and distributed catalogues to the effect that certain brewing materials, plant and office furniture would be sold by him at Bury St Edmunds on a particular day. The conditions included the statement 'The highest bidder to be the buyer.' The plaintiff, had a commission to purchase 'the office furniture' at the sale as advertised. He travelled to Bury St Edmunds and attended the sale and purchased several items. However, the lots described as 'office furniture' were withdrawn from the sale. It was held that the advertising of the sale was not an offer which the plaintiff could accept by making a journey and therefore did not form a binding contract. If the sale was not held, the auctioneer was not bound to indemnify those who had attended.

Hartley v. *Ponsonby* [1857] 7E. & B. 872
A ship left England with a crew of 36. At Port Philip a number of the crew deserted leaving only 19 men, of whom only five were able seamen. The master, in order to induce the remaining crew to complete the voyage, promised to pay them an extra £40 to work the ship to Bombay. The plaintiff received his regular wages but was refused the extra £40. It was held that as it was hazardous and unreasonable for the ship to go to sea with a smaller crew, the seamen were no longer bound to serve. The undertaking of the crew to continue the voyage was therefore a new contract and their promise to serve with a reduced crew was valid consideration for the masters promise to pay them the extra £40.

Re Pinnel's Case [1602] 5 Co. Rep. 117a
Pinnel, the plaintiff, bought an action to recover £8 10s due on a bond on 11 November 1600. The defendant argued that at the plaintiff's request, he had paid him £5 2s 6d on October 1 and Pinnel had accepted in full satisfaction of the debt. The court held that although payment of a lesser sum on the due day in satisfaction of a greater sum cannot be any satisfaction for the whole, payment of a smaller sum at the creditor's request before the due day can be good consideration for a promise to forego the balance, for it is a benefit to the creditor to be paid before he was entitled to payment, and a detriment to the debtor to pay early.

D and C Builders Ltd v. *Rees* [1965] 3 All E.R. 837
The defendant owed £482 13s 1d to the building company for work carried

out, and refused to pay. Eventually the defendant's wife, acting for her husband and knowing that the plaintiffs were in financial difficulty offered £300 in settlement of the debt, saying that if the offer was not accepted, nothing would be paid. The plaintiffs agreed to take a cheque for £300 in full satisfaction of the debt. They then sued for the balance. It was held that the plaintiffs could recover the balance because there was no consideration for the earlier promise to settle for less. Payment by cheque was not a different method of payment which would be consideration.

Hong Kong Fir Shipping Co Ltd v. *Kawasaki Kisen Kaisha Ltd* [1962] 1 All E.R. 474

The plaintiff owned a ship, the Hong Kong Fir which they chartered to the defendants for a 24 month period, commencing February 1957. The agreement held the term that the ship was 'in every way fitted for ordinary cargo service.' On delivery however, it was discovered that the ship's machinery was very old and could not be handled by the inexperienced and incompetent staff which the company had provided. The plaintiffs admitted that they had broken the term in the contract and that the breach for the first seven months of the charter had rendered the ship unseaworthy. In June, the following year, 10 months after the ship became seaworthy, the defendants repudiated the contract on the basis that a breach of condition had occurred. It was held that the admitted breach of an innominate term did not entitle the defendants to repudiate the contract as retrospectively, the delay caused by the breach did not frustrate the commercial purposes of the charter-party. The breach was therefore to be treated as a breach of warranty.

Lewis v. *Averay* [1971] 3 All E.R. 907

Lewis, the plaintiff, advertised his car for sale. A man, a rogue, telephoned, without giving his name and made an appointment to see the car. The man duly arrived and viewed the car and the plaintiff took him to a flat to discuss details. At the flat the man stated that he was the well-known television actor Richard Greene and offered to buy the car for £450 which the plaintiff accepted. The man payed by cheque signing it R.A. Greene, he also produced a special pass of admission to Pinewood Studios bearing the name 'Richard. A. Greene.' The cheque was worthless and consequently dishonoured but the rogue resold the car to Averay, the defendant, who bought the car in good faith. The plaintiff sued the defendant for conversion of the car. It was held that the rogue's fraudulent behaviour did not prevent there being a contract between him and the plaintiff. The rogue had obtained voidable title, but had sold the car to the defendant before the contract had been avoided, therefore the defendant had a good title.

Bisset v. *Wilkinson* [1927] A.C. 177

The appellant, Bisset, wished to sell land in the Southern Island of New Zealand. The holding had not previously been used as a sheep farm and Wilkinson, the respondent, knew this. Bisset had stated that in his belief, the land would carry 2,000 sheep. When Bisset claimed the balance of the purchase price, Wilkinson counter-claimed recission of the contract on the ground of misrepresentation. It was held that Bisset's statement of the capacity of the farm, was merely an opinion which was honestly held. It was not a representation of fact of its real capacity. Therefore, the claim for recission failed.

Locker and Woolf Ltd v. *Western Australian Insurance Co Ltd* [1936] 1 K.B. 408

The appellants, when applying for fire insurance in respect of their premises, failed to disclose that a previous proposal for insurance on their new motor cars had been refused by another insurance company on the grounds of misrepresentation and non–disclosure. It was held that the respondents were entitled to avoid the policy as the non–disclosed previous rejection was a 'material fact' in the proposal for fire insurance even though the rejection referred to an entirely different type of insurance from that which was being sought.

Redgrave v. *Hurd* [1881] 20 Ch. D.1

The plaintiff, a solicitor, advertised in the Law Times, that he wished to take a partner into the business with him. Hurd answered the advertisement and during his interview with the plaintiff, was told that the business was worth about £300 a year. In fact the practice was only worth about £200 a year, but Mr Hurd did not examine the papers produced which would have disclosed this information. Hurd agreed to become a partner, but when he later discovered the true financial position of the business, he refused to complete the contract. The plaintiff sued for breach of contract and Hurd counter–claimed for recission on the grounds of misrepresentation. It was held that Hurd was entitled to rescind as he had been induced to enter into the contract by false representations, lack of diligence in reading the papers did not preclude his claim for relief.

Attwood v. *Small* [1836] 6 Cl. and F m. 232

The appellant offered to sell the respondent mines and iron works. He made exaggerated and unreliable statements about the capabilities of the property which were confirmed, wrongly, by expert agents appointed by the respondents. The respondents were satisfied with the agents report and the contract for sale was completed. Six months later the respondents discovered the statements were inaccurate and tried to rescind the contract on the grounds of misrepresentation. It was held that the respondents could not claim misrepresentation, as they had not relied on the vendor's statements, but had tested their accuracy by independent investigations and declared themselves satisfied with the results.

Smith v. *Baker & Sons* [1891] A.C. 325

The plaintiff, a servant of the defendants, was employed to drill holes in a rock cutting. While he was working a crane was constantly being swung above his head carrying crates of stones. He was aware of this but nevertheless continued to work. A stone fell out of the crate and injured him. He brought an action in negligence against his employer who pleaded Volenti non fit injuria. The House of Lords held it was not enough to know of the risk but the plaintiff must also have consented to it. This was always a question of fact to be discovered from the circumstances. The jury had found in this case that there had been no acceptance of risk, and the House of Lords upheld that view.

Haynes v. *Harwood* [1935] All E.R. 103
The plaintiff, who was a policeman, was injured when he dived in front of the defendant's runaway horses pulling a van in a crowded street. The defendant pleaded the defence of Volenti non fit injuria, i.e. that the plaintiff had acted voluntarily in undertaking the risk. The court held that in an emergency a rescuer who takes reasonable steps to help is not a volunteer.

Hughes v. *Lord Advocate* [1963] 1 All E.R. 705
The plaintiff was a boy aged eight. He was injured while playing in the street with warning lights left by post office engineers outside a manhole on which they had been working. The plaintiff in fact knocked over a paraffin lamp which then spilled and caused an explosion when it ignited fumes in the manhole. The House of Lords held the defendant was liable because the plaintiff was injured as a result of the type or kind of accident that was foreseeable, even though the exact way was not foreseen.

Goldsoll v. *Goldman* [1915] 1 Ch. 292
The defendant carried on business in London selling imitation jewellery. He sold the business to the plaintiff on terms that for two years he would not deal in real or imitation jewellery in any part of the United Kingdom or various parts of Europe. In an action by the plaintiff to enforce the restraint the court held the clause was unreasonable on two counts. The business was largely based in the United Kingdom, therefore the restriction on trading in Europe was too wide, and since the business sold had only been concerned with imitation jewellery the restraint relating to real jewellery was also too wide. However the Court of Appeal held the offending clauses could be severed to leave the restraints limited to the United Kingdom, and to imitation jewellery, as reasonable and valid.

H. Parsons (Livestock) Ltd v. *Uttley Ingham and Co Ltd* (1978) 1 All E.R. 525
The plaintiffs owned a pig farm on which they reared top grade animals. The defendants agreed with the plaintiffs to supply and instal a food hopper which, according to the terms of the contract, had been fitted with a ventilated top. The defendants erected the hopper but failed to notice that the ventilator had been left in the closed position on installation. The food inside the hopper became mouldy and as a result of eating it, 254 pigs contracted a rare intestinal infection and died. The plaintiffs sued for the loss of the pigs. It was held that there was 'a serious possibility' of the resulting damage occurring – the defendants should have foreseen such an event if the ventilator to the feed hopper remained closed. The defendants were therefore liable for the loss of the pigs.

Page One Records Ltd v. *Britton* [1967] 3 All E.R. 822
The plaintiffs, business managers, were appointed by the defendants, The Troggs pop group, to manage their careers for five years. The plaintiffs were to use their professional expertise to promote the group and would, in return, receive 20% of money earned by the plaintiffs during the five-year period. The Troggs became very successful, earning up to £400 a night but the group wished to repudiate the management contract before the agreed period had expired. The plaintiffs sued for damages for breach of contract

and also applied for an interlocutory injunction to restrain The Troggs from engaging anyone other than the plaintiff as their manager. It was held that an injunction would compel The Troggs to employ the plaintiff. This was considered unworkable because it involved enforcing a contract for personal services where the relationship would involve both parties seeing each other amicably for another four years, which by now would be impossible, therefore no injunction was granted.

Chapter 3

Jones v. *Lipman* [1962] 1 All E.R. 442
In the words of Russell J in this case: 'The defendant company is the creature of the first defendant, a device and a sham, a mask which he holds before his face in an attempt to avoid recognition by the eye of equity'.

The case is an illustration of the preparedness of the courts to over-ride the usual policy of recognizing the separate legal personality of a company (i.e. 'lifting the veil of incorporation'). The defendant had sold his house to the plaintiff, but before the transaction had been completed he sold it again to a company of which he was one of the two shareholders and directors. Despite the usual approach, a decree of specific performance was granted to enforce the sale to the plaintiff.

Multinational Gas and Petrochemical Co v. *Multinational Gas and Petrochemical Services Ltd* [1983] 2 All E.R. 563
It was held in this case that, in accordance with the decision in *Salomon* v. *Salomon* [1897], there would be separate legal personality in a company, and that this extends to wholly owned subsidiaries in a group. These were not to be regarded as agencies of a holding company, unless there was a specific agency agreement.

DHN Food Distributors v. *London Borough of Tower Hamlets* [1976] 3 All E.R. 462
This case concerns the concept of group identity. There was a holding company which operated through two wholly owed subsidiaries. Certain of their business premises were compulsorily aquired by the local council. Naturally, compensation would be payable for such an action. This was to fall into two catagories: the value of the land and the disturbance to the business. There was reluctance to pay under this second head on the basis that the claimant (the holding company) had no interest in the land. This is another aspect of the corporate personality idea. However, in this case, the veil of incorporation was lifted on the basis that since group accounts were required by company legislation, then the courts should be prepared to recognize a group identity in this, another, context.
On the other hand, this case is not widely regarded as authority for a general principle of group identity. It seems to depend upon the circumstances of each individual case.

Re A and BC Chewing Gum Ltd [1975] 1 All E.R. 1017
In this case a winding up was ordered because changes had been made in the Articles of Association which had the effect of preventing the

petitioners from participating in the management of the company. These petitioners, Topps Chewing Gum, held one third of the ordinary shares in A and BC on the basis of a shareholders' agreement that they would share in management. This reasoning seems very close to an argument based in partnership law.

Lee v. *Lee's Air Farming Ltd* [1960] 3 All E.R. 420

The plaintiff was a widow. Her husband had been killed while flying the plane that he used in the business of crop spraying. He died in 1956. In 1954 he had formed a company to carry on business as crop spraying contractors. He owned 2999 of the 3000 shares in the company. He was the governing director. He was the chief pilot. He had arranged his own salary. The plaintiff sued the company under a Workers Compensation Act for the loss of her husband. She needed to establish that her husband was the employee of the company so that a master–servant relationship existed under which she would be entitled to compensation. This she was able to do because of the legal principle of separate corporate personality.

Chapter 4

Commercial Plastics Ltd v. *Vincent* [1964] 3 All E.R. 546

CP Ltd were engaged in the business of manufacturing thin P.V.C. sheeting which was used in the manufacture of adhesive tape. The company produced about 80% of the total plastic sheeting produced in the UK, and it represented about 20% of their total output. V was employed in research by CP Ltd. His contract of employment contained the following clause: 'In view of the highly technical and confidential nature of this appointment, you have agreed not to seek employment with any of our competitors in the PVC field for at least one year after leaving our employ.' On leaving the company V went to work for a competitor, and CP Ltd sought to enforce the restraint clause. Held the clause was too wide and went beyond protecting the company's legitimate interests and the injunction was refused. The court said there were certain things which an ex-employee could not be prevented from using, e.g. his skill, aptitude and general technical knowledge with regard to the production of a commodity and also the business organization and methods of his employer. However, confidential information which gives the possessor a competitive advantage and gained during employment could legitimately be protected by a reasonable restraint clause.

Faccienda Chicken Ltd v. *Fowler and others* [1985] I.R.I.R. 69

F was employed as sales manager for the plaintiff company. F's plan to sell fresh chickens from refrigerated vans was put into operation by the company. The van driver/salesmen were furnished with details about the customers, including names and addresses, prices of goods and the quality and quantity of goods sold. In 1980 F left the company and set up his own rival business operating on the same routes and serving the same kind of customer. Eight other employees joined F's company, but none of them was subject to an express agreement restricting their services after leaving the company's employment. The plaintiffs sued F for breach of contract, i.e. breach of the implied term of good faith. Held that, although F had made use of sales information obtained during his employment, this could not be a breach of contract after he had left the company. Implied terms die with the termination of the contract. Had the company had a reasonable written restraint clause in the contract the clause would have been enforceable after the contract was terminated for the term stipulated in that restraint clause.

Taw v. *Novtek* [1951] 68 R.P.C. 271
Taw owned a registered trade mark for motor lamps, and so did Novtek. Both products used a comparison with the eyes of a cat. This was an action for the infingement of a trade mark and for passing off. The mark was held to have been infringed, but the action in passing off failed. This was because no confusion had been established. The distribution chains of each of the products was different.

Stenhouse Ltd v. *Phillips* [1974] A.C. 391
P was employed by S, an insurance company, and his contract contained long and detailed restraint clauses preventing him from competing with the company and with its subsidiaries should he leave S's employment. As the clauses were contained in separate paragraphs, severance was made easier, but the restraint was held to be too wide, as ' . . . the employee is entitled to use to the full any personal skill or experience even if this has been acquired in the service of the employer . . . ' There must be a legitimate interest to protect, and restraint clauses cannot just be used to prevent employees from working after the contract is terminated.

United Sterling Corporation Ltd v. *Felton and Monnion* [1974] I.R.L.R. 314
M was employed by USC Ltd as a production manager. The company had recently developed two new production processes for polystyrene. Whilst on holiday M met a former employee of USC Ltd, F, who was in contact with a rival company, Hammond Plastics, and M was offered a job. M was suspended by USC Ltd and on his return to England was dismissed; USC Ltd also sought an injunction to prevent him taking on his new post. The injunction was refused on the grounds that there was no evidence to suggest that the information gained by M had been expressly disclosed in confidence to M by his employer, also he was entitled to use to the full any knowledge and personal skills which he had acquired in USC Ltd's employ. The case also illustrates that it is necessary for a restraint clause to be in writing to be enforced after the termination of the contract.

Chapter 5

Bellhaven Brewery Co Ltd. v. *McLean* [1975] I.R.L.R. 370
The Brewery had been issued an Improvement Notice requiring them to securely fence transmission machinery and other dangerous parts of the company's plant, by fixing interlocking devices attached to doors or gates. These devices would automatically switch off the electricity and compressed air as soon as the gates or doors were opened. The company claimed that not only were the interlocking devices too expensive to install, but that a high

level of supervision and an intelligent staff meant that such devices were not needed. The company argued they could comply with the Health and Safety at Work etc. Act by merely erecting safety screens. The Tribunal dismissed the appeal against the notice on the grounds that the risks of injury involved far outweighted the financial cost to the company, and therefore it was considered reasonably practicable to comply with the Improvement Notice.

Bridlington Relay Ltd v. *Yorkshire Electricity Board* [1965] 1 All E.R. 264
The plaintiffs provided a television broadcast relay service to subscribers in Bridlington, to whom the defendants supplied electricity. The defendants erected a power line which the plaintiffs considered a potential source of interference with their business, so they applied for an interlocutory injuction to stop the defendants from using the power line. Held that the plaintiffs business was of a particularly sensitive nature, so the court therefore held that they could not complain of an interference which would not be unreasonable to a less sensitive occupier.

Harrison v. *Michelin Tyre Co Ltd* [1985] 1 All E.R. 918
H, a tool grinder employed by the defendants, was injured in the course of his employment while standing on the duck-board of his machine talking to a fellow employee. The injury occurred when S, another employee, indulged in some horseplay and caused H to fall. H sued his employers for compensation for his injury claiming they were vicariously liable for S's actions. The employer claimed that S had taken himself outside of the course of his employment and was on a 'frolic of his own'. Held the test of whether an employee was acting in the course of his employment was whether a reasonable man would say either that the employee's act was part and parcel of his employment (in the sense of being incidental to it) even though it was unauthorized or prohibited by the employer, or that it was so divergent from his employment as to be plainly alien to his employment, and wholly distinguishable from it. Applying this test, a reasonable man would say that even though S's act was of a kind which would never have been countenanced by the employer, it was none the less part and parcel of his employment. Accordingly the employers were vicariously liable for S's negligence.

Otterburn Mill Ltd v. *Bullman* [1975] I.R.L.R. 223
Otterburn Mill operated four carding machines which were not guarded. A factory inspector visited, made an inspection of the company and ordered that guards be fitted. On the company's failure to effect recommendations, the inspector issued a deferred Prohibition Notice giving three months for the guards to be fitted or else the machines would not be able to be used. Whilst the company accepted that the unguarded machines posed a danger to the operators, they appealed against the time limit on the grounds that they could not afford to fence them all at once, and if they could not be used the mill would have to close down. Held the company would have to guard the machines, but it was accepted by the tribunal that the company would be seriously embarrassed if production was cut down or halted, export orders could not be met and labour would have to be laid off. The company was therefore granted an extension of twelve weeks for guarding one of the machines.

Pannett v. *McGuiness* [1972] 3 All E.R. 137
The defendants were engaged in demolishing a warehouse. When the work was almost complete the workmen took down hoardings and made a fire with them. Three workers were employed as watchmen to keep their eye open for children who had been regularly trespassing on the site. The plaintiff, aged five, who had been chased off the land several times, fell into the fire and was seriously burned. The men were absent from the site at the time and the fire was therefore left unguarded. Held that the defendants were liable. They were occupiers who owed a duty of care to the child even though he was a trespasser. The hazardous nature of the situation meant that the defendants should have taken steps to provide proper supervision as they knew that children regularly trespassed on it.

Chapter 6

Wings Ltd v. *Ellis* [1984] 1 All E.R. 1046
W. Ltd were tour operators. Their brochure mistakenly indicated that a particular hotel was air conditioned. On discovering the mistake W. Ltd gave instructions to amend their brochures and inform travel agents. However, a customer booked a holiday at the hotel without having been informed of the error and subsequently complained to the Trading Standards Officer. A successful prosecution was brought under section 14 of the Trades Description Act 1968 alleging the making of a false statement knowingly or recklessly. On appeal the Court of Appeal held W. Ltd not guilty on the grounds that liability is not strict, where the relevant state of mind arises after the original publication the prosecution must prove a failure to take all reasonable steps to correct the error. This is a question of fact.

Arcos Ltd v. *Ronaasen and Son* [1933] A.C. 470
A Ltd. agreed to sell to R. a quantity of timber specified to be half an inch thick. On delivery the timber was found to be ⅝ in. thick and R sought to reject it for breach of condition of correspondence with description. An official arbitrator found the timber had almost certainly been shipped at the correct size and had probably swollen in transit. Nevertheless A. Ltd were held entitled to reject, correspondence with description is a very strict condition (S.13 Sale of Goods Act [1893].

Re Moore and Co and Landauer and Co [1921] All E.R. 466
Sellers agreed to sell tinned fruit in cases each containing thirty tins. The correct quantity was delivered but about half the cases contained only twenty four tins. It was held the buyer was entitled to reject the entire consignment for breach of correspondence with description contrary to S.13 Sale of Goods Act 1893.

Rogers v. *Parish (Scarborough) Ltd* [1987] unreported
R. bought a new Range Rover from P. The car suffered a number of small technical problems in the engine and bodywork which persisted. R. sought to reject for breach of merchantable quality under S. 14(2) Sale of Goods Act 1979. The court held that in assessing merchantable quality it was necessary to take into account standards of comfort, handling and appear-

ance related to the price paid and the plaintiff's reasonable expectations. On the facts the court found for R.

Sumner Permain and Co v. *Webb and Co* [1922] 1 K.B. 55
W., manufacturers of mineral water, contracted to sell some of their product to S.P. for resale by S.P. in Argentina. Unknown to S.P. the water contained a chemical prohibited in Argentina and on arrival there the water was condemned as unfit for human consumption. In an action by S.P. against the sellers it was held the sellers were in breach of S. 14(1) of the Sale of Goods Act 1893 which implied a term that goods shall be fit for the particular purpose for which they were intended, and of section 14(2) implying a general term of merchantable quality.

Brown and Son Ltd. v. *Craiks Ltd.* [1970] 1 All E.R. 823
B. Ltd ordered cloth from C. Ltd intending to use it for dress making. C. Ltd believed the cloth was for general industrial purposes. The cloth was not suitable for dress making and B. Ltd. sought to repudiate and claim damages for breach of the condition of merchantable quality (S. 14(2) S.G.A. 1893). The court held the goods were of merchantable quality being quite suitable for several industrial purposes, although not the buyer's particular purpose.

Bartlett v. *Sydney Marcus* [1965] 2 All E.R. 753
B. bought a secondhand car from S.M. on terms that there was a small problem with the clutch for which a price allowance had been made. After three weeks and three hundred miles the car broke down and was found to be in need of expensive repairs. B. claimed to recover his costs of repair alleging a breach of the implied term of merchantable quality (S. 14(2) S.G.A. 1893). On the facts the court found there was no such breach, the car was secondhand and had been fit to drive.

Vacwell Engineering v. *B.D.H. Chemicals* [1969] 3 All E.R. 1681
B.D.H. supplied chemicals to V.E. for use in the manufacture of transistors. A newly developed chemical was supplied which exploded on contact with water and caused substantial damage. Neither of the parties was aware of this hazard and no warning had been given. V.E. sued for breach of 14 (1) Sale of Goods Act 1893 alleging that the goods were not fit for the particular purpose for which they were bought and that they had relied on the sellers' skill and judgement. Damages were awarded.

George Mitchell v. *Finney Lock Seeds* [1983] 2 All E.R. 737
G.M. ordered seed from F.L.S. The seed supplied was of a different variety from that ordered and of inferior quality. The crop failed. G.M. brought an action for breach of contract claiming damages of £61,513 despite an exclusion clause in the contract purporting to limit liability to a refund of the purchase price, in this case £201.60. The court held the exclusion clause was not fair and reasonable and was therefore not enforceable under S. 55 Sale of Goods Act 1979. The court had regard to F.L.S.'s practice of not relying on the exclusion clause in other disputes, their negligence and their ability to take out insurance.

Chapter 7

Brennan v. *J.H Dewhurst Ltd and French* [1983] I.R.L.R. 357
Dewhursts, a chain of butchers shops, advertised for a butcher's assistant at one of its shops in Torquay. Applications were to be made to the manager Mr French but the appointment was to be made by the District Manager. B was interviewed by Mr French and she felt she was asked discriminatory questions. She did not get the job. B claimed she had been discriminated against both in the arrangements made for offering employment, i.e. the questions asked at the interview, contrary to S.6(1)(a) of the S.D.A. and by being refused employment contrary to S.6(1)(c). The EAT upheld B's complaint even though Mr French did not have the power to appoint he was acting as a filter for applicants before presenting a short-list to the District Manager. Discriminatory questions are unlawful under S.6(1)(a) S.D.A.

Coleman v. *Skyrail Oceanic Ltd* [1981] I.C.R. 864
C., a female booking clerk in S's travel agency bcame engaged to a male employee in a rival business. She promised not to divulge confidential information to him. The day after her wedding she was dismissed on the assumption that her husband was the breadwinner, and because of her employer's fears of leakage of confidential information. Held that C had been unlawfully discriminated against on the grounds of both sex and marital status. It was clear that a man would not have been treated in a similar way by S. In the Court of Appeal it was said: 'An assumption that men are more likely than women to be the primary supporters of their spouses and children is an assumption based on sex. Therefore the dismissal of a woman based upon an assumption that husbands are breadwinners and wives are not will amount to discrimination under the SDA.

Hivac Ltd v. *Park Royal Scientific Instruments Ltd* [1946] 2 All E.R. 350
Five employees of the plaintiff company spent their Sundays working on highly specialized tasks for the defendants who manufactured midget valves in direct competition with the plaintiff. The plaintiffs sought, and were granted, an injunction against the defendants to stop the practice, notwithstanding that there was no evidence of actual misuse of confidential information, because the employees concerned were in breach of the implied duty of fidelity. As per Lord Greene MR:

> 'It would be most unfortunate if anything we said should place an undue restraint on the right of the workman, particularly a manual workman, to make use of his leisure for his profit. On the other hand, it would be deplorable if it were laid down that a workman could, consistently with his duty to his employer, knowingly, deliberately and secretly set himself to do in his spare time something which would inflict great harm on his employer's business.'

Hurley v. *Mustoe* [1981] I.R.L.R. 208
Mrs H. had four children, and for ten years she had worked as a waitress for four nights a week while her husband looked after the children. She

applied successfully for a waitressing job with M's bistro, but after only one night's work she was dismissed by M. as he had a policy not to employ women with children. She was unable to bring an unfair dismissal claim so H. brought an action under the Sex Discrimination Act 1975. The EAT held that as M. did not apply his policy equally to men and women there had been direct sex discrimination. It was also held that in general a condition excluding all members of a class on the ground that some members are undesirable (i.e. some married women with children do take a lot of time off work) cannot be supported. The policy was therefore also one of indirect discrimination.

Igbo v. *Johnson Matthey Chemicals Ltd* [1986] I.R.L.R. 215

I. wished to take extended leave and she signed a document which stated that she agreed to return to work by a certain date, and if she failed to return by that date her contract of employment would be automatically terminated. She failed to return on the due date and the employers treated the contract as at and end. I. claimed she had been unfairly dismissed. The Court of Appeal held s.140(1) of EPCA stipulated that any provision in a contract which purports to exclude or limit the operation of any provisions of the Act will be void. This agreement purported to take away her right to claim unfair dismissal and was therefore void. (The case of *British Leyland* v. *Ashraf* was over-ruled).

Morton Sundour Fabrics Ltd v. *Shaw* [1967] 2 I.T.R. 84

S. worked for the appellant company as foreman in their velvet department. The employers decided that they were going to shut down the velvet department and informed S. in early March that this would occur ' . . . sometime in the course of 1966'. Within a few days of being informed S. obtained alternative employment with another company, and then claimed a redundancy payment from his employer. Held that S. had not been 'dismissed' within the meaning of S.1. Redunancy Payments Act 1965, for in order to terminate a contract of employment the notice of termination must specify the date on which the contract would come to an end, or at least contain sufficient facts from which that date can be ascertained. 'Advanced warning' of termination 'sometime in the future' was not a termination of the contract.

Chapter 8

Trevor v. *Whitworth* [1889] 12 App. Cas. 409

This case provides the common law basis for the rules concerning the purchase by a company of its own shares. The action concerned the unsuccessful claim of a former shareholder to the remainder of the price of shares which he had sold to the company before it went into liquidation.

Lord Watson said. . . . one of the main objects contemplated by the legislature, in restricting the power of limited companies to reduce the amount of their capital as set forth in the memorandum, is to protect the interests of the outside public who may become their creditors.

Re Introductions [1969] 3 All E.R. 697
This case is concerned with the ability of a company to vary its activities, consistently with the scope and ambit of its objects clause. The company here had been involved with the Festival of Britain, with deckchairs at a seaside resort, and after a period of inactivity, involved with pigs. The case concerned the ability of the company to borrow money. This was held to be an incidental power. Harman L.J. said: '. . . a power or an object conferred on a company to borrow cannot mean something in the air; borrowing is not an end in itself and must be for some purpose of the company'.

March Cabaret Club and Casino v. *London Assurance* [1975] 1 Lloyds Rep. 169
The club was badly damaged by fire. A claim was made against the defendant insurers, but it was resisted. This was on the basis that the insured had been under a duty to disclose, and had failed to disclose, that he had been convicted of handling stolen goods. The court found for the defendants. They did not have to pay.

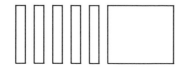

Table of Cases

Page numbers in bold type refer to case summaries
section, pages 213–25

A and BC Chewing Gum Ltd, Re [1975] 90, **217**
Amalgamated Investment & Property Co. v. *John
Walker & Sons* [1976] 60
Annabel's (Berkeley Square Ltd) v. *Shock* (1972) 109
Anderson & Sons Ltd v. *Rhodes (Liverpool) Ltd*
[1967] 169
Anderson v. *Daniel* [1924] 57
Archbolds (Freightage) v. *Spanglett* [1961] 57
Arcos Ltd v. *Ronaasen & Son* [1933] 150, **221**
Ashbury Railway Carriage & Iron Co. Ltd v. *Riche*
(1875) 85, 201
Associated Dairies Ltd v. *Hartley* [1979] 120
Attwood v. *Lamont* [1920] 116
Attwood v. *Small* (1838) 56, **215**

B&S Contracts & Design Ltd v. *Victor Green
Publications Ltd* [1984] 48
B.A.C. Ltd v. *Austin* [1978] 186
Baldry v. *Marshall* [1925] 153
Balfour v. *Balfour* [1919] 41
Barclay v. *City of Glasgow D.C.* [1983] 183
Bayoomi v. *British Railways Board* [1981] 166
Barnet v. *Chelsea and Kensington Hospital Mgnt
Committee* [1969] 72
Barrett v. *Associated Newspapers* (1907) 110
Bartlett v. *Sydney Marcus* [1965] 153, **222**
Beale v. *Taylor* (1967) 150
Bellhaven Brewery Co. Ltd v. *McLean* [1975] 121, **219**
Bentham v. *North East Regional Airport Committee* –
unreported 167
Bent's Brewery Co. Ltd v. *Hogan* [1945] 172
Bernstein v. *Pamsons Motors* [1987] 151
Bick v. *Royal West of England School for the Deaf*
[1976] 167
Bisset v. *Wilkinson* [1927] 56, **214**
B.L. v. *Armstrong Patents Ltd* [1986] 104

Blyth v. *Birmingham Waterworks Co.* [1856] 71
Bollinger v. *Costa Brava Wine Co.* [1960] 109
Bolton v. *Mahadeva* [1972] 60
Bolton v. *Stone* [1951] 71, 72, 120
Bradford Corporation v. *Pickles* [1895] 65
Brennan v. *Dewhurst Ltd* [1983] 168, **223**
Bridlington Relay Ltd v. *Yorkshire Electricity Board*
[1965] 138, **220**
Bristol Tramways v. *Fiat* [1910] 153
British Crane Hire Corporation v. *Ipswich Plant Hire*
[1974] 50
British Leyland Ltd v. *Ashraf* [1978] 183
British Railways Board v. *Herrington* [1972] 136
Brown & Son Ltd v. *Craiks Ltd* [1970] 153, **222**
Bulmer v. *Bollinger* [1974] 20
Butler Machine Tool Co. Ltd v. *Ex-Cell-O-
Corporation Ltd* [1979] 46
Byrne & Co. v. *Van Tienhoven & Co.* (1880) 44

Capital Fire Insurance Association, Re [1883] 89
Carlill v. *Carbolic Smoke Ball Co. Ltd* [1892] 42, 208
Car & Universal Finance v. *Caldwell* [1063] 56
Caparo Industries PLC v. *Dickman* [1989] 74
Cehave N.V. v. *Bremer Handelgesellschaft, The
Hansa Nord* [1975] 153
Chappell & Co. v. *Nestle & Co.* [1960] 48
Chaproniere v. *Mason* [1905] 153
Chessman v. *Price* (1865) 92
Christie v. *Davey* [1893] 138
Coleman v. *Skyrail Oceanic Ltd* [1981] 164, **223**
Collen v. *Wright* (1857) 202
Commercial Plastics Ltd v. *Vincent* [1964] 114, 115,
218
Condor v. *Barron Knights* [1966] 59
Connor v. *Halfords* [1972] 187
Cope v. *Sharp* [1912] 68
Corner v. *Buckinghamshire C.C.* [1978] 179
Couturier v. *Hastie* (1852) 55
Cutter v. *Powell* (1795) 60

D & C Builders v. *Rees* [1966] 48, **213**
Daniels & Daniels v. *R White & Sons* [1938] 139
Davidson v. *Kent Meters Ltd* [1975] 187
De Berenger v. *Hamel* (1829) 92
Dennis & Co. v. *Campbell* [1977] 172
Department of Trade v. *St Christopher Motorists' Association* [1976] 208
DHN Food Distributors v. *London Borough of Tower Hamlets* [1976] 81, **217**
Donoghue v. *Stevenson* [1932] 70, 73
Dunlop Tyre Co. Ltd v. *New Garage and Motor Co. Ltd* [1915] 62

Easson v. *L N.E.R.* [1944] 75
Edwards v. *National Coal Board* [1949] 119
Emmerson v. *Commissioners for Inland Revenue* [1977] 179
Entores Ltd v. *Miles Far East Corporation* [1955] 6
Equal Opportunities Commission v. *Robertson* [1980] 167
Esso Petroleum v. *Harpers Garages* [1967] 58
Esso Petroleum Co. v. *Southport Corporation* [1956] 68

Faccenda Chicken Ltd v. *Fowler* [1985] 114, 116, **218**
Factage Parisien Ltd, Re (1865) 90
Fisher v. *Bell* [1960] 4, 42
Fitch v. *Dewes* [1912] 116
Fluss v. *Grant Thornton Chartered Accountants* (1987) unreported 166
Fountaine v. *Carmarthen Rail Co.* (1868) 201
Fox v. *Findus Foods Ltd* [1973] 187
Froom v. *Butcher* [1975] 69
Frost v. *Aylesbury Dairy* [1905] 153
Futty v. *D & D Brekkes Ltd* [1974] 185

Galley v. *National Coal Board* [1958] 172
Gardner, F. C., Ltd v. *Beresford* [1978] 172, 186
Garland v. *British Rail Engineering Ltd* [1982] 18
Garrard v. *James* [1925] 201
Garrett v. *Boots* (1980) 147
General Auction Estate & Monetary Co. v. *Smith* [1891] 201
Godley v. *Perry* [1960] 153
Goldsall v. *Goldman* [1915] 58, **216**
Grant v. *Australian Knitting Mills* [1936] 153
Greer v. *Sketchley Ltd* [1979] 116
Greig v. *Community Industry & Ahern* [1979] 164
Griffiths v. *Peter Conway* [1939] 153
Griffiths & Robertson & Strathclyde Regional Council (1985) unreported 165
Gubala v. *Crompton Parkinson Ltd* [1977] 165

Hadley v. *Baxendale* [1843–60] 62
Haig v. *Bamford* (1972) 73

Haley v. *London Electricity Board* [1965] 70
Halsey v. *Esso Petroleum Co. Ltd* [1961] 137
Hanlon v. *Allied Breweries (UK) Ltd* [1975] 171
Harris v. *Birkenhead Corporation* [1976] 136
Harris v. *Nickerson* (1873) 42, **213**
Harrison v. *Michelin Tyre Co. Ltd* [1985] **220**
Hartley v. *Ponsonby* (1857) 47, **213**
Hathaway v. *FWD Merchants Ltd* [1975] 187
Hay (or Bourhill) v. *Young* [1942] 71
Haynes v. *Harwood* [1935] 67, **216**
Hedley Byrne & Co. Ltd v. *Heller & Partners Ltd* [1964] 73, 133, 169
Herbert Morris v. *Saxelby* [1916] 114
Heron II, The [1969] 62
Hilton v. *Burton (Rhodes) Ltd* [1961] 132
Hivac Ltd v. *Park Royal Scientific Instruments Ltd* [1946] 172, **223**
Hoenig v. *Isaacs* [1952] 60
Hollywood Silver Fox Farm Ltd v. *Emmett* [1936] 138
Home Counties Dairies Ltd v. *Skilton* [1970] 116
Home Office v. *Dorset Yacht Co. Ltd* [1969] 133
Home Office v. *Holmes* [1984] 165
Hong Kong Fir Shipping v. *Kawasaki Kisen Kaisha* [1962] 51, 59, **214**
Horsey v. *Dyfed C. C.* [1982] 165
Hughes v. *Lord Advocate* [1963] 71, **216**
Huppert v. *Univ. of Cambridge & U.G.C.* (1986) 165, 166
Hurley v. *Mustoe* [1981] 167, **223**
Hussein v. *Saintes Complete House Furnishers Ltd* [1979] 165

Igbo v. *Johnson Matthey Chemicals Ltd* [1985] 183, **224**
Interfolio Picture Library Ltd v. *Stiletto Visual Programmes Ltd* [1968] 52
Interlego AG v. *Tyco Industries* [1988] 105
Introductions, Re [1969] 201, **225**
Isle of Wight Tourist Board v. *Coombes* [1976] 172

Jackson v. *Rotax Motor & Cycle Co.* [1910] 153
James v. *Waltham Holy Cross U.D.C.* [1973] 187
JEB Fasteners Ltd v. *Marks, Bloom and Co.* [1983] 74
John v. *Rees* [1970] 29
Jones v. *Lipman* [1962] 81, **217**
Jones v. *London Co-operative Society* [1975] 187

Ladbroke [Football] Ltd v. *William Hill [Football] Ltd* [1964] 103
Lancaster v. *Anchor Hotels Ltd* [1973] 187
Lavery v. *Plessey Telecommuncations Ltd* [1983] 180
Lawton v. *BOC Transhield Ltd* [1965] 168
Leavers v. *Civil Service Commission* (1987) 166
Lee v. *Lee's Air Farming Ltd* [1960] 81, **218**
Lewis v. *Avery* [1971] 55, **214**

Lewis Shops Group Ltd v. *Wiggins* [1973] 187
Littlewoods Organisation Ltd v. *Harris* [1978] 116
Lister v. *Romford Ice & Cold Storage Co. Ltd* [1957] 172
Loch v. *John Blackwood Ltd* [1924] 89
Locker & Woolf v. *Western Insurance* [1936] 56, **215**
Lucas, T & Co. Ltd v. *Mitchell* [1972] 116
Lumb v. *Charcon Pipes* [1972] 187
Luxor (Eastbourne) Ltd v. *Cooper* [1941] 171
Lyne v. *Nicholls* (1906) 110

MacMillen Bloedel Containers Ltd v. *Morris* (1984) unreported 168
Mandla v. *Lee* [1983] 165
March Cabaret Club & Casino v. *London Assurance* [1975] 209, **225**
Marion White Ltd v. *Francis* [1972] 116
Maritime National Fish v. *Ocean Trawlers* [1935] 59
Marley v. *Forward Trust Group Ltd* [1986] 172
Marley Tile Co. Ltd v. *Johnson* [1982] 116
Marshall v. *Southampton and S.W. Hants Area Health Authority* [1986] 18, 31, 165
Martin v. *Yeoman Aggregates Ltd* [1983] 185
McAlpine v. *Minimax* [1970] 153
Metroploitan Railway Warehousing Co. Ltd, Re (1867) 89
Middlesborough Assembly Rooms Co. Re (1880) 89
Midland Electric Manufacturing Co. Ltd v. *Kanji* [1980] 183
Ministry of Defence v. *Jeremiah* [1979] 165
Mitchell (George) v. *Finney Lock Seeds Ltd* [1983] 154, **222**
Moorcock, The (1899) 50
Moore & Co. and Landauer & Co. Re [1921] 150, **221**
Morton Sundour Fabrics Ltd v. *Shaw* (1966) 185, **224**
Multinational Gas & Petrochemical Co. v. *Multinational Gas and Petrochemical Services Ltd* [1983] 81, **217**
Murphy v. *Hare Bros Ltd* [1973] 183

National Coal Board v. *Galley* [1958] 172
Nichols v. *Marsland* (1876) 68
Nimmo v. *Alexander Cowan & Sons Ltd* [1968] 119
Northampton B.C. v. *Farthingstone Silos Ltd* (1981) unreported 125

Ojuitku & Oburani v. *Manpower Services Commission* [1982] 165
Okereke v. *The Post Office* [1974] 187
Olley v. *Marlborough Hotel Ltd* [1949] 51
Osborne v. *Bill Taylor of Huyton Ltd* [1982] 121
Otterburn Mill Ltd v. *Bullman* [1975] 121, **220**
Overseas Tankship (UK) Ltd v. *Morts Dock & Engineering Co. Ltd* [1961] 65, 73
Owen v. *Briggs & Jones* [1981] 165

Page v. *Freight Hire (Tank Haulage) Ltd* [1981] 121
Page One Records v. *Britton* [1968] 63, **216**
Pannett v. *McGuiness* [1972] 136, **221**
Parker-Knoll v. *Knoll International Ltd* (1962) 109
Parsons v. *Uttley Ingham* [1978] 62, **216**
Paris v. *Stepney Borough Council* [1951] 71, 72, 120
Patchett v. *Sterling Engineering Ltd* [1955] 112
Penny v. *Wimbledon U.D.C.* [1899] 68
Pharmaceutical Society of Great Britian v. *Boots* [1953] 42
Phonogram v. *Lane* [1892] 84
Pinnel's Case (1602) 48, **213**
Planché v. *Colbourn* (1831) 61
Porcelli v. *Strathclyde Regional Council* [1985] 165
Porter v. *Honey* [1968] 15
Powell v. *Kempton Park Racecourse* [1899] 17
Price v. *Civil Service Commission* [1978] 165
Priest v. *Last* [1903] 153
Produce Marketing Consortium Ltd, Re [1989] 204

R. v. *Allen* (1872) 16
R. v. *Clarkson's Holidays* [1972] 146
R. v. *Swan Hunter Shipbuilders Ltd* [1981] 121
Raffles v. *Wichelhaus* (1864) 54
Ratcliffe v. *Dorset C.C.* [1978] 180
Ready Mixed Concrete (South East) Ltd v. *Minister of Pensions and National Insurance* [1968] 131
Redgrave v. *Hurd* (1881) 56, **215**
Reffell v. *Surrey C.C.* [1964] 135
Reigate v. *Union Manufacturing Ltd* [1918] 171
Richley v. *Faull* [1965] 75
Rickards (Charles) Ltd v. *Oppenheim* [1950] 61
Rigby v. *Chief Constable of Northamptonshire* [1985] 68
Robertson v. *British Gas Corporation* [1983] 172
Robinson v. *Crompton Parkinson Ltd* [1978] 172
Robinson v. *Kilvert* (1889) 138
Rogers v. *Parish (Scarborough) Ltd* [1987] 151, **221**
Roles v. *Nathan* [1963] 135
Rolled Steel Products (Holdings) Ltd v. *British Steel Corporation* [1986] 85
Rose v. *Plenty* [1976] 132
Roselodge Ltd v. *Castle* [1962] 209
Rowland v. *Divall* [1923] 150
Ryan v. *London Borough of Camden* (1982) 136
Rylands v. *Fletcher* (1868) 66

Sadler v. *Whiteman* (1910) 84
Saloman v. *Saloman and Co. Ltd* [1897] 80–1, 200, 201, 204
Saunders v. *Anglia Building Society* [1970] 55
Saunders v. *Richmond Borough Council* [1977] 168
Sayers v. *Harlow U.D.C.* [1958] 69

Seager v. *Copydex Ltd* [1967] 172
Scott v. *London and St Katherine's Docks* (1865) 75
Scott v. *Shepherd* (1773) 65
Shell UK Ltd v. *Lostack Garage Ltd* [1977] 171
Shine v. *General Guarantee Corporation* [1988] 151
Shipton, Anderson & Co. Re [1915] 59
Sibun v. *Modern Telephones Ltd* [1976] 187
Simkiss Rhondda B.C. (1983) 136
Simpkins v. *Pays* [1955] 42
Sinclair v. *Brougham* [1914] 202
Smith and another v. *Hughes and others* [1960] 16
Smith v. *Baker & Sons* [1891] 66, **215**
Smith v. *Bush* [1989] 53, 74
Smith v. *Land House Property Corporation* [1884] 56
Smith v. *Mardale Pipes Plus Ltd – unreported 167*
Smith Kline & French Laboratories Ltd v. *Sterling Winthrop Group Ltd* [1975] 107
Smith, Stone & Knight Ltd v. *Birmingham Corporation* [1939] 81
Snow v. *Milford* (1868) 92
South Portland Cement v. *Cooper* [1974] 136
Spafax v. *Harrison* [1980] 116
Stanley v. *Powell* [1891] 68
Stenhouse v. *Phillips* [1974] 114, **219**
Stevenson, Jordan and Harrison v. *MacDonald* (1952) 131
Stewart v. *West African Terminals Ltd* [1964] 65
Stilk v. *Myrick* (1809) 47
Stevenson Jordan & Harrison Ltd v. *MacDonald & Evans* [1952] 131
Strathclyde Regional Council v. *Neil* [1984] 114
Sumner Permain and Co. v. *Webb and Co.* [1922] 153, **222**
Sumpter v. *Hedges* [1898] 61
Sutton & Gates v. *Boxall* [1979] 187
Systems Floors (UK) Ltd v. *Daniel* [1981] 175

Taw Manufacturing Co. v. *Novtek Engineering Co.* (1951) 108, **224**
Taylor v. *Alidair Ltd* [1978] 187
Taylor v. *Caldwell* (1863) 60

Tesco Stores v. *Nattrass* [1972] 146
Thorn v. *Meggitt Engineering Ltd* [1976] 166
Thorndyke v. *Bell Fruit Company* [1979] 167, 168
Thornton v. *Shoe Lane Parking Ltd* [1971] 51
Thomas v. *Thomas* (1842) 48
Trevor v. *Whitworth* [1887] 199, **224**

United Sterling Corporation Ltd v. *Felton & Mannion* [1974] 114, **219**

Vacwell Engineering Ltd v. *B D H. Chemicals* [1971] 153, **222**
Victoria Laundry (Windsor) Ltd v. *Newman Industries Ltd* [1949] 62

Wagonmound, The see Overseas *Tankship (UK) Ltd* v. *Morts Dock & Engineering Co. Ltd* (1961)
Warner Bros Pictures Inc v. *Nelson* [1936] 63
Ward v. *Tesco Stores* (1976) 135
Watkins v. *Jubilee Club & Institute* (1982) unreported 166
Watt v. *Hertfordshire C.C.* [1954] 71
Wells v. *Cooper* [1958] 71
Wessex Dairies v. *Smith* [1935] 172
Western Excavations (ECC) Ltd v. *Sharp* [1978] 186
Whitely v. *Chappell* [1868] 16
Wigan B.C. v. *Davies* [1979] 186
Wilkie v. *Strathclyde Regional Council –* unreported 167
Wilson v. *Ricketts* [1954] 153
Wiltshire C.C. v. *NATFHE & Guy* [1980] 185
Wilts United Dairies v. *Thomas Robinson* [1958] 110
Wings Ltd v. *Ellis* [1984] 147, **221**
Wood v. *Freeloader* [1977] 171
Woodman v. *Photo Trade Processing* (1981) 156
Wrexham, Mold & Conah's Quay Railway Co. Re [1899] 202
Wright v. *Rugby Borough Council* (1985) unreported. 165

Yewens v. *Noakes* (1880) 130

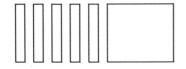

Table of Statutes

Asbesto (Licensing) Regulations 1983 128

Betting Act 1853 17
Business Names Act 1985 84, 86

Chemical Works Regulations 1922 119
Children Act 1972 10
Children and Young Persons Act 1933 10
Children and Young Persons Act 1963 10
Civil Liability (Contribution) Act 1978 67
Coal Industry Nationalization Act 1946 81
Companies Act 1948 85
Companies Act 1985 82, 84, 198–9, 201, 203
Company Directors Disqualification Act 1986 205
Consumer Credit Act 1974 22, 159–60
Consumer Protection Act 1987 43, 66, 97, 99, 117,
    140, 142, 143, 145, 147
Consumer Safety Act 1978 156
Contract of Employment Act 1963 39
Contract of Employment Act 1972 39
Control of Pollution Act 1974 125
Copyright, Designs and Patents Act 1988 103–5, 108,
    113, 117
County Courts Act 1846 27
Courts Act 1971 30

Data Protection Act 1984 8, 40, 189–91

Education Acts 1944–76 10
Education (Work Experience) Act 1973 13
Employers' Liability (Compulsory Insurance) Act
    1969 39, 134, 206
Employers' Liability (Defective Equipment) Act 1969
    39
Employment Act 1980 180, 185, 194–5
Employment Act 1982 40, 185, 194–5
Employment Act 1988 41, 194–5
Employment Protection Act 1975 191–3
Employment Protection (Consolidation) Act 1978 8,
    29, 40, 174–5, 179, 182, 184–7, 194

Equal Pay Act 1970 39, 182
Equal Pay (Amendment) Regulations 1983 40
Estate Agents Act 1979 158
European Communities Act 1972 17

Factories Act 1961 64, 117, 119, 122

Health and Safety at Work etc. Act 1974 4, 9, 39, 64,
    96–9, 117–19, 121–9, 136, 143, 172, 180
Health and Safety Policy Statements (Exceptions)
    Regulations 1975 122

Implied Terms (Sale of Goods) Act 1979 149, 154
Industrial Relations Act 1971 7, 39, 184
Industrial Training Act 1964 173
Insolvency Act 1986 89
Insurance Companies Act 1958 208

Law of Property (Miscellaneous Provisions) Act
    1989 54
Law Reform (Contributory Negligence) Act 1945 68
Law Reform (Frustrated Contracts) Act 1943 60
Limited Partnership Act 1907 83

Misrepresentation Act 1967 57

Occupiers' Liability Act 1957 117, 125, 135–6
Occupiers' Liability Act 1984 136
Offences Against the Person Act 1861 16
Offensive Weapons Act 1959 4
Offices, Shops and Railway Premises Act 1963 117,
    119

Partnership Act 1890 84, 92
Patents Act 1977 100, 112–13, 117
Public Trustee Act 1906 81

Race Relations Act 1976 40, 163
Redundancy Payments Act 1965 39
Rehabilitation of Offenders Act 1974 40, 169

Registered Designs Act 1949   104–5
Resale Prices Act 1976 57
Restrictive Trade Practices Act 1976 57
Road Traffic Act 1972 206

Safety Representatives and Safety Committees
    Regulations 1977 9, 123
Sale of Goods Act 1893 149
Sale of Goods Act 1979 50, 99, 149–54
Servants Characters Act 1792 168
Sex Discrimination Act 1975 15, 18, 40, 163–8, 185
Sex Discrimination Act 1986 18, 31, 40, 163–5, 167
Single European Act 1986 19
Social Security Act 1986 41
Social Security and Housing Benefits Act 1982 40
Street Offences Act 1959 16
Supply of Goods and Services Act 1982 138, 155–6
Supply of Goods (Implied Terms) Act 1973 155

Telecommunications Act 1984 8
Trade Description Act 1968 145
Trade Marks Act 1938 106–8
Trade Marks Act 1984 108
Trade Union Act 1984 195
Trade Union & Labour Relations Act 1974 7, 40,
    191–2
Trading Stamps Act 1964 155
Transfer of Undertakings (Protection of
    Employment) Regulations 1981 20, 40, 193
Transport Act 1981 7
Treaty of Rome 1957 17–19, 57–8
Truck Acts 1831–1940 181

Unfair Contract Terms Act 1977 45, 52, 53, 74, 135,
    156, 169

Wages Act 1986 40, 181

Index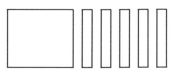

'Acceptable quality' 152
Acceptance 46
Act of God 68
Advertising 145
Advertising Standards Authority 145
Agreement 59
Arbitration 24
Articles of association 85
Averaging 210

Bankruptcy 92
Barristers 33
B.I.M. 9
Breach of contract 59
Breach of duty 71
Byelaws 10

Capability 187
Caveat emptor 55
C.B.I. 9
Civil law 3
Closed shop 193
Collective agreements 172
Commission for Racial Equality 167
Common law 6
Company 86
Company objects 201
Conditions 50
Consideration 47
Consensus ad idem 54
Consultation 193
Consumers' Association 155
Consumer credit 159
Consumer Protection Act 99, 140, 145
Contingency insurance 207
Contract 41
Contract of employment 170
Contributed capital 198

Contributory negligence 68
Conveyance 54
Copyright 102
Corporations 80, 84, 89
County court 27
Course of employment 132
Court of Appeal 30
Court system 25
Credit factoring 202
Creditors 89
Criminal law 3
Crown court 30
Custom 4

Data Protection Act 189
Damages 62, 72
Debentures 81, 200
Debt capital 200
Decisions 20
Declaration 3
Defamation 67
Delegated legislation 8
Designs 104
Designer's duties 125
Direct discrimination 164
Directives 20
Director General of Fair Trading 158
Discharge of contract 58
Disciplinary procedures 178
Disciplinary rules 177
Discrimination 163
Disclosure of information 192
Dispute settlement 22
Duty of care 53, 70, 72

Effective date of termination 185
Equal Opportunities Commission 167
Equal pay 182

Employee inventions 111
Employee references 168
Employee's duties 126
Employer's duties 119
Enforcement 49, 126
Equity 7
Erectors/installers' duties 126
European Community 17
European Court of Justice 31
Exclusion terms 51, 154
Express terms 49, 170

False price indicators 147
Fault liability 66
Fieri facias 49
'Fitness for purpose' 153
Fixed charges 200
Fixed term contracts 183
Flixborough disaster 124
Floating charges 87, 200
Frustration 59, 183

General defences 67
Gross misconduct 177
Guarantee 54, 87

Health and Safety at Work Act 96, 118
Health and Safety Commission 124
Health and Safety Executive 127
High Court 28
House of Lords 30

Illegal contracts 57
Implied terms 49, 149, 171
Importer's duties 125
Improvement notice 127
Independent contractors 130, 133
Indemnity 54

Indemnity insurance 207
Indirect discrimination 165
Industrial tribunals 173
Injunction 3, 63
Injurious falsehood 110
Insolvency 89
Insurable interest 208
Insurance 205
Intention to be legally bound 41
Interviews 168
Inventions 111
Itemized pay statements 182

Job advertisements 167
Joint tortfeasors 67

Legislation 7
Liquidated damages 62
Liquidator 91
Loan capital 200
London Gazette 91

Magistrates' courts 29
Manufacturer's duties 125
Marital status discrimination 166
Maternity rights 180
Memorandum of association 85, 198
Merchantable quality 150
Misconduct 178
Misleading trade descriptions 146
Misrepresentation 56
Mistake 54
Mortgage 200

National Consumer Council 156
N.F.U. 9
Necessity 68
Negligence 69, 139
Neglegent misstatement 73
Negotiation 23
Nominal capital 85
Notice 183
Novus actus interveniens 65
N.S.P.C.C. 9
Nuisance 136

Obiter dicta 5
Occupiers' liability 134
Offer 42
Office of Fair Trading 158
Ordinary shares 199

Partnership 82, 86, 92
Passing-off 109
Patents 100
Performance 60
Personnel function 163
Policy decision 133
Precedent 5
Preference shares 199
Private law 2
Product liability 140
Professional liability 73
Professional indemnity 206
Prohibition notice 127
Public company 82
Public law 2

Quantum meruit 61

Racial discrimination 164
Ratio decidendi 5
Receiver 92
Recission 56
Recommendations 20
Recruitment and selection 163
Redundancy 188
References 168
Registered company 198
Regulations 20
Rehabilitation of offenders 169
Remedies 187
Restraint clauses 113
R.S.P.C.A. 9

Safety policy 122
Self-regulation 148
Seveso disaster 125
Servant 130
Service contracts 154
Sex discrimination 164
Share capital 198

Short listing 167
Sole trader 80, 84
Solicitors 32
Specific performance 3, 63
Spent convictions 169
Standard form contracts 45
Stare decisis 5
'State of the art' defence 141
Statute 7
Statutory authority 68
Statutory interpretation 14
Statutory rights 173
Strict liability 67
Subrogation 210
Suppliers' duties 125
Supply contracts 154

Termination of employment 182, 185
Time off work 179
Tort 64
Tracing 202
Trade Associations 157
Trade descriptions 145
Trade mark 106
Trade unions 191
Tribunals 31

Uberrimae fidei 56, 209
Ultra vires 14, 201
Unfair dismissal 184
Union membership agreement 193

Valid reasons for dismissal 186
Vicarious liability 130
Vitiating factors 53
Volenti non fit injuria 67

Wagering contracts 203
Wages 181
Warranties 50
Winding up 89
Works rules 172
Written statements 173
Wrongful dismissal 184
Wrongful trading 203